Morgenstern's
FINEST ICE CREAM

Nicholas Morgenstern

with photography by Lucia Bell-Epstein

Alfred A. Knopf

New York

2025

THIS IS A BORZOI BOOK PUBLISHED BY ALFRED A. KNOPF

Copyright © 2025 by Nicholas Morgenstern
Photographs copyright © 2025 by Lucia Bell-Epstein
All rights reserved. Published in the United States by Alfred A. Knopf, a division of Penguin Random House LLC, New York, and distributed in Canada by Penguin Random House Canada Limited, Toronto.

www.aaknopf.com

Knopf, Borzoi Books, and the colophon are registered trademarks of Penguin Random House LLC.

Library of Congress Cataloging-in-Publication Data
Names: Morgenstern, Nicholas, author. | Bell-Epstein, Lucia, photographer.
Title: Morgenstern's finest ice cream / Nicholas Morgenstern ; photography by Lucia Bell-Epstein.
Description: First edition. | New York : Alfred A. Knopf, 2025. | Includes index. |
Identifiers: LCCN 2024021288 (print) | LCCN 2024021289 (ebook) | ISBN 9780593534847 (hardcover) | ISBN 9780593534854 (ebook)
Subjects: LCSH: Ice cream, ices, etc. | LCGFT: Cookbooks.
Classification: LCC TX795 .M77 2025 (print) | LCC TX795 (ebook) | DDC 641.86/2—dc23/eng/20240517
LC record available at https://lccn.loc.gov/2024021288
LC ebook record available at https://lccn.loc.gov/2024021289

Grateful acknowledgment is made to the following for permission to reprint previously published material: Jessica Che for the illustrations on pages v, 35, 77, 177, 187, 237, 312, 359, and 360; Julie F. Farias for the essay "The Origins of the Mulie Fajitas Picoso' Classic Sundae"; and Brian Koppelman for the essay "The Koppelman."

Some of the recipes in this book may include raw eggs, meat, or fish. When these foods are consumed raw, there is always the risk that bacteria, which is killed by proper cooking, may be present. For this reason, when serving these foods raw, always buy certified salmonella-free eggs and the freshest meat and fish available from a reliable grocer, storing them in the refrigerator until they are served. Because of the health risks associated with the consumption of bacteria that can be present in raw eggs, meat, and fish, these foods should not be consumed by infants, small children, pregnant women, the elderly, or any persons who may be immunocompromised. The author and publisher expressly disclaim responsibility for any adverse effects that may result from the use or application of the recipes and information contained in this book.

Front-of-cover photograph by Priyaporn Pichitpongchai
Back-of-cover illustration by Jessica Che
Cover design by Jessica Che
Production by Ellen Scordato for Stonesong
Interior Creative Direction: Jessica Che
Interior Design by Stan Madaloni for studio2pt0, llc

Manufactured in China
First Edition

CONTENTS

ABOUT THIS BOOK 1
The Morgenstern's Difference 4
How to Use This Book 6
Ingredients 6
Equipment 7

VANILLA 11
Vanilla Sugar 19
Madagascar Vanilla 20
French Vanilla 22
Vanilla Brûlée 25
Bourbon Vanilla 26
Burnt Honey Vanilla 28
The Hot Fudge Sundae: The Most
    Important Sundae in America 31
Morgenstern's Hot Fudge 32
Whipped Cream 33
King Kong Banana Split 34

CHOCOLATE 37
Chocolate 42
Olive Oil Charred Eggplant 47
Salted Chocolate 50
Blueberry Milk Chocolate 52
Bitter Chocolate 54
Brownie Sundae 59
Sundae Brownies 60
Hotter Fudge 61
"The Origins of the Mulie Fajitas Picoso'
    Classic Sundae" by Julie Farias 64
Mulie Fajitas Picoso' Classic Sundae 66
Rockiest Road 69
Ricky Road 71
Marshmallow Fluff 73
Peanut Butter Caramel 73

STRAWBERRY 75
Smooth and Delicious Strawberry 78
Chunky Strawberry 81
Strawberry Jam 83

Strawberry Pistachio Pesto 86
Strawberries N' Cream 88
Banana Split 91
Crushed Pineapple 92
Strawberry Sauce 94

COFFEE 97
Vietnamese Coffee 101
Coffee Crisp 106
Espresso Honeycomb 108
Coconut Espresso 110
Affogato 113

CARAMEL 115
Caramel Sauce 118
Water Caramel 120
Sesame Caramel 121
Bourbon Caramel 121
Dulce De Leche 122
Crème Caramel 124
Baked Crème Caramel 128
Butterscotch 129
Salted Caramel Pretzel 138

NUTS 143
Peanut Butter Cup 148
Honey Almond Custard 150
Honey Almond Honeycomb 152
Pistachio Black Currant 154
Black Currant Jam 158
Hazelnut Risbo 160
"The Koppelman" by Brian Koppelman 162
The Koppelman 163
Dacquoise 168
Peanut Butter 170
Grape 171
PB Frosting 171
Mascarpone 172
Butter Pecan 174
Buttered Pecans and Pecan Butter 176

BANANA ... 179
Drunken Monkey ... 181
Banana Curry ... 183
Bananas Foster ... 186
Charred Banana ... 188
Macadamia Praline Banana ... 192
Macadamia Praline ... 194

TROPICAL FLAVORS ... 199
Avocado Toast ... 200
Avocado ... 201
Coconut Sorbet ... 205
Pickled Pineapple ... 209
Pineapple Salted Egg Yolk ... 210
Salted Egg Yolk Streusel ... 212
Strawberry Guava Sorbet ... 216
Mango Passion Rice ... 218
Vegan Mango Sundae ... 221
Coconut Whipped Cream ... 222
Mango Passionfruit Caramel ... 222
Mango Chips ... 223
Durian Banana ... 225

CITRUS ... 229
Cardamom Lemon Jam ... 232
Lemon Jam ... 233
Lemon Curd Poppyseed ... 238
Lemon Curd ... 240
Mango Satsuma ... 242
Yuzu Toasted Rice ... 245
Yuzu Jelly ... 248
Kathy's Kalamansi Gin Pop ... 251
Condensed Milk Fluff ... 253

RASPBERRY ... 255
Raspberry Dark Chocolate ... 256
Raspberry Cheesecake ... 258
Graham Cracker Crumb ... 262
Raspberry Swirl ... 262
Raspberry Green Tea Jelly ... 264
Green Tea Jelly ... 266
Raspberry Papaya Sorbet ... 268
Raspberry Milkshake ... 270

PEACHES ... 273
Peaches N' Clotted Cream ... 275
Sour Cream Canned Peach ... 278
Peach Jam ... 281
Peach Sweet Tea ... 282
Honey Lavender Peach ... 285

CLASSICS ... 291
Cookies N' Cream ... 294
Bubble Gum ... 296
S'mores ... 299
Rum Raisin ... 302
Schoolyard Mint Chip ... 305
Grasshopper Sundae ... 308
Chocolate Lace ... 310
Cookie Monster Cake ... 313
Cookie Monster Ice Cream ... 314
M&M's Frosting ... 315
Chocolate Cake ... 316

MISCELLANEOUS ... 319
Raw Milk ... 320
Cinnamon Raisin Toast ... 323
Black Ass Licorice ... 326
Burnt Sage ... 328
Sage Dip ... 331
Tahini and Jelly ... 332
Grape Jelly ... 334
Labneh Sorbet ... 335
French Fry ... 336
Green Tea Pistachio ... 338
Nick's It ... 343
Chocolate Dip ... 347

THANKS ... 348

INDEX ... 352

ABOUT THIS BOOK

People have been eating frozen water for dessert for hundreds of years. It's like a trick; edible magic that never gets old. America's love affair with ice cream goes all the way back to the founding fathers. At my Manhattan flagship store we make 88 flavors of ice cream in-house every day, digging deep into the history of ice cream to find the flavors of tomorrow.

I grew up in San Francisco, raised by a single mom and a down-and-out deadbeat dad. They divorced when I was young and we struggled with just about everything, including putting food on the table. Most of my upbringing found my brother and I staring down plates of my mother's version of healthy; disgusting options such as raw zucchini salads and steamed chicken.

During the summer of 1983, when I was five and my brother was four, our parents put us on a plane to Columbus, OH, where my grandparents lived. They picked us up and we drove three hours south to Marietta, OH, on the bank of the Ohio River. Over the next five summers or so, the same routine ensued. We stayed a month at a time. We'd never been outside of the hippie commune that was San Francisco, where we ate kale and steamed tofu and absolutely no sugar. But back in Marietta, Grandpa Morgenstern ate real food. He survived losing his father at 12 during the Great Depression and that loss and leanness shaped his identity and his attitude about food—EATING IS SERIOUS BUSINESS. I can still hear him saying it, and I still believe it's true. Grandpa Morgenstern served in the Army during World War II, and afterward put himself through school on the GI Bill while working at Broughton's Dairy, where he fell in love with ice cream. Meals with my grandparents were simple but formidable: pork chops, lima beans, and corn; chicken fried steak with tomatoes; burgers (he loved hamburgers!). Appetizers were saltines with butter, a treat I indulge in to this day. But most exciting was this absolute: there was always dessert, and it was always ice cream. My grandfather loved ice cream—butter pecan most of all—and always had three or four flavors on hand. He had ice cream with every meal and so did we. Having ice cream everyday was a reminder that both he and America had made it through something tough, and this was their reward.

I started cooking professionally right out of high school, and immediately gravitated to the intoxicating world of fine dining. I spent years grinding my way up the ranks, as pastry chef of Gramercy Tavern Restaurant—a temple of American dining in New York. I knew nothing other than the twisted psychosis of cooking in this world, and I loved it. But I had reached a ceiling and just as I crested that pinnacle, I realized it was not going to be enough for me. I needed more space to grow, find new challenges, and create my own path.

So I quit my job and squinted into the light of a new reality. I'd been making ice cream for years at this point, ever since I unpacked the first ice cream machine at the Francis Drake Hotel in San Francisco, when I was 18 or 19. Ice cream had been a constant in my life. But when I looked around at the ice cream shops in New York at the time, I felt offended. Offended that something so good was being made so badly.

My savings were minimal, so I had to keep working. I spent the next couple years consulting, helping friends open restaurants, and figuring out what to do next. In 2008, I met a guy who owned a building with a restaurant space in Ft. Greene, Brooklyn. We were an odd pairing; he was an aging banker who owned real estate and clubs; I was an ex–pastry chef looking for a new path and opportunity. He wanted an operations guy, general manager, and chef who would allow him to collect a profit and enjoy a mojito at the bar every night. Being a partner would be my reward.

I chewed on it and finally decided to go with my gut, trusting my work ethic would carry me. We opened an all-day café in the summer of 2008, just as the Great Recession was tearing New York's dining world apart. As the markets crumbled, fine dining was spinning out, and casual dining was in.

At the end of the summer, I asked my business partner (and landlord) if I could sublease a small room in the basement, about 100 square feet. It had a dirt floor and was primarily used as a dumping spot for unused restaurant crap. He laughed when I told him I wanted to make ice cream there. He laughed again when I told him I wanted to put an ice cream cart in front of the restaurant, but he drew up a lease and let me do it. I used my savings to purchase an ice cream machine on eBay for $9,000, pour a foundation, and tile the room.

As winter ended, the business settled in. I had a little time to work on the ice cream cart. I knew Workman Cycles, just across the bridge in Queens, made beautiful push carts but none of them were what I wanted; I needed something unique and functional. I'd just purchased a '73 Datsun 620 pickup that put me in the mood for mechanics, so I sketched out a design and gave myself a week to find the parts and put it together.

On the first spring day, we rolled out the cart. There was still a slight chill in the air; some of the staff wore sweatshirts. The sun came out, and when I opened the yellow and white umbrella, everything felt right. From that first chilly day, people were lined up for our ice cream, and soon other people were opening ice cream carts of their own. We made all the product five feet from the cart; Vietnamese Coffee (page 101), Burnt Honey Vanilla (page 28), Green Tea Pistachio (page338). But the standout was Salted Caramel Pretzel (page 138). At the end of the summer, *The New York Times* ran a piece on all the new ice cream places in the city. We were the last one featured in the article, dubbed "The Holy Grail of Ice Cream."

From that little cart, I went on to open stores in Manhattan, serving hundreds of thousands of scoops of ice cream each year. We serve flavors that are a little different than you can find elsewhere. Our store has a distinct aesthetic: black and white, old school, to contrast with our very modern flavors—to keep the creativity in the cup and on the cone. It's a way of telling our consumers that they're in good hands, that we are trustworthy.

After years of making ice cream, this book is my attempt to share my perspective, highlighting the most important elements of flavor, texture, and nostalgia. Ice cream is, after all, serious business.

RIP Grandpa Morgenstern.

THE MORGENSTERN'S DIFFERENCE

At Morgenstern's we make everything on-site. Does this matter?

I love ordering an ice cream cone, and I never ask for a taste first. I read the menu, feel the anticipation, and then commit. That moment of consideration is why I created Morgenstern's. Before I opened my own shop, I'd order a cone someplace and find myself disappointed, always thinking *this could be better.*

In order to exceed the expectation and anticipation that you feel when you read the menu, we make almost everything we serve ourselves, from ice cream bases to sauces, mix ins, and toppings. This allows us to control the quality of what we serve, and to fine-tune every aspect of our flavors.

In making ice cream, the bottom line is this: eggs are cheaper than cream, sugar is cheaper than eggs, and air is cheaper than anything. Most ice cream companies are driven by profit margins, so they use eggs, cream, and air to control costs. At Morgenstern's, the number one goal is to get the ice cream to taste like the flavor, which means no eggs, low sugar, and less air. It's not that I don't like making money, I just like making great ice cream more.

Eggless
I love eggs, but at Morgenstern's, we rarely use them in our ice cream because their flavor gets in the way of the flavor of my ice cream.

America has never been a place where technique must be showcased, so it's a very American thing to do—to take a shortcut of sorts and make ice cream without eggs. This stands in contrast to the French technique, which uses a crème anglaise with lots of egg yolks added in and then cooked slowly, giving it a smooth texture.

Europeans developed ice cream and elevated it to an art. But Americans turned it into an everyday indulgence. Today, there are many who remain happily married to making ice cream with eggs, but for me it was simple to abandon the French method in my effort to make the best product.

Low Sugar
I've always used sugar the way that chefs use salt: enough to balance flavor. Using less sugar is challenging; sugar, chemically, is one of the key ingredients in making ice cream soft and there is no one that doesn't love soft ice cream. We commit ourselves to making sure that none of our flavors are too sweet but are still soft enough to enjoy on a cone.

Less Air
This might sound obvious, but air doesn't taste like anything. The more you put into your ice cream, the less flavor it will have. You want some air to make it lighter than liquid, but not so much that you lose flavor. We use equipment to churn our ice cream with less air than most traditional American ice creams. By using cream with lower butterfat we trap less air, keeping the flavor "clear," while still maintaining a richness that is consistent with an American scoop.

Mix Ins
A fundamental element of scoops at Morgenstern's is the mix in. This means adding a spoonful of an ingredient to the tub of ice cream just before scooping. This started with pretzels in our Salted Caramel Pretzel (page 138) and condensed milk in our Vietnamese Coffee (page 101) flavors. A tablespoon or two is usually enough for a scoop, but can be adjusted to fit your preference.

HOW TO USE THIS BOOK

The recipes in this book have been taken straight from my production manuals. I have scaled them down—most make about a quart but a few reduce less easily, so be sure to check the yield. I've adjusted them slightly to keep it simple, but these are pretty much the recipes I make and sell at Morgenstern's. That said, I am probably not eating your ice cream, so adjust as you see fit.

INGREDIENTS

Not all ingredients are created equal. A simple rule of thumb is to use the best ingredients where it counts, and use your budget efficiently. The quality of chocolate, fruit, or cream will impact the quality of your ice cream far more than the quality of sugar or salt.

Dairy: I don't use specialty organic dairy. I also don't use a premixed ice cream base. We buy all our cream and milk from a local distributor. The milk is full fat, approximately 2%. The cream I specify for all the recipes has a lower fat content at approximately 36%. This is not widely available, but it can be found. While I started with raw milk, I recommend using something that is pasteurized—save the stuff from your local farmers market or boutique grocery store for your coffee or homemade ricotta. We don't use stabilizers, and because you will probably be making this in a home ice cream machine, the butterfat in a "farm" fresh cream will be more prone to separating and creating fat pockets. Raw, unpasteurized milk can be delicious, however I cannot recommend it as I would not want my publisher to run afoul of the FDA. (They are here to protect you!)

Sugar: I'm on the East Coast, so I use Domino granulated sugar unless otherwise noted. Sometimes it is worth getting special sugar, but very rarely. The only sugar I have ever worked to get is called jaggery, or sometimes palm sugar. There are two types, and the one I love is from Southern India and is made from red dates. It has a unique flavor and aroma unlike anything else I have ever experienced. If you get your hands on it, swap out the sugar in the Raw Milk (page 320) recipe with it. Otherwise, granulated will work for everything in here.

Glucose Syrup: This is a modified sugar syrup that is not as sweet as sugar, and as the name suggests is liquid. If you cannot get this, corn syrup will work. It will help keep your ice cream smooth.

Salt: I prefer a fine grain kosher salt, like Diamond Crystal, for just about everything. Its flavor is consistent, and it is readily available and reasonably priced. Occasionally I will use sea salt from Portugal or Greece if I want something with a sharper salinity. Do not fall into the Maldon sea salt trap. It is overpriced, and merely lends a crispy texture due to a man-made production gimmick. If you want texture from salt, use fleur de sel, which will also add flavor.

Pectin: All the recipes in this book use Sure-Jell pectin. Different pectins respond in very different ways, so I strongly recommend that you don't substitute here.

EQUIPMENT

Tools are important. Knowing what tool to use for what job is important. I'm not going in to every piece of equipment here but assume that you have a sharp knife and a clean cutting board. I like to have towels that have been soaked in hot water and wrung out available for keeping my station clean.

Ice Cream Machine: There are a few methods for freezing ice cream at home. Probably the most common one uses a frozen bowl. In my opinion, the best option is a hand crank rock salt and ice machine. This is probably how ice cream was made for the longest time and these salt and ice machines lingered well into the age of batch freezers, sorta like CD or DVD players today. They require loads of ice and salt. (If you add salt to ice, it miraculously accelerates its melting and thereby drops the temperature temporarily and allows you to churn your ice cream base much faster.)

There are many different models, some with hand cranks, some with motors. All of the recipes in this book were tested using a Nostalgia (4-quart) machine, which cost about $60. I personally like the 2 or 4 quart version made by a company called White Mountain. They've been discontinued, however they are still readily available online. A hand crank model is a pain in the ass, but it will allow you to increase the speed manually at the end of churning your ice cream, which will allow you to emulsify the base and make it smooth right when it is setting, giving you a creamy consistency. If you can find a machine that accommodates a motor and allows you to switch to a hand crank at the end, it will save your arm.

There are also ice cream machines that use a compressor, a piece of equipment that cools a gas (Freon) to keep things cold. It is what keeps your fridge and freezer cold at home. In an ice cream machine, it must work hard to bring temperatures below freezing, fast.

If you are a real psycho and must have an ice cream machine at home, you can either purchase a tabletop machine from Carpigiani or Taylor. The other option would be a Pacojet, which is not technically an ice cream machine, but for making small batches of "ice cream" at home they work well.

Freezer: I hope it goes without saying that you need one of these if you are going to make ice cream. But here I am saying you need one of these to make ice cream. The temperature of your freezer matters, a lot. I like to freeze our ice cream at -20°F and serve it at 5°F. This is tough to do at home, so I recommend checking the temperature in your freezer and setting it to about 0 degrees. This will work for freezing and serving. Adjusting the temperature in a home freezer can take days, with minor movements in the dial requiring hours to change the actual temperature in the freezer. If you want to be sure of the temp, take three or four readings every 24 hours, and don't make any change to the dial before then. Having lots of stuff in your freezer will extend the time it takes for the temp to adjust, but will also keep the temperature in your freezer consistent. Opening and closing the door a lot will obviously increase the temperature, and you cannot overestimate how long it can take for a home freezer to get cold once it is warmed up. Ideally, you should freeze the container that you are putting your ice cream in before you begin churning. As soon as you have filled your container, put a lid on it, and get it in the freezer. KEEP THE DOOR CLOSED. Ideally your ice cream freezes for 24 hours before serving. If you are serving for a party, check the consistency before you are going to serve. If it is too hard, plan on pulling it out of the freezer for a few minutes before scooping.

Mixing Bowls: It is a good idea to have mixing bowls for combining ingredients. I like stainless steel for ease of use and cleaning. Having more than one is helpful for many of the recipes in this book. Mixing bowls are for mixing, not storing. FYI.

Whisks: These are designed to incorporate ingredients together or add air into ingredients when mixing. They are great for combining two ingredients that don't want to get together, like liquids and dry ingredients. I do not whisk any ice cream base while it is cooking, this is not the time to add air to your ice cream.

Spatulas: An essential tool in making ice cream. You can substitute with a wooden spoon if you have no choice, but a spatula will be more effective, especially to keep the base from sticking to the pot.

Measuring Cups and Spoons: Measuring is important. It is a good idea to have a set of measuring spoons and cups that can be read easily. It is also good to be able to get ingredients in and out of them thoroughly and easily.

Digital Scale: A small digital scale is great. Make sure you check the calibration periodically (weigh something with a clear absolute value like a pound of butter and see that it matches the scale's reading).

Digital Timer and Thermometer: I also like a digital timer to keep track of how long processes take (baking, mixing, cooking, and freezing). It is also very helpful to have a digital thermometer for checking the temperature of what you are cooking, as well as a thermometer to measure the temperature inside your freezer.

Grater: Sometimes you will need to grate the zest off citrus, or grate spices, like nutmeg or even cinnamon bark. For this I recommend a micro plane, but a box grater will work.

Mesh Strainers: Every one of our bases go through a fine-mesh strainer before it is frozen. This filters out any lumps and ingredients that have been steeped and need to be removed like mint leaves or vanilla pods. Occasionally I will strain something through a large hole strainer before the fine-mesh strainer to accelerate the process and get some of the big stuff out before using the fine strainer. A stainless steel 2-ounce ladle can help in pressing the bottom of the strainer to get all of the flavor out of a steeped ingredient. If you are committed to making ice cream at home, you will need to invest in a fine-mesh strainer. If not, get ready to eat lumpy ice cream.

Containers: For cooling the ice cream base before it is churned, a stainless steel bowl or container will work best to cool quickly and keep clean. I like clear plastic containers with lids for storing any ice cream bases. Glass works, but it is heavy and obviously prone to breaking. I spin all of our ice cream into half gallon plastic buckets with a sealed lid. Keeping ice cream in a sealed container is more important than most people imagine. It keeps out other odors and flavors, and also keeps the ice cream from drying out and developing a crust on top.

Ice Cream Scoops: For me, there is only one scoop for scooping ice cream. It is a nonmechanical scoop made by a company called Zeroll. They come in different sizes and create beautifully smooth scoops of ice cream. Do not put them in the dishwasher, ever.

Ice Bath: We use an ice bath to cool the ice cream bases after they are cooked, before they get churned. As a rule of thumb I like to use equal parts ice and water. The container that holds your ice bath needs to be large enough to submerge whatever container you are cooling.

In conclusion, I am not going to tell you to have fun. Eating ice cream is fun. Making it is serious business. Keep your station clean, pay attention, and follow through. And absolutely no screaming for ice cream.

MADAGASCAR VANILLA

FRENCH VANILLA

BOURBON VANILLA

BURNT HONEY VANILLA

VANILLA

IN THIS CHAPTER, I AM PAYING HOMAGE TO THE MOST IMPORTANT FLAVOR OF ALL: VANILLA. As any ice cream aficionado will tell you, the measure of an ice cream shop is its vanilla ice cream. When I am ordering ice cream for myself, I get vanilla on a cake cone. It is uncomplicated and pure and for me, it is the taste of where it all begins, historically and in my own memory. It's what our parents ordered for us when we were children because we couldn't make up our minds and we rely on it as adults who still can't make up our minds. But me, I've made up mine: Vanilla is my favorite.

Vanilla ice cream was brought to the U.S. from Paris in the 1790s by Thomas Jefferson, a legendary gourmand. A short time later, in the mid-nineteenth century, Edmond Albius (an enslaved Black twelve-year-old in the French colony of St. Suzanne, Reunion) discovered that vanilla orchids could be manually pollinated to propagate the crop and thereby revolutionized the cultivation of vanilla, launching an entire industry. Vanilla—or imitation vanillin—can now be found in fragrances, lotions, soaps, sodas, and deodorants, not to mention its longtime bedfellow, chocolate. Almost all chocolate contains vanilla, or more likely vanillin.

Vanilla has enjoyed its position at the top of the ice cream food chain, quietly but consistently being rated the number one most ordered flavor in America every year for the past 50 years, according to the International Dairy Foods Association. At Morgenstern's, I have been absorbed with, even mildly obsessed with, making the best vanilla possible from the very beginning, with a rotating roster of different versions from Burnt Honey Vanilla (page 28) to Bourbon Vanilla (page 27), and, of course, our classic Madagascar Vanilla ice cream (page 20). If you want to know what an ice cream shop is made of, order a scoop of vanilla. It will tell you everything you need to know.

MADAGASCAR THE COUNTRY, NOT THE MOVIE

The term "vanilla" has come to mean plain and ordinary, but the life of a Madagascar vanilla bean is anything but.

The only edible part of any flower in the orchid family, vanilla is also the most popular fragrance in the world. The Aztec Empire is said to have started cultivating vanilla around the fifteenth century, and conquistador Hernán Cortes introduced it to Europe shortly after. Between the 1500s and the 1800s, Mexico was the primary producer of vanilla, but in 1819, it was introduced to the island of Reunion, off the southeast coast of Africa. Today, most vanilla comes from nearby Madagascar, an island teaming with flora and fauna not found anywhere else. Its climate is ideal for cultivating complex ingredients: cocoa and coffee, peppers and papayas. But nothing thrives like the vanilla bean, which has been harvested there for hundreds of years. Cured under the heat of the sun in hand-made wooden boxes to develop flavor, at night they are locked up in a safe house like fine jewels in a jewelry shop window.

After saffron, vanilla is the most expensive spice out there, but these are tough times to be a Madagascar vanilla bean. The supply is affected by cyclones, draught, political unrest, and theft. During the vanilla blight in 2015, international distributors sent private militia to Madagascar to safely ferry their crops off the island. Would vanilla taste the same if it didn't cause such international intrigue? What would vanilla be if it grew like dandelions anywhere it pleased?

For better or worse, in blind taste tests imitation vanilla—vanillin—is preferred over the real thing. A paltry 1 percent of the vanilla consumed around the world is from real pods. But for me, there is no alternative. Real vanilla is volatile and alive. The flavor is rich and buttery, like bourbon and pecans. The best beans are plump and oily, long, and tight and their flavor can't be replicated in a laboratory. They are not just a dried orchid stamen but the embodiment of America's favorite flavor.

BUYING VANILLA

Vanilla is a commodity product, and the buying process is wacky. And by "wacky," I mean that the price is affected by factors outside of anyone's control. On top of world events and weather, middlemen distributors see vanilla as a high-margin product and take advantage of the volatility in the market to make as much profit as possible. For the uninformed buyer, purchasing vanilla is like buying a used car; it's very likely that you don't know what you're looking at and you must rely on the salesperson. As has been the case for many years, today, vanilla consumption is on the rise, and production is on the decline. Because half the world's vanilla comes from one very volatile place, the price is almost impossible to predict and plan for. If you are as committed to buying the real thing, as we are at Morgenstern's, you've got to have a strategy.

1. Sourcing the pods

Do not buy vanilla beans from a purveyor who also sells Crisco. This goes for grocery stores as well as boutique specialty shops. If you are not buying vanilla by the pound, unfortunately your best source is going to be the online marketplace.

The beans should be soft and totally pliable. If a bean breaks, it's garbage, having long ago lost its aromatic perfume. They should have a strong, rich and intoxicating aroma of sweet wood and kerosine. I like beans that are plump, though I am often presented with ones that are big and fat, but with few seeds inside. This will be hard to screen prior to purchasing without being able to handle the bean, but if it looks too fat, or too skinny for its length, it is probably short on the precious seeds, where the flavor is.

2. Sourcing the paste

A good vanilla paste is a great shelf-stable substitute for the real thing. A cross between extract and fresh vanilla beans, the paste is loaded with vanilla flavor and seeds. It is made by grinding up whole vanilla beans with a sugar syrup. You can buy a few ounces of paste for much less than what the fresh beans will cost you. It should be thick and clumpy and dark brown/black. Vanilla paste can typically be found at specialty shops and fine pastry providers online. Use this in place of beans, about 1 tablespoon in place of 1 bean.

3. Sourcing the extract

Vanilla Extract is made by soaking vanilla beans in alcohol. It is something that most people keep in the cabinet at home indefinitely. However, for the best flavor, it should be used within five years. Write the date on the bottle when you buy it. I prefer to get extract from companies that are already selling beans and producing both paste and extract. They are more likely to be making a quality version.

HOW WE PROCESS VANILLA AT MORGENSTERN'S

Most of us encounter vanilla as imitation extract, made in a lab. Sadly, in blind taste tests 9 out of 10 people prefer imitation vanilla over the real thing. Be that as it may, I can assure you, once you've handled a fresh vanilla bean, you will not want to use anything else. The process to extract vanilla from the bean is laborious and requires diligence. Please do persevere.

I love beans from Madagascar best. I taste beans from all over the world every year, from Indonesia to Mexico, Tahiti, and Ghana. I always come back to Madagascar. The flavor is consistently clean, clear, and true, but it does not come cheap. When the global vanilla supply was decimated around 2015, prices quadrupled. This forced me to look closely at what we were doing with every part of the pod. The following is my solution—what we have been doing since—to curb waste and add more vanilla flavor to our ice creams.

We begin all of our vanilla ice creams with fresh Madagascar vanilla beans. We flatten them out on a cutting board and split them lengthwise, scraping out all the fresh seeds from within using the back of a paring knife. We add those seeds to the pot when making ice cream. That sticky paste that is stuck to your fingers? It is the strongest essence of vanilla, so DON'T WASTE IT! Scrape it carefully from your fingers into the pot as well. (So clean hands before you begin, please.)

We take the remaining pods and cover them with sugar (65g per pod) and seal them tightly in a large container. As we add in more pods, we top off the container with more sugar. The pods should not sit in sugar for more than a month so do not use a container that will take longer than a month to fill.

Next, we turn out the filled container onto a large tray. We pour the vanilla pods and sugar mixture into a commercial kitchen processor, but a home model will also work, and grind it all until we have a wet powder. We sift that powder through a drum sifter to separate the vanilla sugar from the scrap (larger pieces of the pods that did not grind up completely). This sugar is used in every recipe for vanilla ice cream at Morgenstern's; the floral sticky vanilla flavor from the soaked pods adding depth to every ice cream we add it to.

That scrap isn't headed for the garbage, though. The next step is to take those discarded pieces and put them in 1-liter bottles. We then top off those bottles with Old Grand-Dad Kentucky Bourbon and let the pod pieces soak for 12 to 24 months (the longer the better), at which point, we blend them in a commercial blender (a home blender will also work), straining to create vanilla extract. This extract is better than any I have ever purchased. Make your own extract. You will be proud. Your friends will be proud. Or just buy imitation, it's not like anyone knows the difference anyway.

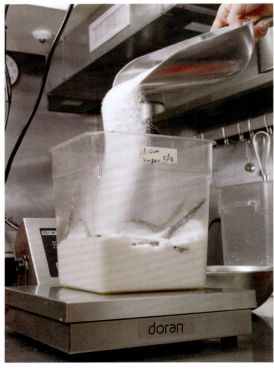

VANILLA SUGAR

If you don't have loads of vanilla beans curing in buckets of sugar for months on end, this process below will work to make a fragrant vanilla sugar.

Makes 1 cup

Vanilla Bean	1
Granulated Sugar	1 cup (200g)

Split the vanilla bean in half lengthwise with a sharp knife. Scrape the seeds into a large container with a lid, making sure to include any paste that sticks to your fingers or to the knife. Add the sugar and the scraped-out pod. Using an immersion blender, combine the seeds, pod, and sugar together into a powder. The vanilla sugar will keep for 6 months in a tightly sealed container, preferably in a cool dark place.

MADAGASCAR VANILLA

WE SERVE FIVE TO SEVEN TYPES OF VANILLA ICE CREAM EVERY DAY, but the Madagascar Vanilla is the standard against which they are all judged. This recipe is all about the holy pairing of dairy and vanilla and the most important element is using the highest quality beans. Do whatever you have to do, pay the price, you won't be disappointed. I have been making this recipe for over a decade, since long before I started Morgenstern's. Once I found a dealer who would bring me beans straight from Madagascar, I had to write a recipe to do justice to their quality. Beautifully creamy, with low butterfat and low sugar, this recipe highlights the clean clear flavor of the vanilla bean. (Spoiler, this is my favorite flavor.)

Makes approximately 1 quart

Whole Milk	1½ cups (367g)
Heavy Cream	1½ cups (357g)
Glucose Syrup	2 tablespoons (40g)
Vanilla Bean	1
Granulated Sugar	½ cup (100g)
Whole Milk Powder	¼ cup (30g)
Vanilla Sugar (page 19) or Granulated Sugar	2 tablespoons (25g)
Kosher Salt	¼ teaspoon (2g)
Vanilla Extract	¼ teaspoon (2g)

Place the milk, cream, and glucose syrup into a 4-quart saucepan.

Split open the vanilla bean and scrape the seeds into the saucepan. Reserve the scraped-out pod to make Vanilla Sugar (page 19).

Heat the mixture over medium heat, stirring with a rubber spatula or wooden spoon to keep it from burning, until small bubbles appear around the edges and the temperature reaches 180°F.

In a large bowl, whisk together the granulated sugar, milk powder, Vanilla Sugar, and salt.

Slowly pour the hot cream mixture into the bowl, stirring constantly.

Pour the mixture back into the pot and cook over medium heat, stirring constantly, until the temperature returns to 180°F.

Remove the pot from the heat, immediately stir in the vanilla, then strain through a fine-mesh strainer into a clean container.

Fill a large bowl with ice and cold water to make an ice bath.

Put the container into the ice bath and let the base cool to 38°F, stirring occasionally.

Freeze in an ice cream maker according to the manufacturer's instructions.

FRENCH VANILLA

I'VE SAID THAT I DON'T USE EGGS IN MY RECIPES AT MORGENSTERN'S. However, this is an exception. The French have contributed tremendously to the world through food, especially in sweets and pastries, and most ice cream out there is made using their crème anglaise recipe. So in this recipe, I salute that contribution and highlight the marriage of cream, vanilla, and cooked egg yolks. Richer and more luxurious than its Madagascan cousin, this flavor reimagines the American classic with a French accent.

Makes approximately 1 quart

WHOLE MILK	1⅓ CUPS (330G)
HEAVY CREAM	1⅓ CUPS (325G)
GLUCOSE SYRUP	1 TABLESPOON (20G)
VANILLA BEAN	1
EGG YOLKS	8
GRANULATED SUGAR	½ CUP (100G)
VANILLA SUGAR (PAGE 19) OR GRANULATED SUGAR	2 TABLESPOONS (25G)
KOSHER SALT	¼ TEASPOON (2G)
LEMON JUICE	¼ TEASPOON (2G)

In a 4-quart saucepan, place the milk, cream, and glucose syrup. Split open the vanilla bean and scrape the seeds into the saucepan. Reserve the scraped-out pod to make Vanilla Sugar (page 19).

Heat the mixture over medium heat, stirring with a rubber spatula or wooden spoon to keep it from burning, until small bubbles appear around the edges and the temperature reaches 180°F.

In a large bowl, whisk together the egg yolks, granulated sugar, Vanilla Sugar, and salt.

Slowly pour the hot cream mixture into the bowl, stirring constantly.

Pour the mixture back into the pot and cook over medium heat, stirring constantly until it returns to 180°F.

Remove the pot from the heat, immediately stir in the lemon juice, and then strain through a fine-mesh strainer into a clean container.

Fill a large bowl with ice and cold water to make an ice bath.

Put the container into the ice bath and let the base cool to 38°F, stirring occasionally.

Freeze in an ice cream maker according to the manufacturer's instructions.

VANILLA BRÛLÉE

THIS IS A BIT OF A PARTY TRICK AND A CROWD PLEASER. Caramelized sugar and egg custard go together like tomatoes and mozzarella. To make this treat, pack a pre-frozen coffee cup or ramekin with French Vanilla (page 22) ice cream, and leave it in the freezer to harden, the longer the better. Generously coat the surface with granulated sugar and immediately cook the sugar with a blow torch until it caramelizes. Serve immediately.

BOURBON VANILLA

Long before we decided to make our own vanilla extract using bourbon, I was in love with the idea of making a Bourbon Vanilla ice cream. Before I opened my shop, I was just running my ice cream cart in front of the restaurant I owned in Brooklyn. Bourbon was having a moment (yet again) and my bar manager had a real hard-on for the stuff. He lined up all the bourbons from the back bar, plus some other samples, and we made 12 different test batches with different bourbons, and a couple of rye whiskeys. Oddly the more refined (expensive) bourbons were far too subtle. The ryes were mostly too hot. Sitting in plain sight was Old Grand-Dad with a flavor profile that was right down the middle, not too hot, or too sweet, and with enough kick to let you know there was bourbon in those barrels.

Makes approximately 1 quart

Whole Milk	1⅔ cups (414g)
Heavy Cream	1⅔ cups (403g)
Glucose Syrup	2 tablespoons (40g)
Vanilla Bean	1
Granulated Sugar	⅓ cup (69g)
Whole Milk Powder	¼ cup (30g)
Vanilla Sugar (page 19) or Granulated Sugar	2 tablespoons (25g)
Kosher Salt	¼ teaspoon (2g)
Old Grand-Dad Bourbon	2 tablespoons (30g)

In a 4-quart saucepan, combine the milk, cream, and glucose syrup. Split open the vanilla bean and scrape the seeds into the saucepan. Reserve the scraped-out pod to make Vanilla Sugar (page 19).

Heat the mixture over medium heat, stirring with a rubber spatula or wooden spoon to keep it from burning, until small bubbles appear around the edges and the temperature reaches 180°F.

In a large bowl, whisk together the granulated sugar, milk powder, Vanilla Sugar, and salt.

Slowly pour the hot cream mixture into the bowl, stirring constantly.

Pour the mixture back into the pot and cook over medium heat, stirring constantly, until it returns to 180°F.

Remove the pot from the heat, immediately stir in the bourbon, and then strain through a fine-mesh strainer into a clean container.

Fill a large bowl with ice and cold water to make an ice bath.

Put the container into the ice bath and let the base cool to 38°F, stirring occasionally.

Freeze in an ice cream maker according to the manufacturer's instructions.

BURNT HONEY VANILLA

I don't remember why I thought burning honey would be a good idea. It might have been that we were on the heels of making one of our most popular flavors of all time (Salted Caramel Pretzel, page 138) and I was looking for another hit. Caramel got me thinking about when I worked at a French restaurant, where we caramelized honey for a pain perdu recipe. Cooking the soaked bread in the honey gave it a rich and robust identity. So I scraped the vanilla seeds, and added the scraped-out pods, into a pot of hot honey. It was love at first sight watching the pods and seeds cooking away in the boiling honey. There is something satisfying about knowing the beans can take the heat and will combine their essence with the honey's. There is no place for them to go. For this recipe, I recommend a relatively light, neutral honey, like clover or orange blossom. It's getting hammered, so no honeysuckle needed here.

Makes approximately 1 quart

VANILLA BEAN	1
HONEY (SEE HEADNOTE)	½ CUP (173G)
WHOLE MILK	1½ CUPS (367G)
HEAVY CREAM	1½ CUPS (357G)
WHOLE MILK POWDER	¼ CUP (30G)
KOSHER SALT	¼ TEASPOON (2G)
VANILLA EXTRACT	¼ TEASPOON (2G)

Split the vanilla bean open with a sharp knife and scrape the seeds into a 4-quart saucepan. Reserve the scraped-out pod to make Vanilla Sugar (page 19).

Add the honey and bring to a boil over medium heat. Boil for 5 minutes.

Remove the pan from the heat and slowly add the milk and cream. Heat the mixture over medium heat, stirring with a rubber spatula or wooden spoon to keep it from burning, until small bubbles appear around the edges and the temperature reaches 180°F.

In a large bowl, whisk together the milk powder and salt.

Slowly pour the hot cream mixture into the bowl, stirring constantly.

Pour the mixture back into the pot and cook over medium heat, stirring constantly, until it returns to 180°F.

Remove the pot from the heat, immediately stir in the vanilla, and then strain through a fine-mesh strainer into a clean container.

Fill a large bowl with ice and cold water to make an ice bath.

Put the container into the ice bath and let the base cool to 38°F, stirring occasionally.

Freeze in an ice cream maker according to the manufacturer's instructions.

THE HOT FUDGE SUNDAE

The Most Important Sundae in America

Most sundaes are made with vanilla ice cream, especially the most important one of all, the hot fudge sundae. The history is long, with lots of twists and turns, but one thing remains the same, this is the most important sundae in America. Oddly, I regularly meet people who have never had one, and if you fall into that group, I strongly urge you to find the best place nearby and sit down to enjoy one as soon as possible. You won't forget it. Or use the recipe that follows.

Created in Hollywood in 1906, few things conjure visions of America like a hot fudge sundae. It is the platonic ideal of an ice cream sundae, the picture-perfect possibility of everyday indulgence.

My last meal on earth ends with this: Vanilla ice cream layered with hot fudge, covered with whipped cream, more hot fudge, and showered in chopped, salted Spanish Red skin peanuts, and, of course, a cherry on top. Hot and cold, vanilla and chocolate, crunchy and smooth, salty and sweet, it's got it all. Add a whiskey old-fashioned and good night.

Serves 2

....

Warm Morgenstern's Hot Fudge (page 32), reheated in a jar in a pot of simmering water, or in the microwave
½ cup (125g)

Madagascar Vanilla (page 20)
1 pint (300g)

Whipped Cream (page 33)   ½ cup (80g)

Chopped Picosos' Peanuts, salted (hand chopped, please)   ½ cup (77g)

Maraschino Cherries (with stems)   2

....

The assembly of the sundae is just as important as the ingredients. Using two footed sundae glasses, drizzle some fudge around the edge of each glass unevenly. Fill each glass with two scoops of vanilla ice cream to reach just below the rim. Add more hot fudge. Pipe a beautiful corkscrew of Whipped Cream on top ending with a point. Pour just enough fudge over the cream to drip down the glass. Do not add TOO much, or it will melt the whipped cream. Generously cover the cream with the chopped peanuts. Gently perch one maraschino cherry with a stem at the peak. The stems tend to fall off of these puckered red cherries, and the No. 5 red dye will stain your fingers, but please don't serve a hot fudge sundae with a stemless cherry.

MORGENSTERN'S HOT FUDGE

Hot fudge is one of the most important ingredients in any ice cream parlor. Originally invented to serve with vanilla ice cream, typically, milk, cream, and egg yolks are included for a rich creamy sauce. However, for this sundae I've come to believe that the dairy does not add to the flavor of the fudge once combined with the ice cream with which it will be paired, so I have developed a recipe that is just water, cocoa, chocolate, sugar, and corn syrup. The key here is to boil the cocoa and water mixture together to create a smooth, rich, and stable base for the chopped chocolate. This will make the fudge silky and shiny—essential for a storybook hot fudge sundae.

Makes 1¼ cups

Cocoa Powder	⅔ cup (60g)
Granulated Sugar	½ cup (100g)
Light Corn Syrup	2 tablespoons (40g)
Water	1 cup (235g)
Chopped Chocolate (64% cocoa)	½ cup (90g)

Combine the cocoa powder, sugar, corn syrup, and water in a 4-quart saucepan over medium heat and simmer for 20 minutes, stirring constantly with a whisk. The fudge will be thick and bubbly when it is ready.

Remove from the heat and add the chocolate, stirring until the chocolate has melted.

Strain through a fine-mesh strainer into a bowl or clean storage container and let cool before using.

The fudge will hold for 2 weeks in the fridge in a sealed container. It can be reheated in a jar in a pot of simmering water, or in the microwave.

WHIPPED CREAM

WHIPPED CREAM IS IMPORTANT.

A sundae is not a sundae without perfectly whipped cream, and although there's more than one way to whip cream, I think this one's the best when making sundaes. For the perfect hot fudge sundae, the cream needs to be light and airy so you can make a beautiful spiral leading to a peak on which to rest a cherry. It should be lightly sweetened and "whipped" in a whip cream charger (such as an iSi canister). If you don't have a charger, you can put softly whipped cream into a pastry piping bag, with a star tip. Once the cream is whipped, it must be kept cold before serving.

Makes 1 quart

WHIPPING CREAM (36% BUTTERFAT)   2 CUPS (475G)

POWDERED SUGAR   1 TABLESPOON (7G)

Place the cream and the sugar into the canister and seal.

Shake the canister for 1 minute to dissolve the powdered sugar.

Add the charger and shake the canister a few times to distribute the cream and the gas.

Keep cold in the fridge for up to 3 days.

PICOSOS' PEANUTS "A DELIGHT WITH DRINKS!"

Founded in 1966 by the Ibarra brothers in Helotes, Texas, Picosos' have been hand roasting and salting Spanish Reds to perfection for over half a century. Unlike the mealy Runner Peanut, these Spanish Red peanuts have a firm crunch and are never bitter; their red skin clings to the nut adding texture when roasted. In Texas these are sold in gas stations, grocery stores, bars, icehouses—icehouses are a cross between a saloon and a convenience store and Picosos' can be found in small wooden bowls on the bars of most of them. Packaged in tins for bars and in bags for snacking, I met many Texans with a small bag in the glove box. I was introduced to them on a trip to San Antonio with my friend and colleague Julie Farias, a native, at the Texas Ice Service on Blanco Street. We had some beers and I crunched on the peanuts at the bar. "Those are Picosos', they are like a state treasure," Julie said. We grabbed a few bags for the road. Later on that same trip we stopped by Dairy Queen and I got my favorite sundae of all time, the Peanut Buster Parfait. When I was halfway through it, I added a handful of Picosos'. The rest is history. Picosos' aren't fancy or precious, and they are not, as their tagline says, only a delight with drinks; they are also the perfect nut for the perfect sundae.

KING KONG BANANA SPLIT

Before opening Morgenstern's, I hadn't thought that much about the history and provenance of the banana split. I served one on the menu of a very, very pretentious restaurant once, with caramelized bananas, three scoops of ice cream of choice, candied walnuts, and hot fudge, both served on the side, both gilded with gold leaf. It was ridiculous. It was also very popular. Years later, when we were opening Morgenstern's, I decided to do another over-the-top version of the banana split. This would not be available to go. It would be served in a special Japanese glass banana boat. Five scoops of ice cream, Pickled Pineapple, Sesame Caramel sauce, Whipped Cream, and of course, a cherry on top. When I mentioned this to the food editors of *New York* magazine in advance of our opening, they loved it, but asked if we could make the banana split with the five different vanilla ice creams that we would be serving in the shop. That sounded interesting. They took a photo and made it a centerfold in that weeks issue. I attribute the opening day success of our shop, and the subsequent snowball of business, to that image. Thanks, Rob and Robin.

While the split in the photograph featured all of our vanilla ice creams at the time, we never served it that way. In real life, I prefer it with the flavors listed below, they give you a better sampling of what we do at Morgenstern's.

Serves 2

Ripe Banana	1	Pickled Pineapple (page 209), liquid strained	
Bourbon Vanilla (page 26)	1 scoop	Whipped Cream (page 33)	
Salted Chocolate (page 50)	1 scoop	Sesame Caramel (page 121)	
Vietnamese Coffee (page 101)	1 scoop	Luxardo Cherries	
Green Tea Pistachio (page 338)	1 scoop		
Strawberry Guava Sorbet (page 216)	1 scoop		

Peel and split the banana lengthwise and add it to a large Japanese glass banana boat. Line up 3 scoops of ice cream on the bottom, with two more on top. Add some generous portions of Pickled Pineapple between the banana and the dish. Add Whipped Cream to the top of the ice cream scoops and then drizzle with Sesame Caramel. Top with 3 Luxardo cherries.

CHOCOLATE

OLIVE OIL CHARRED EGGPLANT

SALTED CHOCOLATE

BLUEBERRY MILK CHOCOLATE

BITTER CHOCOLATE

ROCKIEST ROAD

RICKY ROAD

CHOCOLATE

If vanilla is the default ice cream choice, chocolate is the default indulgence. If you want something sexy and compelling, but don't want to think about it too much, chocolate is just exciting enough to check that box.

I should be sick of chocolate. I worked for a chocolate manufacturing company for years early in my career, melting, tempering, and filling chocolate molds by hand. It does not matter how skilled you are, when you work with chocolate, it will get on your hands, then into your blood. Twelve-hour shifts, day after day, week after week, I felt like I was submerged in it. I would come home, take a long shower and, for better or worse, still be told I smelled of chocolate when I got into bed.

The word alone conjures a long list of applications. With its endless, varied identities, you'll find chocolate in everything from face masks to candy, candles to cake. But when it comes to chocolate in ice cream, you're talking about a very specific medium. Most chocolate ice cream tastes like instant hot cocoa; its bland flavor is probably why kids love it. If you are going to make chocolate ice cream that really tastes like chocolate, you have to put your back into it. You'll need to use a few different chocolates, cocoa powder, and SALT. Do not forget the salt.

A LITTLE BIT ABOUT CHOCOLATE

I can't get into the true origins of chocolate here, as that would be its own book. I will abbreviate, and tell you that in the beginning chocolate was mostly consumed as a beverage by the Mayans (and later the Spaniards.) Eventually the Spaniards figured out how to separate the cocoa mass from the cocoa butter to create cocoa cake or pure cocoa, and then added cocoa butter back into the cocoa cake with sugar to make the beta version of what we today know as chocolate. This process has evolved, with ups and downs, and what we enjoy now is very different from what the ancients consumed as a beverage built around ritual hundreds of years ago. This was very exciting for everyone swapping tea for bitter hot cocoa, but the real revolution in chocolate came with sugar, and later milk (powder) which combined with cocoa to create the everyday craving that is still being satiated today.

Chocolate flavor has lots of different determining parts: what type of cocoa bean it is made from (there are three), where the beans were grown, how they were fermented and processed, and how much cocoa solids or cocoa liquor the chocolate has in it.

Cocoa Content
This commonly shows up on packaging as a percentage, like 76%. Basically the 76% is the chocolate bit, and the other 24% is the sugar, cocoa butter, milk powder or solids for milk chocolate, along with some other bits and bobs, like vanilla, lecithin, and maybe salt.

Origin
The next factor to consider in chocolate selection is the origin of the bean. Single-origin chocolate is chocolate that is made with cocoa pods grown in the same place. It is very common for chocolate to be made with beans from different places to help balance flavor and, more importantly, costs. Single-origin chocolates can have flavors that are more clear or pure. This may not come as a surprise, but my favorite single-origin chocolate comes from Madagascar. It has the perfect balance of bright acidity and mellow alkaline sweetness and the cocoa content is right in the middle at 64%. However, that does not mean that they are better. Great chocolate manufacturers take the blending process very seriously and are using high quality beans from all over the world. I do not personally love all single-origin chocolate as the flavor can be strong, one dimensional, and overpowering.

Dark Chocolate
When it comes to chocolate, dark chocolate is the default. This is strange to me because we consume so much more milk chocolate in the United States. I would argue that if you gave most Americans the choice between milk chocolate ice cream and dark chocolate ice cream, they are going to choose milk chocolate. In fact I know this to be true because our salted (milk) chocolate ice cream outsells our

chocolate ice cream 2 to 1. Having said that, for the chocolate purist, there is nothing like dark chocolate. It is rich and complex, and far less sweet. Dark chocolates come in a very broad range of cocoa contents from about 45% on the low end, all the way up to 99%, which is unsweetened. At Morgenstern's we use 55%, 58%, 62%, 64% (my favorite), 72%, 88%, and 99%. I use these individually (especially if they are single-origin) as well as together for different flavor combinations, and for applications with different ingredients. I love using a combination of lighter cocoa content chocolate with a small percentage of high cocoa content in our dark chocolate ice cream.

Milk Chocolate

After the 64% Madagascar chocolate, my next favorite is a 49% dark milk chocolate, also from Madagascar. Traditionally milk chocolate is about 33% cocoa, but chocolate makers are starting to make higher cocoa content milk chocolates. At the shop we use 38% and 49%. These are milky sweet and balanced, with strong cocoa undertones, perfect for ice cream making. These high cocoa content bars scratch the milk chocolate itch, with more chocolate back bone than their candy shelf cousins.

White Chocolate

White chocolate is a weird product. It is not technically chocolate, as it is made from cocoa butter, milk solids, and sugar, sans cocoa mass. Lots of people argue that the flavor of chocolate comes from the cocoa mass, which is probably true. Whether you think it is chocolate or not, the real trouble with white chocolate is that it's usually poorly made, using lots of sugar and additives that make it sweet and waxy. It's Easter Bunny chocolate, not taken seriously. If you can get a high-quality white chocolate, its actually pretty interesting, especially if you start to cook it and caramelize some of the sugar in the recipe. Historically, I don't work with white chocolate, though I have been brought around to it recently. It has its place and complements things like citrus or olive oil, but you will not find a recipe for it here. Call me biased, I don't care.

Cocoa!

Rich, pure, and luxurious chocolate. For years, that was all I used in all of the chocolate ice creams at Morgenstern's. There are too many bad ice creams made with large quantities of cocoa powder and little to no chocolate, so I left cocoa out of the equation entirely. Cocoa always seemed cheap to me, great for instant hot chocolate or box cakes (I love both), but not good enough for ice cream. After years of working toward the platonic ideal of (dark) chocolate ice cream, one that was deep and rich and satisfying, I was stumped. Something was missing. It was obvious after I took a look at one of our most popular recipes for chocolate sorbet which was loaded with cocoa powder. As we started to add cocoa to the base, little by little, it became clear that this was the way to balance the recipe. Good quality unsweetened cocoa adds a depth and mellow bitterness to ice cream that cannot be achieved with chocolate alone. Use it with judicious intention and it performs wonders.

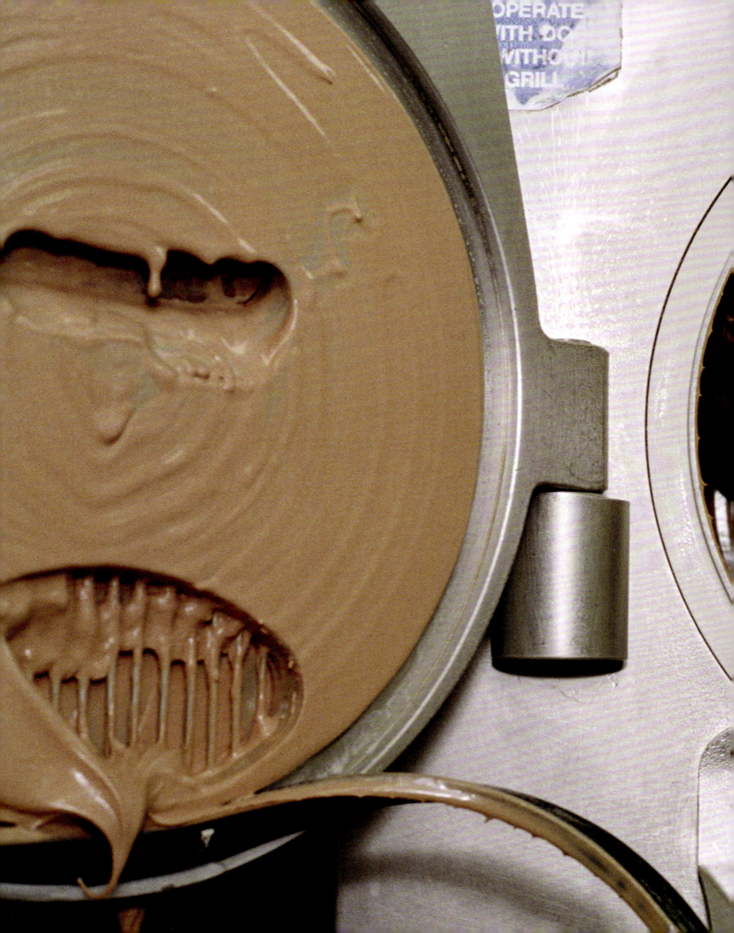

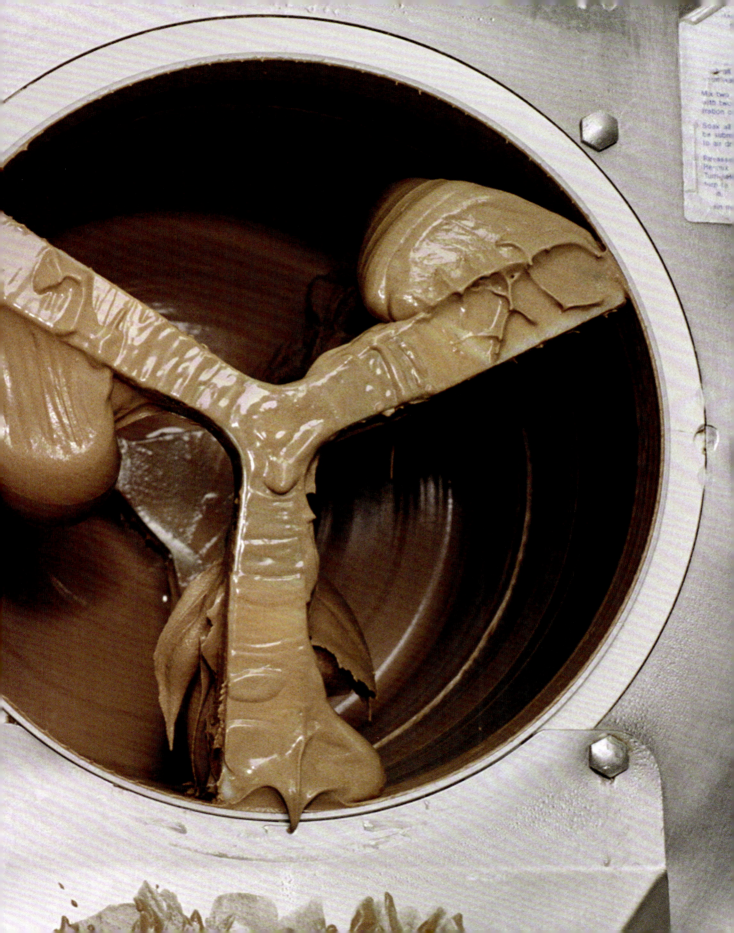

CHOCOLATE

When I started out making ice cream, I began with all the different flavors I wanted to eat myself. So I made all the vanillas, the caramels, and the coffees. Of course, I made chocolate ice cream, but instead of the standard dark chocolate, I made a new flavor, Salted Chocolate (page 50), something unusual and addictive in its own way. Sometimes an ingredient is overhyped so much that I reflexively ignore it. Once I circled back and took a closer look at dark chocolate ice cream, I realized I had a chocolate blind spot—and this recipe was born.

Makes approximately 1 quart

Heavy Cream	1½ cups (357g)
Whole Milk	1⅓ cups (330g)
Glucose Syrup	1 tablespoon (20g)
Granulated Sugar	¾ cup (150g)
Whole Milk Powder	2 tablespoons (15g)
Cocoa Powder	2 tablespoons (12g)
Kosher Salt	¼ teaspoon (2g)
Chopped Dark Chocolate (64% cocoa)	¼ cup (45g)
Chopped Dark Chocolate (62% cocoa)	½ cup (90g)

Combine the cream, milk, and glucose syrup in a 4-quart saucepan. Heat the mixture over medium heat, stirring with a rubber spatula or wooden spoon to keep it from burning, until small bubbles appear around the edges and the temperature reaches 180°F.

In a large bowl, whisk together the sugar, milk powder, cocoa powder, and salt.

Slowly pour the hot cream mixture into the bowl, stirring constantly.

Pour the mixture back into the pot and cook over medium heat, stirring constantly, until it returns to 180°F.

Remove from the heat, add the chocolates, and blend with an immersion blender until smooth. Immediately strain through a fine-mesh strainer into a clean container.

Fill a large bowl with ice and cold water to make an ice bath.

Put the container into the ice bath and let the base cool to 38°F, stirring occasionally.

Freeze in an ice cream maker according to the manufacturer's instructions

CHOCOLATE FOILS

At Morgenstern's, we don't dump a lot of stuff into our ice creams, which is traditionally the way that chocolate ice cream is pimped out—by adding lots of extras to it. While I appreciate Rocky Road, I don't need ice cream that has a core of jelly, peanut butter, cotton candy, etc. Aren't we past the super slurpy Big Gulp archetype—why not just dump a bag of sugar into your mouth? Chocolate is a dynamic entity, powerful and subtle at the same time. It warrants an appropriate dance partner. It deserves a strong foil. For me, these are collaborators that enhance, surprise, and delight, adding depth to an already exciting ingredient.

Chocolate needs to be balanced differently in ice cream than when creating chocolate bonbons or a chocolate dessert. With every flavor at Morgenstern's we are balancing the flavor of dairy with sugar, salt and acid. This balancing is even more important with chocolate forcing us to turn up the volume on a few key elements to create new flavors.

Salt & Chocolate
A delicious match. I would argue that, when it comes to chocolate ice cream, salt and milk chocolate are the most important combo. It's really salty and sweet, as milk chocolate has as much as double the sugar of dark chocolate. Adding salt balances this sweetness. Salt enhances all chocolate experiences, especially chocolate ice cream.

Tart & Chocolate
Most chocolate is quite acidic, which makes the combination of chocolate and acid unexpected. Adding acidity to chocolate creates a new flavor dynamic: an exciting combination of bright with bitter, toasty with sharp. We love blueberry or lemon and milk chocolate, orange and dark chocolate, and even pineapple and white chocolate.

Char & Chocolate
The chocolate industrial complex has done an amazing job of making burned chocolate taste sweet and luxurious. Most chocolate in the world is made from cocoa beans that have been over fermented, burned, and then blended with lots of sugar and other garbage to cover up the taste. I personally love the flavors of char and bitter, especially with chocolate. It takes the richest notes and turns them up a notch, uplifting the cocoa flavor to its full, heady potential. We love burning all the sugar in a recipe, or cooking the chocolate in the oven until the edges burn, deliciously personified in charred eggplant (see page 47) with super dark chocolate (72% cocoa or more). Both bitter caramel and burned bananas also go beautifully with milk chocolate.

OLIVE OIL CHARRED EGGPLANT

I LOVE EGGPLANT. It's a sponge that soaks up flavors. I'm not the first or last person to do eggplant with chocolate, but maybe the first in ice cream? Doesn't matter, chocolate and eggplant go together. This recipe takes you to the deeper, darker reaches of where chocolate goes if you push its alkaline limits. You must use the darkest, most astringent high cocoa content chocolate possible. I love using long thin Japanese eggplants for this, as the ratio of skin to flesh is higher. Fresh olive oil is critical to bind everything together, but use something mellow, nothing green or spicy. This recipe takes time, and commitment, but the technique is worth it, and can be applied to other ingredients; roasting fruit with oil and chocolate brings out a unique flavor.

Makes approximately 1 quart

Chopped Dark Chocolate (75% cocoa) ½ cup (90g)

Eggplant (I prefer Japanese, but any kind will do) 3½ ounces (100g) (approx. 1 small eggplant)

Olive Oil 3 tablespoons (35g)

Kosher Salt, plus more for the eggplant ¼ teaspoon (2g)

Whole Milk 1¼ cups (306g)

Heavy Cream 1¼ cups (298g)

Glucose Syrup 1½ tablespoons (30g)

Granulated Sugar ⅔ cup (138g)

Whole Milk Powder 2 tablespoons (15g)

Cocoa Powder 2 tablespoons (12g)

Preheat your oven to 300°F.

Melt the chocolate in a double boiler, or in a microwave, if you must, and set aside.

Prepare the eggplant: If your eggplant is large, quarter and then slice into about ½-inch-thick pieces. If using a smaller eggplant, like a Japanese, Chinese, or Fairy Tale, you can just slice it into ½-inch-thick rounds. Toss the eggplant with the olive oil and a pinch of salt and lay the pieces out in a single layer in a shallow baking dish. Pour all of the melted chocolate over the top and spread it so that it covers all of the eggplant.

Bake in the oven for 15 to 20 minutes, until the chocolate is bubbling and starts to char a bit at the edges. Set aside while you make the ice cream base.

In a 4-quart saucepan, heat the milk, cream, and glucose syrup over medium heat, stirring with a rubber spatula or wooden spoon to keep it from burning, until small bubbles appear around the edges and the temperature reaches 180°F.

In a large bowl, whisk together the sugar, milk powder, cocoa powder, and the ¼ teaspoon of salt.

Slowly pour the hot cream mixture into the bowl, stirring constantly.

Pour the mixture back into the pot and cook over medium heat, stirring constantly, until it returns to 180°F.

Remove from the heat and immediately strain through a fine-mesh strainer into a clean container.

Scrape all of the eggplant chocolate mixture into the container and blend into the strained ice cream base with a blender or immersion blender.

Fill a large bowl with ice and cold water to make an ice bath.

Put the container into the ice bath and let the base cool to 38°F, stirring occasionally.

Freeze in an ice cream maker according to the manufacturer's instructions.

SALTED CHOCOLATE

How many expectant fathers have been sent to Morgenstern's moments before closing, in the dead of winter, to pick up four pints of Salted Chocolate ice cream? Enough to make it an anecdote in this book. We use salt in all of our ice cream, but especially with chocolate, and absolutely with milk chocolate. You need the salt to balance the sweetness of the chocolate, not to combat it. The resulting balance is addictive.

Makes approximately 3¼ cups

··································

Whole Milk	1¼ cups (306g)
Heavy Cream	1¼ cups (290g)
Glucose Syrup	1 tablespoon (20g)
Granulated Sugar	½ cup (100g)
Whole Milk Powder	2 tablespoons (15g)
Kosher Salt	¾ teaspoon (6g)
Chopped Milk Chocolate (38%)	¾ cup (130g)

··································

Heat the milk, cream, and glucose syrup in a 4-quart saucepan, over medium heat, stirring with a rubber spatula or wooden spoon to keep it from burning, until small bubbles appear around the edges and the temperature reaches 180°F.

In a large bowl, whisk together the sugar, milk powder, and salt.

Slowly pour the hot cream mixture into the bowl, stirring constantly.

Pour the mixture back into the pot and cook over medium heat, stirring constantly, until it returns to 180°F.

Remove from the heat and add the milk chocolate to the pot. Using an immersion blender, blend until fully melted and incorporated, then immediately strain through a fine-mesh strainer into a clean container.

Fill a large bowl with ice and cold water to make an ice bath.

Put the container into the ice bath and let the base cool to 38°F, stirring occasionally.

Freeze in an ice cream maker according to the manufacturer's instructions.

BLUEBERRY MILK CHOCOLATE

Years ago, I started to get asked to judge pie baking contests. I love pie; however, I am not necessarily more qualified than anyone else to judge it. This has been pointed out to me more than once, but never more memorably than by an older gentleman from Michigan, who insisted that the best a la mode pie combo was blueberry pie with chocolate ice cream. I was dubious. This was not a combo I had ever considered, but once I tried it, it was obvious: fruit and chocolate are great together, and while strawberry, raspberry, or orange are the usual choices, blueberry is special, its fruity acidity compliments the chocolate beautifully.. This flavor has become a cult classic on our list. If you have good tart fresh blueberries, it will be even better.

Makes approximately 1 quart

Heavy Cream	1½ cups (357g)
Whole Milk	½ cup (123g)
Glucose Syrup	1½ tablespoons (30g)
Granulated Sugar	⅔ cup (138g)
Whole Milk Powder	2 tablespoons (15g)
Kosher Salt	¼ teaspoon (2g)
Chopped Milk Chocolate (38% cocoa)	¾ cup (135g)
Blueberry Puree	1 cup (245g)
Lemon Juice	2 tablespoons (10g)

Heat the cream, milk, and glucose syrup in a 4-quart saucepan over medium heat, stirring with a rubber spatula or wooden spoon to keep it from burning, until small bubbles appear around the edges and the temperature reaches 180°F.

In a large bowl, whisk together the sugar, milk powder, and salt.

Slowly pour the hot cream mixture into the bowl, stirring constantly.

Pour the mixture back into the pan and cook over medium heat, stirring constantly, until it returns to 180°F.

Remove from the heat, add the chocolate, and blend with an immersion blender until smooth, then immediately strain through a fine-mesh strainer into a clean container.

Fill a large bowl with ice and cold water to make an ice bath.

Put the container into the ice bath and let the base cool to 38°F, stirring occasionally.

Mix in the blueberry puree and lemon juice and freeze in an ice cream maker according to the manufacturer's instructions.

BITTER CHOCOLATE

THIS RECIPE IS VEGAN, so not technically ice cream. But with its intense bitter chocolate flavor and rich luxurious texture, it is already in a class of its own. The key is the burnt sugar, which is extremely bitter, but brings a backbone of flavor and texture which complements the two types of high cocoa content chocolate and helps balance the flavor of the coconut cream. You can make this with a lower cocoa content chocolate, but it will not have the same rich chocolate flavor or texture.

Makes approximately 3½ cups

....

RICE MILK	1¼ CUPS (306G)
COCONUT CREAM	1 CUP (240G)
ALMOND MILK	⅓ CUP (85G)
GLUCOSE SYRUP	2 TABLESPOONS (40G)
LIGHT AGAVE SYRUP	1½ TABLESPOONS (32G)
GRANULATED SUGAR	½ CUP (100G)
COCOA POWDER	2 TABLESPOONS (15G)
KOSHER SALT	¼ TEASPOON (2G)
CHOPPED DARK CHOCOLATE (72% COCOA)	½ CUP (90G)
CHOPPED DARK CHOCOLATE (88% COCOA)	⅓ CUP (55G)

....

In a 2-quart saucepan, heat the rice milk, coconut cream, almond milk, glucose syrup, and agave over medium heat, stirring with a rubber spatula or wooden spoon to keep it from burning, until small bubbles appear around the edges and the temperature reaches 160°F.

Place the sugar in a 4-quart saucepan large enough to accommodate the rice milk and coconut cream mixture.

Cook the sugar on medium high heat, stirring constantly with a wooden spoon. It will begin to liquify and caramelize. Stir the sugar so that it cooks evenly, scraping any stuck sugar caramel from the pot and or spoon. Once the sugar is all liquid, cook until it smokes slightly at the edges. It will be a dark amber/black color. Remove from the heat and carefully add a quarter of the coconut mixture. BE CAREFUL! It will steam violently and can burn your hands or face. Swirl the coconut mixture until it is incorporated and then add another quarter of the mixture. Swirl to incorporate and add the final half of the mixture.

Heat the mixture over medium heat, stirring with a rubber spatula or wooden spoon to keep it from burning, until small bubbles appear around the edges and the temperature reaches 180°F.

In a large bowl, whisk together the cocoa powder and salt.

Slowly pour the hot mixture into the bowl, stirring constantly.

Pour the mixture back into the pot and cook over medium heat, stirring constantly, until it returns to 180°F.

Remove from the heat, add the chocolates, and blend with an immersion blender until smooth.

Immediately strain through a fine-mesh strainer into a clean container.

Fill a large bowl with ice and cold water to make an ice bath.

Put the container into the ice bath and let the base cool to 38°F, stirring occasionally.

Freeze in an ice cream maker according to the manufacturer's instructions.

ON BROWNIES

The brownie has existed in America for about 100 years as the more chocolatey counterpart to one of the most American portable treats, the chocolate chip cookie. Brownies are great. Leave them in your pocket for a day while running around at school, and the resulting confection is better than when you got off the bus that morning. Delicious. Ice cream has been topping brownies for almost as long as they have both been served in America. Unfortunately, brownie sundaes seem to have fallen out of favor, not portable enough for a cup or cone, and a cop-out on restaurant dessert menus. Which is strange, as making brownies, fudge sauce, and whipped cream are all very easy. (Be warned; if you do find one on a restaurant dessert menu, the probability that all the components came from the Sysco freezer truck is high. I'd avoid it.) Cold ice cream melting into a warm brownie topped with whipped cream and hot fudge running over will make you an afterschool hero.

BROWNIE SUNDAE

This is a very simple sundae with a few key ingredients. The brownie is the most important element, and I prefer something fudgy as in the recipe following. It should be moist and served at just above room temperature. You can warm it in the oven for 30 seconds or so if you like, but it should hold its shape and not melt the ice cream too fast.

Serves 1

Sundae Brownies (page 60)	1 square	Toasted Sliced Almonds	2 tablespoons
Vanilla Ice Cream (your choice)		Hotter Fudge (page 61)	
Whipped Cream (page 33)		Maraschino Cherries	1

Place the brownie on the plate, add 1T hot fudge on top of the brownie followed by 1T toasted almonds, add one scoop of ice cream on top, a nice rosette of Whipped Cream, about a tablespoon of chocolate fudge, , add 1T toasted almonds and of course a maraschino cherry with stem on top.

SUNDAE BROWNIES

THIS IS NOT THE DURABLE after school lunchbox brownie. This is barely set melted chocolate suspended in eggs and a little flour. Add vanilla ice cream and hot fudge and you have the Second Coming. These are best baked early in the morning, allowed to cool to room temperature, and then eaten that afternoon or evening. They can be warmed slightly before serving.

Makes one 12 x 9 pan of brownies

NONSTICK SPRAY	
CHOPPED DARK CHOCOLATE (72% COCOA)	1¼ CUPS (225G)
UNSALTED BUTTER	⅓ CUP (85G), CUT INTO PIECES
EGGS	2
GRANULATED SUGAR	¾ CUP (150G)
CORNSTARCH	3 TABLESPOONS (30G)
COCOA POWDER	1 TABLESPOON (6G)
BITTER CHOCOLATE (88% COCOA), CUT INTO CHUNKS	⅔ CUP (115G)

Preheat your oven to 325°F. Coat a small baking tray, approximately 12 x 9 x 1-inch, with nonstick spray, cover with a piece of parchment paper, and spray the paper.

In a double boiler (or the microwave, if you must) heat the chocolate and butter until they have melted. Do not burn them.

Whisk the eggs and sugar together in a large bowl until the sugar has dissolved.

Add the chocolate/butter mixture and whisk to combine.

Sift the cornstarch and cocoa powder over the top and gently fold in using a rubber spatula.

Fold in the chocolate chunks and pour the mixture into the prepared tray.

Bake for 20 to 25 minutes, until the brownies just start to release from the edge of the pan.

Cool to room temperature. Turn the entire pan out onto a cutting board and remove the parchment paper. Cut into 3 x 3-inch squares and keep in an airtight container. They will be delicious for 24 hours.

HOTTER FUDGE

Unfortunately, most of our collective exposure to fudge comes from shelf-stable plastic squeeze bottles. Raw eggs, cream, and loads of bitter chocolate make this recipe stick to the roof of your mouth and clog your arteries—much better. Make it at the end of the year, before resolutions. This fudge comes out thick and gooey. It will have the consistency of peanut butter when it is cooled.

Makes about 1½ cups

Water	½ cup (118g)
Granulated Sugar	3 tablespoons (37g)
Unsalted Butter	3 tablespoons (45g)
Chopped Dark Chocolate (58 to 64% cocoa)	1¼ cups (225g)
Egg Yolks	3
Light Corn Syrup	2 tablespoons (40g)

Bring the water, sugar, and butter to a boil in a 4-quart medium saucepan over medium heat. Simmer for about 10 minutes, or until the mixture has reduced and thickens. Remove from the heat and add the chocolate and blend completely, scraping down the sides of the pot. Add the egg yolks and mix to incorporate, again scraping down the sides of the pot. Add the corn syrup, stir, and strain the fudge through a fine-mesh strainer into a glass jar with a lid. Cool and cover. The fudge sauce will keep in the refrigerator for up to 2 weeks.

CHOCOLATE CANDIES AND THEIR PLACE IN ICE CREAM

Almost all the candy I eat has chocolate in it. Mostly I'm eating SNICKERS in the afternoon for a little energy boost, but I also love candy for the weird fun nostalgia of it, as a mix in for ice cream, and a fertile ground for flavor inspiration. The most important thing to acknowledge is the texture that candy bars add. Most of them are chocolate—with something crunchy, almost always proprietary if they are popular. If you can't beat 'em, join 'em.

Hershey's Bar
Created in the 1900s by the confectioner bearing the same name, Hershey's has become synonymous with chocolate for most of us in America. I have to admit I love Hershey's squares; the familiar soft snap of the bar with its signature sweet and slightly sour milky flavor profile exerts a nostalgic pull that still resonates with me today. As far as I'm concerned, if you are making s'mores with something else, you are doing it wrong.

Culturally, it is looked down upon to prefer sweet creamy milk chocolate over more potent dark chocolate, but the fact is most Americans prefer sweeter chocolate, which means milk chocolate. Most milk chocolate, especially Hershey's, is made with very low cocoa content, around 30%.

The flavor of the Hershey's chocolate bar has informed many, many people's taste for chocolate. It is good to remember this when thinking about how we eat chocolate now. That unusual and unexpected combo of sweet and sour endures today. It might have something to do with the popularity of our salted chocolate flavor.

Reese's Pieces
Everyone loves a Reese's Peanut Butter Cup, and I can assure you that if you're running an ice cream shop, they will be one of the most popular flavors on your menu if added to vanilla or peanut butter ice cream. But pause for a moment and consider one of my favorite candies of all time, Reese's Pieces. These make an outstanding mix-in for peanut butter ice cream, and I would argue the candy shell offers a better texture for the peanut butter flavor. One of my favorite versions of peanut butter ice cream uses both Reese's Pieces and Reese's Peanut butter cups.

Almond Joy

While I love this candy bar, and always will, it is not appropriate as a mix in for ice cream. The coconut candy filling gets hard and flaky, losing its signature chew. But as a flavor inspiration it is as classic as it gets, coconut ice cream with chocolate and toasted almonds is like a coconut rocky road.

Butterfinger

Made famous in the '90s with Bart Simpson's "nobody better lay a finger on my Butterfinger" commercials, there is nothing quite like a Butterfinger: chocolate covered peanut butter corn flake and molasses taffy filling. The filling is what makes this bar so special, and while it works as an ice cream filling, the best version I have ever had is mixed into a milk shake, or blizzard. Those peanut buttery bits are the perfect compliment for softened ice cream.

Heath Bar

A classic ice cream mix in, chocolate covered toffee pieces crushed and mixed into Kahlúa coffee ice cream make an outstanding mudslide stand in.

Junior Mints

This is a weird one, and warrants an explanation (read the essay on page 64). A hazardously melty candy, many people prefer the texture of a frozen Junior Mint, making them an ideal mix in. Their menthol minty flavor can be a hurdle that many people don't appreciate, so I recommend incorporating them carefully, and sometimes silently. They make a delicious surprise at the bottom of a cone.

"THE ORIGINS OF THE MULIE FAJITAS PICOSO' CLASSIC SUNDAE"
by Julie Farias

Nicholas and I were working together at FiveNinth. Days off were rare. When I did have one, I usually planned a day of sleeping late, grabbing some pizza and bourbon, and snacking on Junior Mints as I binge-watched *The Sopranos* with a barely working AC. (Note: this is me not complaining about a minute of this.)

Between FiveNinth and Bay Ridge, in Red Hook, there was a liquor store called LeNell's, which had the most fantastic bourbon selection that any poor sous chef could afford. The owner, LeNell, would come up with the best suggestions according to price, mood, or food. She knew that I had a limited income and a sophisticated palate (champagne taste on a Budweiser budget). When I said, "I'm gonna eat Junior Mints and hole up in my bedroom to watch *The Sopranos*, what do you recommend?" she gave me a bottle of Old Grand-Dad Bonded. It was cheap and had a cinnamon-like taste on the palate that ended with a slightly sweet finish that was perfect, according to LeNell, for Junior Mints and *The Sopranos*. What I didn't know at the time was what bonded (aged to 100 proof, according to government standards) meant. This will be important later in the story.

I started my day off sipping, the precursor to day-drinking, while changing the sheets, and generally getting everything ready for my well-planned agenda. I got wasted . . . like super wasted. I was eating my soft, melty Junior Mints paired with that Old Grand-Dad, loving every drunk minute of it. I passed out before *The Sopranos* ended.

When I woke up, which was probably around four in the morning, the bed was wet. Shit, I peed myself, I thought, but then I looked at the sheets, and I realized it was worse: I shit myself?! There was dark goo all over my ass. I freaked the fuck out. I was not fully awake, and of course, I was still drunk. It took me a second to realize I fell asleep on the box of Junior Mints, and they melted all over my ass. I also spilled what was left of the bourbon, which I had placed between my legs when I had passed out. After I realized what had happened, my first thought was, of course, only you would do this: exhausted, drunk on a bonded bottle of bourbon, hanging out in a dark room in the summer.

You would think I would've been embarrassed, but I'm the kind of person that is pretty self-aware about the stupid shit I do, and pretty much everyone around me knows that. So when I went back to work at FiveNinth, Nicholas, with the rest of the team around, asked how my day was—and I spilled it, literally. Well, it was a good day off—I'd discovered an excellent pairing, with a crazy story that is all mine.

MULIE FAJITAS PICOSO' CLASSIC SUNDAE

The story on page 64 informed this recipe. Incorporating Junior Mints into a sundae can be tricky but rewarding. They offer an unexpected burst of menthol relief. This sundae has evolved a bit over the years. The core is the Old Grand-Dad Bourbon Vanilla ice cream, a classic on our menu from the beginning. It is very soothing and a bit sweet, mostly familiar. The taste of American bourbon and vanilla beans is a match made in, well America. We originally made this sundae with hot fudge but transitioned to Bourbon Caramel to keep things smooth. We add Whipped Cream, showers of salted Picosos' peanuts and, of course, those Junior Mints.

Makes 2 sundaes (Serves 4)

....

BOURBON CARAMEL (PAGE 121)   1 CUP (8OZ)

JUNIOR MINTS

BOURBON VANILLA (PAGE 26)   2 CUPS (16OZ)

WHIPPED CREAM (PAGE 33)

PICOSOS' PEANUTS, SALTED, HAND-CHOPPED

....

I prefer a tall glass for this sundae, but let's be honest, cereal bowls might be more appropriate, chilled if possible. Swirl an excessive drizzle of caramel into each glass, or bowl, at least 2 tablespoons. Put a handful of Junior Mints at the bottom. Put two scoops of ice cream into each dish, on top of the Junior Mints. Drizzle with more caramel, add more Junior Mints and a generous portion of Whipped Cream. Add 2 tablespoons of peanuts. Add one more scoop of ice cream, more caramel, and Junior Mints. Finish with Whipped Cream, caramel sauce, and more peanuts. Pour a glass of Old Grand-Dad and enjoy. Don't shit the bed.

ROCKY ROAD

Like most ice cream innovations, the origins of Rocky Road are unclear. Dreyer's or Fenton? Both are from Oakland, California; both have candy making in their DNA. I'm inclined to go with Fenton, the small parlor that stayed small. As the story goes, Melvin Fenton, grandson of the founder, created the flavor in 1929 inspired by a popular candy bar made with marshmallows and walnuts. Given the omnipresence of the staid Neapolitan ice creams of the era, the new flavor was a big deal. Rocky Road is one of the first in a long line of ice cream flavors incorporating candy. It was one of the first to incorporate "mix-ins," and certainly the most popular.

Rocky Road is the darker, sexier answer to Vanilla Chip, or Swiss Almond, and for me the only acceptable kitchen sink ice cream. The combination of almonds, dark chocolate, and marshmallows in rich chocolate ice cream is hard to resist. To this day, it's still one of my favorite flavors.

ROCKIEST ROAD

A CLASSIC ROCKY ROAD should always contain nuts and marshmallows. At Morgenstern's, I also add chocolate chunks and, for good measure, a swirl of fudge. Some people prefer the original recipe, with toasted walnuts, but for me walnuts are overpowering with their bitter skin which makes them unappealing. Marshmallows are the other critical element in Rocky Road. Traditionally these would be squishy, but for a crispy, crunchy texture that melts in your mouth. I use dehydrated marshmallows.

Makes 2 sundaes (Serves 4)

FOR THE ICE CREAM BASE

Whole Milk	1⅓ cups (330g)
Heavy Cream	1⅓ cups (325g)
Glucose Syrup	1½ tablespoons (30g)
Granulated Sugar	¾ cup (150g)
Whole Milk Powder	2 tablespoons (15g)
Cocoa Powder	2 tablespoons (12g)
Kosher Salt	¼ teaspoon (2g)
Chopped Dark Chocolate (64% cocoa)	¼ cup (45g)
Chopped Dark Chocolate (62% cocoa)	½ cup (90g)

MIX-INS

Chopped Toasted Almonds	¼ cup (35g)
Chocolate Chunks	¼ cup (45g)
Dehydrated Mini Marshmallows	½ cup (25g)

Make the ice cream base: Combine the milk, cream, and glucose syrup in a 4-quart saucepan, and heat the mixture over medium heat, stirring with a rubber spatula or wooden spoon to keep it from burning, until small bubbles appear around the edges and the temperature reaches 180°F.

In a large bowl, whisk together the sugar, milk powder, cocoa powder, and salt.

Slowly pour the hot cream mixture into the bowl, stirring constantly.

Pour the mixture back into the pot and cook over medium heat, stirring constantly, until it returns to 180°F.

Remove from the heat, add the chocolates, and blend with an immersion blender until smooth. Immediately strain through a fine-mesh strainer into a clean container.

Fill a large bowl with ice and cold water to make an ice bath.

Put the container into the ice bath and let the base cool to 38°F, stirring occasionally, and freeze in an ice cream maker according to the manufacturer's instructions.

Add the mix-ins once the product has finished freezing, stirring them in gently.

RICKY ROAD

In 2020, *Rick and Morty* was the most streamed show in the world. As I was muddling through the pandemic and we were slowly rebuilding, Warner Bros., and Adult Swim, reached out and asked us to make flavors that embodied some of the show's animated characters. Food, including ice cream, features prominently in many of the episodes and after watching and rewatching every episode in front of a computer with a notepad, I had lots of ideas. However one stood out as so obvious, I could not believe I had not thought of it myself; Rocky Road + Peanut Butter. Chocolate and peanut butter has long been a magical combination and what could be better than introducing that to the Rocky Road concept of marshmallows and nuts? Like Voltron combining forces, this flavor is a new warrior of the dessert class.

Makes approximately 1 quart

....

For the ice cream base

Whole Milk	1⅓ cups (330g)
Heavy Cream	1⅓ cups (325g)
Glucose Syrup	1½ tablespoons (30g)
Granulated Sugar	¾ cup (150g)
Whole Milk Powder	2 tablespoons (15g)
Cocoa Powder	2 tablespoons (12g)
Kosher Salt	¼ teaspoon (2g)
Chopped Dark Chocolate (64% cocoa)	¼ cup (45g)
Chopped Dark Chocolate (62% cocoa)	½ cup (90g)

Mix-Ins

Marshmallow Fluff (page 73)	½ cup (40g)
Peanut Butter Caramel (page 73)	¼ cup (76g)
Chopped Picosos' Peanuts, salted	¼ cup (35g)
Chocolate Chunks	¼ cup (45g)

....

Make the ice cream base: Combine the milk, cream, and glucose syrup in a 4-quart saucepan, and heat the mixture over medium heat, stirring with a rubber spatula or wooden spoon to keep it from burning, until small bubbles appear around the edges and the temperature reaches 180°F.

In a large bowl, whisk together the sugar, milk powder, cocoa powder, and salt.

Slowly pour the hot cream mixture into the bowl, stirring constantly.

Pour the mixture back into the pot and cook over medium heat, stirring constantly, until it returns to 180°F.

Remove from the heat, add the chocolates, and blend with an immersion blender until smooth. Immediately strain through a fine-mesh strainer into a clean container.

Fill a large bowl with ice and cold water to make an ice bath.

Put the container into the ice bath and let the mixture cool to 38°F, stirring occasionally.

Freeze in an ice cream maker according to the manufacturer's instructions.

Add the mix-ins once the product has finished freezing, stirring them in with a spatula to gently incorporate.

MARSHMALLOW FLUFF

Know that making this fluff is a commitment. And it produces a lot more than you'll need for the Ricky Road. If you want something easier, flip to another recipe. That said, the leftovers do make a good topping for most ice creams.

Makes about 3 cups

Granulated Sugar	1 cup (200g)
Light Corn Syrup	¾ cup (246g)
Water	⅓ cup (84g)
Egg Whites, at room temperature	3 (96g)
Heavy Cream	1 tablespoon (15g)

In a 1-quart saucepan, combine the sugar, corn syrup, and water.

Cook the sugar mixture over high heat to 240°F.

Using a stand mixer fitted with the whisk attachment, whisk the egg whites on medium speed until soft peaks form.

Slowly pour the hot sugar syrup down the side of the bowl into the whipping whites.

Whip on high speed until cool.

Once cool, reduce the speed to low, add the cream, and mix until incorporated.

The fluff will hold in a sealed container but should be used immediately..

PEANUT BUTTER CARAMEL

Makes ⅓ cup

Caramel Sauce (page 118)	2½ tablespoons (38g)
Creamy Peanut Butter	2½ tablespoons (35g)
Kosher Salt	pinch of

Combine the Caramel Sauce, peanut butter, and salt in a mixing bowl until smooth.

SMOOTH AND DELICIOUS STRAWBERRY

CHUNKY STRAWBERRY

STRAWBERRY PISTACHIO PESTO

STRAWBERRIES N' CREAM

STRAWBERRY

Vanilla and chocolate are obvious bedfellows and find themselves perpetually intertwined throughout the dessert landscape. In the beginning there was vanilla and then came chocolate; a match made in heaven. Light and dark. Sweet and bitter. High and low. For the last 65 years, these two have firmly held the first and second spots for popularity and sales volume of ice cream flavors in America. Vanilla first and chocolate second. Star-crossed lovers indeed, so what comes next? Bingo. Strawberry. Strawberry is so perpetually overshadowed by chocolate and vanilla; I am still surprised that it has also consistently come in third place for decades. The third wheel is a funny place to be, because it's somewhat of a rebel spot, not attached, not unattached.

Strawberry ice cream lovers are the more low-key members in any group, and quiet about their favorite flavor. The chocolate ice cream lovers are the schmoozers of the bunch, but strawberry lovers are less in-your-face. Like it's a little bit of a secret for them. Most I've met are a little eccentric in their tastes and prefer to keep to themselves, though there must be a lot of them. They are in on their own secret, and they know something that the vanilla and chocolate lovers don't. The bronze medal is still a medal after all.

SMOOTH STRAWBERRY SEASON

My first job in food after I graduated from culinary school was in Heidelberg, Germany, working as a civilian for the US military. Food was a different experience in Germany in the late '90s: Turkish street food was king and, of course, there was hefeweizen beer and bratwurst and schnitzel and potatoes, potatoes, potatoes! Late nights drinking lots of beer and whiskey at techno clubs is one thing, but going to a German Ice Café—small ice cream shops in every town, most of them owner operated—is something not really celebrated the way that it should be.

I spent a day working in one, lazily cutting strawberries. The owner had already started freezing a plain ice cream base, and once it was partially frozen, he added the fresh strawberries and immediately began extracting. He reached straight into the machine and gave me a taste of the ice cream before it was fully frozen: it was a revelation of juicy chilled strawberries and sweet cream.

But before I left, I tasted the flavor again. The strawberries had frozen into ice chunks and the flavor was gone. It was a good reminder to me that, working with fruit in ice cream is very different from working with caramel or chocolate or coffee. Fruit will freeze and become hard and tasteless. Plus, you're adding acidity. Consistency is critical here, even more so for the strawberry ice cream lover who demands a creamy, smooth, and delicious product.

Which brings me to fresh strawberries. Like everything else in New York City, fruits and vegetables are a racket. Life in NYC has deluded its residents into believing that the Union Square farmers' market is amazing. Is it better than the Soviet-style shopping experience of supermarket chains like Gristedes or Key Food? Sure, but it does not compare to the farmers' markets in France, California, or Tokyo, which are loaded with produce from all over the world, with different varieties of bananas stacked next to different varieties of avocados, grapes, musk melons, cabbages, dates, and apricots. The Union Square farmers' market boasts overpriced eggplant, potatoes, parsley, and apples and apples and apples, all of which are occasionally good. I think it makes us feel better to buy produce from the market, and, of course, it's a scene, with lots of energy, and seeing all of that fresh, vibrant food feels novel alongside the piles of garbage lining the streets of the concrete jungle.

For a short period between June and July, New York farmers' markets are home to the Tristar, a hybrid of the wild mountain Utah berry and strains from California and New Jersey, which is mostly grown in the Northeast. A few of the vendors are known for their Tristars, and they sell out in the first few hours each morning.

Tristars are tiny little doll house berries about the size of a marble with a mini beret of a stem. These small berries, once bursting with fruity strawberry juiciness, are now a shadow of their former glory. Over the years, the quality has fallen off dramatically, and what you'll find at stalls these days are often mediocre, small, and watery, boasting one dimensional flavor at an outrageous price.

For years, I avoided making strawberry ice cream at all because working with these Tristar strawberries was such a frustrating exercise. So rather than participate in this ongoing con, at Morgenstern's, all of our strawberry ice cream is made with puree from France. Not only is the flavor more vibrant and well-balanced, it is consistent.

SMOOTH AND DELICIOUS STRAWBERRY

Most of my early pastry experience came working in fine dining French kitchens, which shaped the way I think about desserts. In these restaurants, desserts are high art, whimsical expression of fancy on a plate. They are meant to delight and more important, satisfy the need to indulge. When fruit is in season, it is prepared in different ways that bring out and highlight specific flavor profiles. These years of working in French kitchens conditioned me to understand that fruit is best served in two ways: fresh on the plate, or as a sorbet. What I absorbed was this: Do not sully your fresh fruit with eggs and dairy. There are exceptions but to me it made perfect sense to leave the fruit unadorned if possible. It was this recipe that made clear to me how critical it is to make ice cream without eggs. Eggs add their own flavor and richness, which can be delicious, but get in the way of the subtle nuances that fruits bring to an ice cream. This same logic applies to most other subtle flavors, eggs get in the way.

Makes approximately 3¼ cups

Whole Milk	½ cup (367g)
Heavy Cream	½ cup (119g)
Glucose Syrup	2 tablespoons (40g)
Granulated Sugar	¾ cup (150g)
Whole Milk Powder	⅓ cup (40g)
Kosher Salt	¼ teaspoon (2g)
Strawberry Puree	1 cup (245g)
Lemon Juice	1 tablespoon (15g)

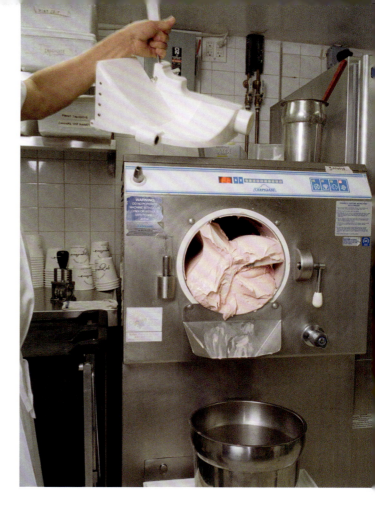

Place the milk, cream, and glucose syrup into a 4-quart saucepan, and heat the mixture over medium heat, stirring with a rubber spatula or wooden spoon to keep it from burning, until small bubbles appear around the edges and the temperature reaches 180°F.

In a large bowl, whisk together the sugar, milk powder, and salt.

Slowly pour the hot cream mixture into the bowl, stirring constantly.

Pour the mixture back into the pot and cook over medium heat, stirring constantly, until it returns to 180°F.

Remove the pan from the heat and immediately strain through a fine-mesh strainer into a clean container.

Fill a large bowl with ice and cold water to make an ice bath.

Put the container into the ice bath and let the base cool to 38°F, stirring occasionally.

Stir in the strawberry puree and lemon juice and freeze in an ice cream maker according to the manufacturer's instructions.

CHUNKY STRAWBERRY

THIS RECIPE CONTRADICTS EVERYTHING I SAID in the headnote for Smooth and Delicious Strawberry, but sometimes you gotta break things up. Most strawberry ice cream is smooth, which only adds to its deliciousness. This is a rich egg custard loaded with a chunky strawberry jam. Unlike the icy frozen chunks I experienced in Germany, here olive oil and egg yolks make this ice cream rich and unctuous, a terrific foil for the sweet acidity of the strawberry jam. Adding pieces of fresh fruit to an ice cream base poses the most basic challenge when it comes to keeping things consistent. (I have already given my opinion of the inconsistent but beloved Union Square Greenmarket Tristar strawberry (see page 76).) But for this flavor, I make an exception. During peak strawberry season, I order cases of strawberries from farms in California. In my opinion these are the best you can get in the United States: big, juicy, and rich. We give them a rough chop and set them with a bit of sugar to make a chunky strawberry jam. We add this into our ice cream as it comes out of the batch freezer to create a rich, frozen, chunky texture. The sugar keeps the strawberries from becoming too icy, but still firm and kind of crunchy.

Note: The jam should ideally be made at least 24 hours before the ice cream is going to be frozen to allow it to cool and set. You can add it the same day if you have no choice, but don't add it hot.

Makes approximately 1 quart

Whole Milk	1⅓ cups (330g)
Heavy Cream	1⅓ cups (325g)
Glucose Syrup	1 tablespoon (20g)
Egg Yolks	7
Granulated Sugar	¾ cup (150g)
Kosher Salt	¼ teaspoon (2g)
Olive Oil	⅓ cup (65g)
Strawberry Jam (recipe follows)	½ cup

In a 4-quart saucepan, heat the milk, cream, and glucose syrup over medium heat, stirring with a rubber spatula or wooden spoon to keep it from burning, until small bubbles appear around the edges and the temperature reaches 180°F.

In a large bowl, whisk together the egg yolks, sugar, and salt.

Slowly pour the hot cream mixture into the bowl, stirring constantly, until well combined.

Pour the mixture back into the pan and cook over medium heat, stirring constantly, until it returns to 180°F.

Remove from the heat, add the olive oil, and immediately strain through a fine-mesh strainer into a clean container.

Fill a large bowl with ice and cold water to make an ice bath.

Put the container into the ice bath and let the base cool to 38°F, stirring occasionally.

Freeze in an ice cream maker according to the manufacturer's instructions.

When the ice cream has finished freezing, stir in the Strawberry Jam. Do not overmix.

STRAWBERRY JAM

Makes 2 cups

Strawberries, trimmed and roughly chopped	3 cups (520g)
Water	3 tablespoons (45g)
Granulated Sugar	¼ cup (50g) plus 1 tablespoon (12g)
Kosher Salt	pinch of
Sure-Jell Original Powdered Pectin (2g; measured by weight rather than volume, if possible)	½ teaspoon
Lemon Juice	1 teaspoon (5g)

Place the strawberries, water, and the ¼ cup (50g) of sugar in a 2-quart small saucepan, and simmer over medium heat to 210°F.

Thoroughly mix the remaining 1 tablespoon (12g) of sugar, the salt, and pectin in a small bowl.

Slowly stir the pectin mixture into the hot jam while whisking constantly.

Return to a full boil, then keep at a lively simmer over medium heat until the liquid starts to thicken, and the surface is covered with thick, viscous bubbles, 6 to 8 minutes.

Remove from the heat and stir in the lemon juice.

Cool to room temperature and then transfer to a container with a seal, cover, and refrigerate for 24 hours before using. The jam will keep in the fridge for 2 weeks.

STRAWBERRY PISTACHIO PESTO

When I opened the shop, I only had one fruit flavored ice cream on the menu; Durian Banana (page 225). Every other fruit flavor was a sorbet. I was content with this until, Gabe Ricter, a longtime employee, gingerly approached me and admitted that he regularly ate a pint of Häagen-Dazs Strawberry ice cream after his closing shift, and selflessly asked if I would ever consider making my own, "for the greater good." At that point I didn't care about fruit ice cream, especially something as obvious as strawberry. Gabe is a highly-intelligent but soft-spoken guy, not prone to rock the Morgenstern's boat. He would not have said anything if he did not think it was important. I was too focused on salted caramel and coffee to see something so obvious.

It was October, and there were no strawberries to be had. We ordered a case of strawberry puree and made a batch. The ice cream was good, but a bit boring for my taste. I've always loved a dessert pesto sauce, made with no garlic or herbs, but sugar and olive oil. We blended up some pistachios and added it to the menu. It was an instant hit and has not come off since.

Makes approximately 1 quart

Whole Milk	1½ cups (367g)
Heavy Cream	½ cup (119g)
Glucose Syrup	2 tablespoons (40g)
Granulated Sugar	¾ cup (150g)
Whole Milk Powder	⅓ cup (40g)
Kosher Salt	¼ teaspoon (2g)
Strawberry Purée	1 cup (245g)
Balsamic Vinegar	1 tablespoon (15g)
Lemon Juice	1 teaspoon (50g)
Pistachio Pesto	approx. ¼ cup

Combine the milk, cream, and glucose syrup in a 4-quart saucepan, and heat the mixture over medium heat, stirring with a rubber spatula or wooden spoon to keep it from burning, until small bubbles appear around the edges and the temperature reaches 180°F.

In a large bowl, whisk together the sugar, milk powder, and salt.

Slowly pour the hot cream mixture into the bowl, stirring constantly.

Pour the mixture back into the pot and cook over medium heat, stirring constantly, until it returns to 180°F.

Remove from the heat and immediately strain through a fine-mesh strainer into a clean container.

Fill a large bowl with ice and cold water to make an ice bath.

Put the container into the ice bath and let the base cool to 38°F, stirring occasionally.

Add the strawberry purée, balsamic vinegar, and lemon juice and freeze in an ice cream maker according to the manufacturer's instructions.

For the pistachio pesto: Preheat your oven to 325°F. Toss 1 cup (140g) pistachios with 1 tablespoon (20g) corn syrup until fully coated, then spread evenly on a baking sheet. Bake for 12 to 15 minutes, until lightly golden brown, then remove from the oven and let cool completely. In a food processor, blend the pistachios with ⅓ cup (65g) olive oil and a pinch of kosher salt until chunky. You can store the pesto for up to 3 weeks in a sealed container at room temperature.

Gently stir in the Pistachio Pesto, to taste, to create ribbons, just before serving.

STRAWBERRIES N' CREAM

For whatever reason, strawberry milk is not for me, and that is what strawberry ice cream reminds me of. What I do love, though, is a bowl of strawberries, and some slightly sweetened whipped cream. This flavor was not possible until we added a freeze-dryer to our operation. Freeze-drying removes all the moisture from the fruit, while leaving behind an ultralight shell of concentrated strawberry flavored crisps. The key to this recipe is the incorporation of the freeze-dried fruit into the ice cream when it comes out of the ice cream machine. The fruit absorbs some of the liquid from the base, making a soft and flavorful strawberry that is not icy whatsoever, but very flavorful.

Makes approximately 1 quart

Heavy Cream	1⅔ cups (403g)
Whole Milk	1½ cups (367g)
Glucose Syrup	2 tablespoons (40g)
Granulated Sugar	¾ cup (150g)
Whole Milk Powder	¼ cup (30g)
Kosher Salt	¼ teaspoon (2g)
Freeze-Dried Strawberries	1 cup (20g)

In a 4-quart saucepan, heat the cream, milk, and glucose syrup over medium heat, stirring with a rubber spatula or wooden spoon to keep it from burning, until small bubbles appear around the edges and the temperature reaches 180°F.

In a large bowl, whisk together the sugar, milk powder, and salt.

Slowly pour the hot cream mixture into the bowl, stirring constantly.

Pour the mixture back into the pan and cook over medium heat, stirring constantly, until it returns to 180°F.

Remove from the heat and immediately strain through a fine-mesh strainer into a clean container.

Fill a large bowl with ice and cold water to make an ice bath.

Put the container into the ice bath and let the base cool to 38°F, stirring occasionally.

Freeze in an ice cream maker according to the manufacturer's instructions. Stir in the freeze-dried strawberries.

BANANA SPLIT

I would love to know how many of these are served each year. It is a dedicated patron who commits to sit down to a plated dessert of this indulgence. As with all iconic ice cream inventions, there is a debate as to when, where, and by whom the banana split was invented. Generally, David Strickler gets the credit; as do Latrobe, Pennsylvania, and the year 1904. Besides the banana, obviously, the thing that sets the classic split apart is the strawberry ice cream with strawberry sauce. Serve in a banana split boat. It does not have to be fancy—though there are lots of fun versions out there, from clear glass to yellow banana shaped porcelain.

Serves 1

Banana, perfectly ripe, no green or brown on the peel	1
Chocolate (page 42)	1 scoop
Smooth and Delicious Strawberry (page 78)	1 scoop
Madagascar Vanilla (page 20)	1 scoop
Crushed Pineapple (page 92)	1 tablespoon
Strawberry Sauce (page 94)	1 tablespoon
Morgenstern's Hot Fudge (page 32)	1 tablespoon
Whipped Cream (page 33)	
Granulated Almonds, toasted	2 tablespoons
Maraschino Cherry (with stem)	1

Peel and split your banana lengthwise and place it in a banana split boat, leave some space between the slices. A moat of melted ice cream and fudge at the bottom of a banana split boat is a sad vision, so I prefer to keep the ice cream scoops at or around 2 ounces each, enough that you can finish an entire split on your own, and enough to share if you must. Start with the strawberry, putting it in the middle with the vanilla and chocolate flanking either side. Add a tablespoon of strawberry sauce on the strawberry ice cream, a tablespoon of pineapple on top of the vanilla, and fudge on the chocolate. Put a rosette of whipped cream on each and shower the chocolate and vanilla with the almonds. Finally add a cherry to the top of the strawberry whipped cream. Serve immediately. Everyone I have ever put this in front of smiles.

CRUSHED PINEAPPLE

For our King Kong Banana Split (page 34), we pickle our pineapple and serve it in large chunks to be enjoyed bite by bite. For a traditional banana split, though, the pineapple should be chopped, or crushed. I prefer to dice it finely to create a textured sauce, which is best if done in advance. I add a vanilla bean to round out the acidity, but nothing else. Pineapple adds a bright bite to the vanilla in your banana split. Why "crushed"? I don't know. I suppose it sounds better than "chopped," even though that's what it often is. Dole makes a crushed pineapple, which is delicious if a little one dimensional. It'll do if you can't get your hands on a fresh pineapple.

Makes apvproximately 2 cups

....

Pineapple, ripe	1
Vanilla Bean	½

....

I recommend a well sharpened chef's knife for this job. Be prepared to resharpen it when you are done, as cleaning a pineapple is like stripping bark from a branch. Cut the top and bottom off the pineapple and trim the sides, top to bottom, working your way around until everything is clean. Carefully remove the "eyes" (dark spots in the flesh left behind from the skin). Cut the pineapple lengthwise in quarters. Trim the core completely from each quarter and discard. Slice and dice the pineapple. Once you have a pile on your cutting board scrape the seeds of the vanilla bean—reserve the scraped-out half pod for Vanilla Sugar (page 19)—on top and chop the pieces like you'd chop herbs, until you have a chunky pulp. Do not even think about using a blender; that will give you pineapple purée, not crushed pineapple. This will keep covered in the refrigerator for up to 3 days, but can turn rancid sooner depending on how ripe the pineapple is. As with anything, taste it before serving.

STRAWBERRY SAUCE

For this we are going to use fresh strawberries. I know I extolled the virtues of strawberry purée earlier on but hear me out. Fresh strawberry purée is all about the seeds. Those annoying little beads found in the far reaches of your gums late at night after you brush. When you use fresh strawberries and blend them with a little sugar, salt, and a little acid, those guys are what ground the frothy mix. They let you know that this sauce was alive not that long ago, and they have sacrificed themselves for your banana split. Enjoy them.

Makes 1 cup

Strawberries, chopped	1½ cups (250g)
Vanilla Sugar (page 19) or Granulated Sugar	2 tablespoons (25g)
Kosher Salt	pinch of
Lemon Juice	

In a 2-quart saucepan, bring the strawberries and Vanilla Sugar to a simmer over medium heat and cook for 5 minutes.

Remove from the heat, add the salt, lemon juice, to taste, and blend until smooth.

Cool and cover. The sauce keeps in the refrigerator for up to 4 days.

NEAPOLITAN

Most of the ice cream that came to the New World in the nineteenth century arrived direct from Napoli, Italy, where one of the regional specialties was three or four different flavors combined in a mold and served in slices. These slices were cut so that the customer received equal amounts of each flavor. The most common combos were vanilla, chocolate, and strawberry, and over time, the term "Neapolitan" has come to mean these three flavors. (Although pistachio may have been the original third partner, later swapped out for the more popular strawberry).

I still love a Neapolitan ice cream sandwich, though I must admit chocolate and vanilla are the first to go, with strawberry last, melting and left out, the perpetual third wheel.

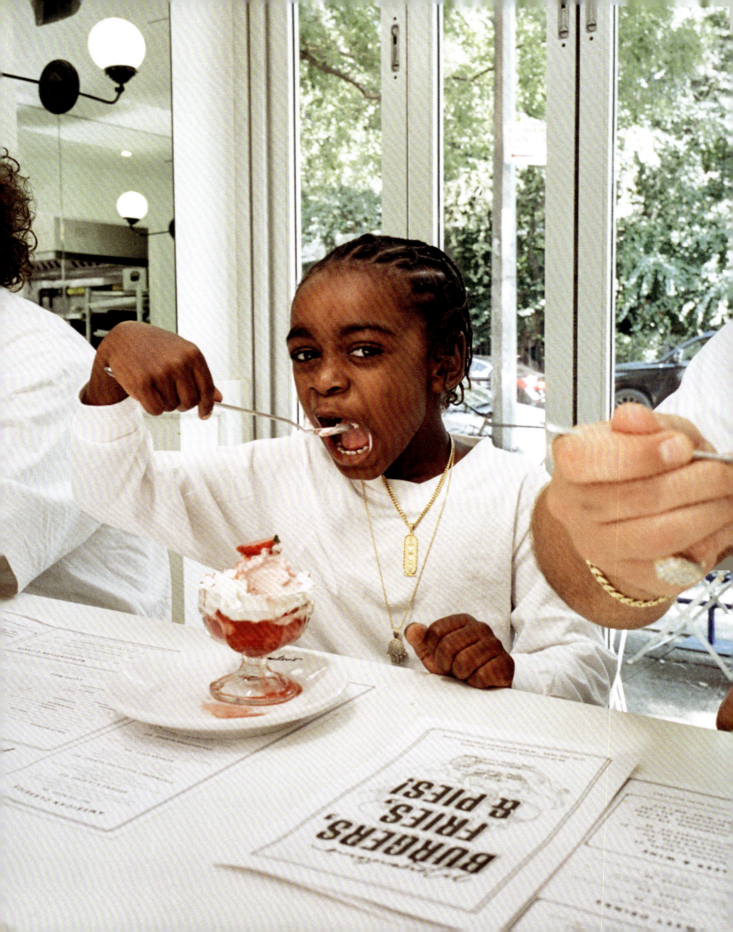

VIETNAMESE COFFEE

COFFEE CRISP

COCONUT ESPRESSO

COFFEE

When I started selling ice cream in 2009, everything was served from a cart that had space for six flavors. The restriction created a framework, and coffee was always in the mix—along with vanilla, chocolate, caramel, a chef's choice, and a sorbet. Although we now have 14 categories on our menu, coffee is still one of the top five best sellers. The range of possible flavors from the mysterious coffee bean is enormous, creating ever more interest among consumers, and more experimental combinations for us, at Morgenstern's, to explore.

When it comes to sourcing coffee for ice cream, there are two things that matter the most: where the beans are coming from and who is roasting them, and these factors are not mutually exclusive. Trust your palate. Brewed coffee, whether espresso or drip, will taste much different in the cup than it will in the scoop. For a very long time, coffee roasting culture has prized ultra-high acid coffees. That's the profile of most of the stuff that wins barista competitions coming—largely—out of Ethiopia. But when making ice cream, I prefer coffee with robust rich flavors over bright acidity. I am more interested in, for instance, an Italian style, roasted a little bit darker, with a richer, more chocolate syrupy kind of flavor. A little bit dustier or dirtier, not as bright and clear. That might sound counterintuitive, but once you add it to ice cream, that's the coffee that stands up to the cream, milk, and sugar.

Mine was the first restaurant in New York to have a La Marzocco—that's the super high-end espresso machine—and I was trained by Counter Culture coffee roasters out of Durham, NC, who taught me how to brew a proper cup of drip coffee, pull a shot of espresso, and steam milk. Then I applied that knowledge to ice cream making. All the usual criteria that make a great cup—in addition to the balance of how much coffee you add—will (usually) make a great scoop.

COFFEE BREWS

There are a few different ways to add coffee to ice cream. I prefer to use brewed coffee, ground beans, shots of espresso, or some combination of the three, I never use extract, and rarely use instant.

Brewed

Drip coffee is a great way to add a subtle coffee flavor to ice cream. We will often remove some of the milk from a recipe and replace it with drip coffee. This is the least labor intensive and gives a coffee flavor very similar to coffee ice cream you might get from Häagen-Dazs. I think of this as a caffè latte, where the coffee is very milky and sweet; the most subdued coffee flavor on our menu.

Ground

Grind your coffee! This is the most effective way to give a strong coffee punch to an ice cream. The coffee should be ground fresh, as close to the time the ice cream base is being cooked as possible. We usually have the cream heated before we grind. The fresher the coffee, the stronger the flavor. This is very expensive but the flavor is superior, and it is worth it. We use a ratio that is similar to drip coffee, about 200 grams of coffee for each liter of water. When you are using this much ground coffee, it is important not to leave it in the cream for more than 5 minutes as it will create an astringent taste like an over-steeped cup of black tea. It's superior because you've used cream and milk in place of what would otherwise be water in your drip coffee ratio or recipe. You're brewing the coffee grounds in the dairy, so you wind up with a very robust coffee flavored ice cream. This method allows you to experience the essence of what coffee can taste like in an ice cream. Most places don't do this because it's labor-intensive and expensive.

Espresso

The flavor of espresso in ice cream is different than either of the other methods, with much brighter, tighter acidity. This is only worth using if you have an espresso machine, or access to real espresso. Home espresso pods will not work, and you want espresso that is as fresh as possible. If you use good espresso, it will be unmistakably espresso, not coffee. We typically add about a ¼ shot of espresso per scoop of ice cream.

Instant Espresso

There is one other wildcard in the mix that may not seem like it belongs. I have never used instant coffee or espresso for an ice cream base, but I have used it for toppings, specifically the Espresso Honeycomb (page 108) listed in the Coffee Crisp recipe on page 106. Instant Espresso is made by brewing the coffee or espresso and then freeze-drying it, which preserves the flavor and extends the shelf life. It also has the added benefit of being water soluble which means that it dissolves on the tongue, making it terrific as an ingredient that can be used for candy or other toppings like nuts or chocolate.

VIETNAMESE COFFEE

THIS ICE CREAM IS A STRONGER, MORE ROBUST COFFEE EXPERIENCE than drinking a cup of drip coffee. In a way, it's more like drinking a cappuccino, but instead of making the coffee ice cream with espresso, you're making it with ground coffee. In Vietnam, they brew rich syrupy coffee, which is typically served on ice and cut with condensed milk. It's purposely a very concentrated coffee, because it's meant to be poured over ice, which dilutes it, giving it a very unique flavor and unctuous texture. I try to emulate it here with the most popular coffee flavor on our menu.

Note: Condensed milk is a shelf-stable milk which has had more than half of the water removed, and sugar added. It was created a couple of hundred years ago and still endures today. Typically sold in cans, it can last for many years without refrigeration, if it remains unopened. This makes it ideal for coffee or tea in countries where refrigeration is not widely available. It is found, both iced and hot in Vietnam, where it's an everyday coffee staple. This is a delicious addition to many ice creams, and mandatory for this one.

Makes approximately 3½ cups

Heavy Cream	1½ cups (357g)
Whole Milk	1⅓ cups (330g)
Glucose Syrup	2 tablespoons (40g)
Granulated Sugar	¾ cup (150g)
Whole Milk Powder	¼ cup (30g)
Kosher Salt	¼ teaspoon (2g)
Coffee Beans	¾ cup (84g)
Sweetened Condensed Milk, for serving	

Combine the cream, milk, and glucose syrup in a 4-quart saucepan, and heat the mixture over medium heat, stirring with a rubber spatula or wooden spoon to keep it from burning, until small bubbles appear around the edges and the temperature reaches 180°F.

In a large bowl, whisk together the sugar, milk powder, and salt.

Slowly pour the hot cream mixture into the bowl, stirring constantly.

Pour the mixture back into the pan and cook over medium heat, stirring constantly, until it returns to 180°F.

Remove from the heat, coarsely grind the coffee beans, stir in, and immediately strain through a fine-mesh strainer into a clean container (you may have to strain it twice).

Fill a large bowl with ice and cold water to make an ice bath.

Put the container into the ice bath and let the base cool to 38°F, stirring occasionally.

Freeze in an ice cream maker according to the manufacturer's instructions.

Mix 1 teaspoon of condensed milk into each scoop just before scooping.

COFFEE TIME

In 1989, my stepfather opened one of the first "gourmet" coffee carts in San Francisco, at UCSF hospital. I would help him push the 1,500-pound cart one block uphill and connect the water and power. The coffee was French Roast, Hazelnut, or Beaujolais, and the steamed milk in the caffè latte was burned and spooned over the espresso like soap suds from an overfilled washing machine. To me, these drinks were novel and exciting, but over time I grew suspicious of seeing all those doctors rushing in and out of the lobby, drinking 4, 6, or 8 double shots of espresso each day. Clearly, they were addicted.

For me, though, coffee is compelling because it's so dynamic. From the day that it's roasted to the day that it's brewed, the nature of the bean is changing. It has all these volatile compounds that are maturing and evolving throughout its life cycle, and every change affects the flavor. These compounds, ping-ponging around inside the beans, are what makes us so obsessed with coffee. Addicted to it, in fact.

There were lots of drugs and alcohol in every kitchen I ever worked in, and while I liked to have a drink now and then, I made it through my career without smoking, doing many drugs, or even drinking coffee. In the early days, I employed a rigid self-discipline to get through the 80-hour weeks. Coffee was not very good in those days—it's much easier to abstain when it's bad—and most of the cooks or managers seemed to be guzzling the stuff diluted with sugar and cream by the quart. This was pre-Third Wave coffee. Especially in New York, coffee had not yet reached the elevated status that it has today. In some circles, people were into good coffee, but it wasn't like now, where on every corner in the city you can find someone who has a $10,000 espresso machine. Back then, people in New York City mainly drank coffee from their bodega, strong and stale.

And it wasn't just brewed coffee that didn't get the respect it deserved. At the four-star restaurants where I worked in the 1990s and early aughts, we bought coffee beans for making coffee ice cream from the same distributor where we were buying our plastic wrap and latex gloves. To buy coffee from a commodity distributor is the equivalent of buying diamonds from Home Depot. And then they would not even grind the beans before using them to make coffee ice cream. Everyone knows that if you make a cup of coffee, you don't make it with ungrounded beans—you have to grind coffee to unlock the flavor—and the same goes for making ice cream. But that's what they were doing back then, even in some of the best restaurants in America.

HÄAGEN-DAZS

My mother was fanatical about what we ate, as well as her own diet, but once in a while, she would allow a specific indulgence: a small scoop of Häagen-Dazs coffee ice cream, with skim milk poured over it. Häagen-Dazs coffee ice cream is pretty mild and milky on its own, and (very, important to my mother) not too sweet, and the skim milk coated the outside of the ice cream and froze, creating a slightly icy shell, further diluting the sweetness. The taste became a benchmark for a certain coffee ice cream flavor for me, which I started to call caffè latte, like a cup of coffee with two-thirds milk added. Light on flavor, and caffeine, but as it is reminiscent of my mother's only indulgence (besides eschewing sugar, she did not drink or smoke), I try to keep the flavor on the menu. I strongly recommend pouring a couple tablespoons of skim milk over a scoop of ice cream.

COFFEE CRISP

Coffee Crisp is a Canadian candy I was introduced to by an ex-girlfriend who hailed from the North. It is essentially coffee-flavored candy, covered in chocolate. I have never been to Canada, but apparently it is a national treasure up there. The first time I tried one I was immediately reminded of a British honeycomb candy called Hokey Pokey, which has a very unique, crisp texture. I combine the two candies: The bitterness from the instant espresso helps cut the sweetness of the honeycomb which adds a terrific sweet crispy crunch to the ice cream. The honeycomb must be kept in an airtight container and added to the ice cream right before it is scooped, otherwise it will dissolve and lose its crispness.

Makes approximately 3¼ cups

Whole Milk	1½ cups (367g)
Heavy Cream	1½ cups (357g)
Glucose Syrup	2 tablespoons (40g)
Granulated Sugar	¾ cup (150g)
Whole Milk Powder	¼ cup (30g)
Kosher Salt	¼ teaspoon (2g)
Coffee Beans	½ cup (55g)
Espresso Honeycomb (page 108)	

Combine the milk, cream, and glucose syrup in a 4-quart saucepan, and heat the mixture over medium heat, stirring with a rubber spatula or wooden spoon to keep it from burning, until small bubbles appear around the edges and the temperature reaches 180°F.

In a large bowl, whisk together the sugar, milk powder, and salt.

Slowly pour the hot cream mixture into the bowl, stirring constantly.

Pour the mixture back into the saucepan and return to medium heat, stirring constantly, until it returns to 180°F.

Remove from the heat, grind the coffee beans, stir them in, and immediately strain through a fine-mesh strainer (you may need to strain it twice) into a clean container.

Fill a large bowl with ice and cold water to make an ice bath.

Put the container into the ice bath and let the base cool to 38°F, stirring occasionally.

Freeze in an ice cream machine according to the manufacturer's instructions.

Add 1 tablespoon of crushed honeycomb for each scoop.

ESPRESSO HONEYCOMB

Makes about 5 cups

Granulated Sugar	1 cup (200g)
Glucose Syrup	¼ cup (80)
Honey	2 tablespoons (45g)
Baking Soda	2 tablespoons (29g)
Instant Espresso	5 tablespoons (20g)

Combine the sugar (spread the sugar so it's covering the entire bottom of the pan), the glucose syrup, and honey in a 4-quart saucepan, and bring to a boil over medium heat.

Once boiling, let the mixture caramelize for about 5 minutes, stirring occasionally, or until golden brown.

Add the baking soda and instant espresso to the pot and stir to dissolve the baking soda.

Off heat, allow the mixture to rise for 20 seconds, it will rise about 1 inch. Then carefully pour it out onto a nonstick tray.

Allow the honeycomb to cool completely.

As soon as it's cool, break it up into bite-size pieces, and store it in an airtight container. The honeycomb will keep for 2 weeks.

COCONUT ESPRESSO

THIS WAS ONE OF THE FIRST VEGAN FLAVORS WE MADE. For me, American ice cream does not exist without dairy; however, the demand for nondairy ice cream is strong in a place like New York City, where alternative diets have taken over. There are all kinds of challenges with making ice cream without dairy. It is impossible to replicate the smooth creamy texture of butterfat. Typically, this is attempted using nut or coconut milk with the addition of stabilizers and/or starch. In the best versions, this usually results in a smoother, but still icy and slightly gummy product not worth serving.

When we started testing, we used nut milks and combined them with some coconut cream or coconut milk, but the milks available in the market are high in water with the lowest amount of nut possible. This yielded an icy product. So, we started to use just coconut cream or coconut milk to create flavors. Coconut products are great for creating a smooth texture, with fat content similar to that of dairy. The challenge, though, is the unmistakably strong flavor of coconut. If we were going to use coconut milk, it would be the predominant flavor, so we'd need to use bold ingredients that could stand up to it. Espresso was a natural fit, with lots of clear acidity to balance the natural coconut alkalinity. This flavor is delicious on its own, but outstanding as an affogato with a sprinkle of salt on top.

Makes approximately 1 quart

COCONUT CREAM	2¼ CUPS (540G)
COCONUT MILK	1⅓ CUPS (80G)
AGAVE SYRUP	½ CUP (168G)
GLUCOSE SYRUP	2 TABLESPOONS (40G)
GRANULATED SUGAR	1 TABLESPOON (12G)
KOSHER SALT	¼ TEASPOON (2G)
ESPRESSO	½ CUP (118G)

Put the coconut cream, coconut milk, agave, glucose syrup, sugar, and salt in a 4-quart saucepan, and heat the mixture over medium heat until it reaches 180°F, stirring constantly.

Remove from the heat and immediately strain through a fine-mesh strainer into a clean container.

Fill a large bowl with ice and cold water to make an ice bath.

Put the container into the ice bath and let the base cool to 38°F, stirring occasionally.

Stir in the espresso and freeze in an ice cream machine according to the manufacturer's instructions.

ESPRESSO

When we put an espresso ice cream on the menu, we pull hundreds of shots to make each recipe. It is exhausting, time-consuming, and would never make sense for a large-scale production. The difference in taste, however, is remarkable. If you are an espresso fan, this flavor is for you. The rich, bright acidic flavor of the espresso stands out very clearly, much more forcefully, than in any other coffee ice cream I have ever tasted.

You can make this by ordering a few double shots of espresso at your local coffee shop. The brighter and louder the roast, the better. Bring them home in a cup or thermos and use them within 24 hours.

COFFEE AND CREAM

Commercial coffee creamers are a huge piece of business in the US, and only getting bigger. Without saying anything about their quality, I can say that they are popular. Food being loaded with ingredients we cannot pronounce has never stopped us from pouring it down our gullets. I bring this up for two reasons, number one—people love this stuff in all its oddly flavored forms, and surely something can be extracted from that. Number two, it can be delicious, but use caution, it has tons of garbage in it. I have a tip. The next time you are at your parent's house thinking about adding that hazelnut mocha Coffee-Mate to your morning brew, check the freezer and see about adding a spoonful of butter pecan ice cream instead. An inverted affogato if you will, a pick-me-up of the American style.

AFFOGATO

Affogato is the adult version of an ice cream float: espresso over ice cream.

The only improvement I can recommend is adding about 2 tablespoons of fudge (see page 61) to your espresso shot before you pour it over your ice cream. This will not only add a rich chocolate mocha flavor, but also viscosity and richness. This combination is outstanding with an egg custard flavor, to take it to another level.

DULCE DE LECHE

CRÈME CARAMEL

BUTTERSCOTCH

SALTED CARAMEL PRETZEL

CARAMEL

I don't like sugar too much, or I should say, I don't like too much sugar. If you're going to eat sugar, it should be worth it; personally, I have a soft spot for all kinds of sweets, from a SNICKERS bar to beignets at Café Du Monde, to the chocolate soufflé at La Grenouille (the best chocolate soufflé in America). What I don't like is anything that is too sweet, like Kool-Aid, or grocery story birthday cake frosting. All of these treats get their sweetness from the same place: granulated sugar made from sugar cane or beets. Sugar takes a lot of forms, mutating itself from granules to syrup and back to granules again, but it's most luxurious when it's cooked into a smooth creamy caramel.

Caramel first made its appearance in American candies thanks to the Lancaster Caramel Company, the first business from Milton S. Hershey. He began his candy career with a couple of copper kettles, eventually growing it to an operation employing 800 people, dedicated to making Hobson Kisses, Roly-Polys, Melbas, Empires, McGintys, and Icelts—all versions of cooked sugar—enjoyed by the caramel-loving public of America hundreds of years ago.

Over the years the popularity of caramel seemed to slowly give way to chocolate as America's favorite candy treat. These days, caramel can still be found inside your chocolate candies, and still shows up as a topping on whipped cream atop your caramel latte. And it has returned to the spotlight, thanks to the addition of sea salt, which has catapulted it back into the modern ice cream zeitgeist.

COOKED SUGAR

What is caramel? Just cooked sugar. The incredible, edible sugar molecule is capable of being modified and manipulated in different ways. Who can resist the satisfying crack of digging a spoon into the top of crème brûlée, or the smooth silkiness of caramel mixing with cooked eggs in custard to make crème caramel or flan? All of these made possible by merely cooking sugar. There are a few stages to cooking sugar and more than one way to create caramel from it. At Morgenstern's, we make two different kinds of caramels—wet and dry, with or without water.

Dry Caramel: We cook sugar in a dry pot or pan, without water, only when we want a bitter or burnt caramel taste. The window of time between uncooked and burnt is very short. Do not attempt this method while watching Game 7 of the World Series. Sugar melts and then caramelizes quickly, so be vigilant, keep the flame on medium, and stir constantly. The sugar will melt and then turn amber; you will know it is ready when a light foam, like a freshly pulled shot of espresso, forms at the edges. Add your cream or butter carefully, fully incorporating each addition before moving on to the next one. This process is challenging and can be stressful, but it's worth it. The fruity, acidic, bitter bite achieved in dry caramel is not possible with wet caramel and it amplifies the richness of dark chocolate particularly well.

Wet Caramel: Adding water to sugar for making caramel allows more time for the sugar to caramelize and softens the bitterness in the flavor. Just add (cold) water. And corn syrup or glucose. Sounds simple. However, there are many ways for this to go wrong, in my experience. After cooking caramel for several years, I still get nasty burns from overcooked sugar. You must always be on your toes when making caramel—either wet or dry—and be present each and every time because in addition to screwing up, you can hurt yourself or someone else.

Chewy Caramel: There is nothing like the stick-to-your-teeth "tackiness" of a chewy caramel candy, but adding caramel to ice cream can be tricky. Its texture depends largely on the temperature at which it will be served. A caramel sauce that is spoonable at room temperature will become chewy when frozen in ice cream.

I cannot tell you exactly how to make a perfect wet caramel. It takes skill, not a recipe. You will have to practice. Here are some pointers that have worked for me:

1. Be safe. The best way to be safe is to pay attention to what the fuck you are doing. You should pay attention at all times in your life, but especially when making caramel. That includes understanding all of the steps: beginning, middle, and end; what can go right, but more important, what can go wrong. Set yourself up for success by taking responsibility for yourself.

2. Start with a clean, dry pot or pan.

3. Use clean sugar that is not contaminated: no stray scraps of paper or grains of rice.

4. Add glucose or corn syrup. This will help keep the sugar from crystallizing. One tablespoon for each pound of sugar will do.

5. Use **cold** water to make a mixture the consistency of wet sand. I also use cold water to rinse any sugar off the insides of the pot. This will give you a layer of water on top of your wet sand.

6. Put the pot on **high heat** from the beginning. It is important to make sure that all of the sugar in the pot comes to a boil. So if you have a hot spot, move the pot around if necessary to bring it all to a boil.

7. Watch for steam. You can walk away as long as you see steam, but once the air is clear above the pot, stay with it. Note: The steam that comes off the pot is violent and can burn you.

8. Do not touch anything until the caramel is amber color. Do not stir the pot. Do not use a pastry brush soaked in distilled water to clean the sides of the pot, as some methods suggest. Leave it alone.

9. Keep an eye out for the proper color of your caramel. Once you see the amber in the pot, turn off the heat and gently swirl the pot. All of the sugar in the pot should be the same color. The sugar is about 335°F once it starts to color, and it will continue to cook.

10. Pay attention. Caramel is deceptive. Looking into a pot of cooking sugar is like looking into deep water. The color will appear darker the deeper the caramel is. Swirl it around to see the color in the shallows. This will tell you how dark it really is. If you are unsure, spoon some onto a plate. Let it cool and check the color and the taste. For ice cream, I take the caramel as far as possible to give the most flavor. Taking it that far requires practice and patience. Taste the caramel as it cools looking out for a rich and ALMOST bitter taste.

11. Add cream, milk, butter, or water. Do this slowly, little by little. Allow the caramel to fully emulsify after each addition. Small amounts should be added frequently in the beginning. Increase the amount as the temperature cools down.

CARAMEL SAUCE

THIS IS OUR MOST BASIC CARAMEL, which we drizzle over ice cream cakes or incorporate into ice cream sandwiches. It is a recipe that is flexible enough to spoon over a scoop, or swirl in and freeze.

Caramel is candy, so get your shit together before you start.

Makes about 1¾ cups

HEAVY CREAM	1 CUP (239G)
UNSALTED BUTTER	3 TABLESPOONS (45G)
GRANULATED SUGAR	1½ CUPS (300G)
WATER	¼ CUP (60G)
SEA SALT	PINCH OF

Heat the cream and butter in a 2-quart saucepan until the butter has melted. Set aside.

In a 4-quart stainless-steel saucepan, combine the sugar and water. Wet your hands with cold water and carefully brush the inside of the pot to remove any stray sugar granules on the edges. Put the pot on high heat and cook, without stirring, until the caramel is a light amber. Turn off the heat and gently swirl until the caramel is dark brown and the color of coffee (no milk). Gently pour a third of the cream/butter mixture into the caramel. BE CAREFUL! It will boil over and steam violently and can burn your hands or face. Gently swirl the pot until the cream mixture is combined and then add another third. Continue until all the cream is incorporated. Stir in the sea salt. Strain into a jar and cool to room temperature.

The sauce can be held in the refrigerator for up to 2 weeks. It can be reheated in a jar in a pot of simmering water, or in the microwave.

WATER CARAMEL

THIS IS A CARAMEL SAUCE MADE WITH WATER INSTEAD OF DAIRY (see Baked Crème Caramel, page 128, for directions). Water is one of the most basic, and often overlooked, vehicles for caramel flavor and texture. I did not know I needed this style of caramel in our ice creams until I made it myself. Now, we use it quite often. A caramel that is loosened with water is the very pure essence of caramel flavor, clear and slippery. It is also versatile and will easily accommodate other water-based ingredients to add flavor, such as orange juice or coffee. This is a great technique for nondairy ice cream additions.

SESAME CARAMEL

SESAME CARAMEL IS THE ZHUZZED UP CARAMEL SAUCE that I created for our King Kong Banana Split (page 34). It has now become one of our more popular toppings. The crunch and pop of black and white sesame seeds are what makes this sauce special. Cook the caramel using the technique listed on page 118. It is helpful to heat the cream and the butter separately before adding to the caramel. Strain the caramel sauce after the dairy has been incorporated. Stir in the sesame seeds last, as many as you'd like. Refrigerate once cool to preserve it. However, serve at room temperature or warm.

BOURBON CARAMEL

Makes 2 cups

HEAVY CREAM	¾ CUP (179G)
UNSALTED BUTTER	3 TABLESPOONS (45G)
GRANULATED SUGAR	1½ CUPS (300G)
WATER	¼ CUP (60G)
SEA SALT	PINCH OF
BOURBON (PREFERABLY OLD GRAND-DAD)	⅓ CUP (75G)

Caramel is candy, so get your shit together before you start.

Heat the cream and butter in a 1-quart pot, over medium heat, until the butter has melted. Set aside.

In a 4-quart stainless-steel saucepan, combine the sugar and water. Wet your hands with cold water and carefully brush the inside of the pot to remove any stray sugar granules on the edges.

Put the pot on high heat and cook until the caramel is a light amber. Turn off the heat and gently swirl until the caramel is dark brown and the color of coffee (no milk). Gently pour some of the cream/butter mixture into the caramel. BE CAREFUL! It will boil over and steam violently and can burn your hands or face. Gently swirl the pot until the cream mixture is combined and then add another third. Continue until all the cream is incorporated. The caramel can be heated over low heat to melt any remaining sugar and incorporate the cream if needed. Add the salt and bourbon and stir to combine.

Using a fine-mesh strainer, strain bourbon into a jar with a lid, and cool to room temperature.

The caramel can be stored in the refrigerator for up to 2 weeks. It can be reheated in the jar in a pot of simmering water, or in the microwave.

DULCE DE LECHE

I LOVE DULCE DE LECHE—a modern interpretation of cajeta, a goat milk sauce—for its rich milk caramel texture. Dulce de Leche is commonly made by boiling cans of condensed milk in water for 4 to 6 hours. It can be a pain in the ass because it takes up a burner that would otherwise be used for making ice cream bases, and the water level needs to be topped up throughout. A lot of the dulce de leche ice creams out there are dulce de leche in name only. You'll often see it added as a flavoring, not as a mix in, which is the best way to use it if you want to achieve the fullest flavor and texture. Room temp is delicious and will give the same unctuous appeal as a spoonful of peanut butter. However, when you add it to an ice cream and freeze it, it will give you the chewiest of chewy caramel textures.

Makes approximately 1 quart

WHOLE MILK	1⅔ CUPS (414G)
HEAVY CREAM	1½ CUPS (357G)
DULCE DE LECHE (SEE NOTE)	½ CUP (152G)
WHOLE MILK POWDER	⅓ CUP (40G)
GRANULATED SUGAR	2 TABLESPOONS (25G)
KOSHER SALT	¼ TEASPOON (2G)

Combine the milk, cream, and dulce de leche in a 4-quart saucepan, and heat the mixture over medium heat, stirring with a rubber spatula or wooden spoon to keep it from burning, until small bubbles appear around the edges and the temperature reaches 180°F.

In a large bowl, whisk together the milk powder, sugar, and salt.

Slowly pour the hot cream mixture into the bowl, stirring constantly.

Pour the mixture back into the pot and cook over medium heat, stirring constantly, until it returns to 180°F.

Remove from the heat and immediately strain through a fine-mesh strainer into a clean container.

Fill a large bowl with ice and cold water to make an ice bath.

Put the container into the ice bath and let the base cool to 38°F, stirring occasionally.

Freeze in an ice cream maker according to the manufacturer's instructions.

Note: You can make dulce de leche by boiling an unopened can of condensed milk in a large pot of water for 4 to 6 hours, adding more hot water as it boils off. The longer you boil it, the darker and richer the flavor will become. Once the can is cooked, allow it to cool completely before opening it. If you don't want to make your own, you can purchase jars of dulce de leche at the grocery store.

CRÈME CARAMEL

A properly baked custard is a beautiful thing. It may seem like a waste to blend it into an ice cream, but it is not: the texture and flavor of cooked eggs and caramel translates into something special. Just adding the caramel and eggs to ice cream without baking them together would not achieve the same rich texture or eggy caramel flavor. It is a lot of work, but well worth it.

Makes approximately 3¼ cups

Heavy Cream	1⅓ cups (325g)
Whole Milk	⅔ cup (170g)
Glucose Syrup	2 tablespoons (40g)
Granulated Sugar	⅔ cup (138g)
Whole Milk Powder	¼ cup (30g)
Kosher Salt	¼ teaspoon (2g)
Baked Crème Caramel (page 128)	⅔ cup (160g)

Combine the cream, milk, and glucose syrup in a 4-quart saucepan, and heat the mixture over medium heat, stirring with a rubber spatula or wooden spoon to keep it from burning, until small bubbles appear around the edges and the temperature reaches 180°F.

In a large bowl, whisk together the sugar, milk powder, and salt.

Slowly pour the hot cream mixture into the bowl, stirring constantly.

Pour the mixture back into the pot and cook over medium heat, stirring constantly, until it reaches 180°F.

Remove from the heat and immediately strain through a fine-mesh strainer into a clean container.

Add the Baked Crème Caramel and blend with an immersion blender until smooth.

Fill a large bowl with ice and cold water to make an ice bath.

Put the container into the ice bath and let the base cool to 38°F, stirring occasionally.

Freeze in an ice cream machine according to the manufacturer's instructions.

BAKED CRÈME CARAMEL

CRÈME CARAMEL IS MADE BY POURING A THIN LAYER OF CARAMEL into the bottom of a baking dish, adding a custard mix, and baking everything in a water bath. When the custard is turned out of the pan, there is a beautiful ombre effect of caramel on top, and custard on the bottom. The flavor of crème caramel is very unique, sweet and nutty. If you add enough of this to your ice cream base, the flavor will intensify. I mix in a water caramel to this recipe to help accentuate the flavor.

It is most common for crème caramel to be baked in individual portions of 4 to 6 ounces. We bake ours in a large metal cake pan of about 30 ounces at a time. If you are going to bake in a large dish, which can be easier for prep and cleanup, keep an eye on your baking, and err on the side of undercooked.

This can be baked the same day, however it is easier to do it the day before, cool it off and hold it in the refrigerator. If you make it the same day, you may want to keep yourself busy for a few hours while the custard bakes and cools a bit.

Makes 1¼ cups (315g; a bit more than you need for the Crème Caramel, page 124, ice cream)

FOR THE CARAMEL

GRANULATED SUGAR	¼ CUP (50G)
WATER	2 TABLESPOONS (30G)

FOR THE CUSTARD

WHOLE MILK	¾ CUP (184G)
HEAVY CREAM	¼ CUP (60G)
GRANULATED SUGAR	¼ CUP (50G)
WHOLE EGG AND EGG YOLK	1 AND 1
KOSHER SALT	PINCH OF

Preheat your oven to 325°F.

To make the caramel: Cook the sugar and water in a 2-quart saucepan, over high heat, until a light caramel forms. Turn off the heat and wait a few minutes for the caramel to get darker and cool.

Pour the caramel into an 8-inch cake pan, tilting the pan to cover the bottom. Set aside.

To make the custard: Combine the milk, cream, sugar, egg, egg yolk, and salt in a medium bowl and whisk thoroughly.

Strain through a fine-mesh strainer into a large clean bowl.

Pour the custard over the caramel.

Place the baking dish inside a larger ovenproof baking dish and fill the larger baking dish with hot water half way up the cake pan and carefully place into the oven.

Bake for 20 to 30 minutes, until there is only a slight jiggle in the middle of the cake pan.

Remove the pan from the water bath and let cool completely. Refrigerate for up to 3 days.

BUTTERSCOTCH

For some reason, Butterscotch seems to have skipped a generation or two in America. Still very popular in England, Americans could care less about this flavor as a candy, and especially an ice cream. But there is something special about its specific buttery caramel flavor, with a smooth round flavor that lingers on your palette, that I love. It is a little bit of work, but worth it for a special occasion. This was very popular with Grandma Morgenstern and is especially delicious with the Bananas Foster (page 186).

Makes approximately 1 quart

Whole Milk	1⅔ cups (414g)
Heavy Cream	1⅓ cups (325g)
Dark Brown Sugar	1 cup (145g)
Unsalted Butter	3 tablespoons (45g)
Glucose Syrup	2 tablespoons (40g)
Granulated Sugar	1 tablespoon (12g)
Whole Milk Powder	¼ cup (30g)
Kosher Salt	¼ teaspoon (2g)
Rum	1 tablespoon (15g)
Vanilla Extract	½ teaspoon (3g)

In a 2-quart saucepan, heat the milk and cream over medium heat, stirring with a rubber spatula or wooden spoon to keep it from burning, until small bubbles appear around the edges and the temperature reaches 180°F. Cover and set aside.

Place the brown sugar, butter, glucose syrup, and granulated sugar in a 4-quart saucepan, and cook over medium heat, stirring constantly with a wooden spoon until melted and bubbling and a medium caramel forms.

Carefully stir in the cream mixture until smooth.

In a large bowl, whisk together the milk powder and salt.

Slowly pour the caramel mixture into the bowl, stirring constantly.

Pour the mixture back into the pot and cook over medium heat, stirring constantly, until it reaches 180°F.

Remove from the heat, add the rum and vanilla and immediately strain through a fine-mesh strainer into a clean container.

Fill a large bowl with ice and cold water to make an ice bath.

Put the container into the ice bath and let the base cool to 38°F, stirring occasionally.

Freeze in an ice cream maker according to the manufacturer's instructions.

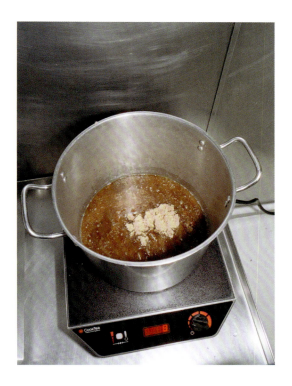

WAFFLE HOUSE

Anytime I'm on the road, I eat at Waffle House. There is something totally epic about sitting at the counter, watching the cooks work the griddle. They are fast, loud, and efficient. Early Sunday morning is best. The kitchen is firing on all cylinders with the dining room full of early churchgoers and late-night revelers. A few years ago, I was on a cross-country road trip through the South, and I found myself at Waffle House more than once. After an oversize breakfast that I could not finish, I was convinced to take a waffle to go. The waffle went in the trunk of my car, where I forgot about it until I returned to New York a few days later. Normally, I'd have tossed it when I found it, but the breakfast was so memorable that I was curious to see how the waffle held up. I thought of the traditional Belgium Liège Waffle, often served many days after it is made. If you've never had a Liège waffle, they are terrific with a dense buttery texture, studded with raw sugar that caramelizes on a heavy waffle iron. I took a bite of my leftover waffle, and realized it still had that signature imitation vanilla sweetness. I chopped it up and made a quick caramel sauce, using butter from Waffle House. I tossed the waffle in the caramel to coat, then pulled the pieces out and let them cool. They were the perfect addition to ice cream—soft inside with crisp butter caramel on the outside, a reminder not to throw away your leftovers. You never know where you're going to find inspiration for an ice cream sundae.

THE HOLY GRAIL

What makes a brand? I was not thinking about this when I started making ice cream on my own. I just made the flavors that I thought would be great. Salted Caramel Pretzel (page 138) was an easy pick, as caramel is a solid one-note flavor, salt adds nuance, and pretzels bring texture—and it wasn't something you found on many menus back when we started. Adding the pretzels before we scooped was defining. When I first started serving Salted Caramel Pretzel from an ice cream cart, located in front of my restaurant, it was an instant hit. We could barely keep up with the demand, sometimes selling ten gallons a day.

Late in the summer of 2009, *The New York Times* ran a roundup of ice cream carts in its "$25 and Under" column. The article was a full page, above and below the fold. As I read through it, I became impatient, reading about all of these other places that were serving ice cream from carts in Manhattan and Brooklyn. Had we been left out? I prepared myself for the disappointment of exclusion and read on. Finally, I came to the last paragraph of the article, by Ligaya Mishan:

> *The holy grail of ice cream turned out to be the salted caramel pretzel and bitter chocolate mint at Greene Ice Cream at the General Greene, 229 DeKalb Avenue (Clermont Avenue), Fort Greene, Brooklyn, (718) 222-1510. It's a dream team that achieves the mystic balance of salt, sweet and crunch. Nicholas Morgenstern, the cart's owner and the restaurant's co-owner and pastry chef, makes Philadelphia style ice cream, without eggs, which yields a satiny texture and more concentrated flavor . . . I'd been knocked out by sugar. I'd sworn never to eat ice cream again. I licked my cup clean.*

I was dumbfounded. I did not feel confident or rewarded. Just happy. Happy that someone had seen what I was trying to do, and that it landed. I would not have had the confidence to open an ice cream shop if it weren't for this flavor, which has come to define our brand.

SALTED CARAMEL PRETZEL

THIS RECIPE IS PRETTY STRAIGHTFORWARD but relies on cooking the caramel as far as it can possibly go before it becomes burnt or even slightly bitter. This can only really be achieved through practice. Once the caramel starts to take on color, pay close attention to the smell, and have your cream close at hand to stop the cooking as soon as you smell any whiff of acrid smoke.

Makes approximately 1 quart

WHOLE MILK	1⅔ CUPS (414G)
HEAVY CREAM	1⅔ CUPS (403G)
GRANULATED SUGAR	¾ CUP (150G)
GLUCOSE SYRUP	1 TABLESPOON (20G)
WHOLE MILK POWDER	¼ CUP (30G)
KOSHER SALT	¾ TEASPOON (6G)
MINI PRETZELS, CRUSHED	6 TABLESPOONS (30 G)

In a 2-quart saucepan, heat the milk and cream over medium heat, stirring with a rubber spatula or wooden spoon to keep it from burning, until small bubbles appear around the edges and the temperature reaches 180°F. Remove from the heat and set aside.

Place the sugar and glucose syrup in a 4-quart saucepan, and add enough water to the sugar to give it the consistency of wet sand. Using a rubber spatula, mix together. Wet your hands with cold water and carefully brush the inside of the pot to remove any stray sugar granules on the edges, as these can crystalize.

Cook the sugar on high heat, keeping an eye on it. Do not stir it or touch the pot. Once it starts to get color at the edges of the pot, turn off the heat and swirl the pot. The sugar will continue cooking and cooling simultaneously. It will be a red amber color when it is ready.

Remove from the heat and carefully add a quarter of the cream mixture. Swirl it until it is incorporated and then add another quarter of the cream. Swirl to incorporate and then add the final half of the cream.

In a large bowl, whisk together the milk powder and salt.

Slowly pour the hot cream mixture into the bowl, stirring constantly.

Pour the mixture back into the pot and cook over medium heat, stirring constantly with a wooden spoon until it returns to 180°F.

Remove from the heat and immediately strain through a fine-mesh strainer into a clean container. Fill a large bowl with ice and cold water to make an ice bath.

Put the container into the ice bath and let the base cool to 38°F, stirring occasionally.

Freeze in an ice cream maker according to the manufacturer's instructions.

Stir in the pretzels just before scooping.

PEANUT BUTTER CUP

HONEY ALMOND CUSTARD

PISTACHIO BLACK CURRANT

HAZELNUT RISBO

PEANUT BUTTER

GRAPE

MASCARPONE

BUTTER PECAN

NUTS

Some of the best ice cream flavors in America have nuts in them—Rocky Road, Swiss Almond, Butter Pecan. The hot fudge sundae, with its signature roasted, salted peanuts, was the first time peanuts were featured prominently in a dessert, in the 1850s. Some of the best ice cream flavors in America have nuts in them—Rocky Road, Swiss Almond, Butter Pecan—typically as what are called "kitchen sink" flavors, where you're adding a lot of stuff to the ice cream.

In recent years, walnuts—originally one of the key elements in Rocky Road, as well as wet walnuts, once another favorite sundae topping—have been pushed aside. Almonds are now standard in Rocky Road and, via Häagen-Dazs, prominently featured in Swiss Almond Fudge.

While nuts show up often in ice cream, these days it's rare to see the *flavor* of nuts highlighted in ice cream. Is a peanut creamier than a pistachio? Does a pistachio taste greener? Nut-flavored ice cream is hard to make. Adding nuts to an ice cream before you freeze it is like adding flavored butter. They provide richness, flavor, and texture, but usually need something to balance them out, so these guys often wind up in a supporting role. Adding nuts also adds fat, which can make the ice cream split, if you don't get the nut to dairy ratio just right.

The best solution is to use nut butters. These give you a concentrated nut flavor but, with the exception of peanut butter, can be expensive. If you want a true nut ice cream, it's going to take commitment—and cost.

Here's the basic cast of characters in nut ice cream.

Peanuts

Although not even technically nuts at all, peanuts top this list thanks to the popularity of peanut butter. No other nut ice cream flavor even comes close. Americans consume about 3 pounds of peanut butter per person each year. In Britain, the estimate is less than 1 tablespoon—and in many parts of the world peanut butter is considered an odd curiosity.

Peanut butter was created in the US late in the nineteenth century, becoming fashionable as a meat alternative a few decades later. Peanut butter cookies, Reese's Peanut Butter Cups, and of course the peanut butter and jelly sandwich are all anchors of American life.

The peanut butter and jelly sandwich transcends class and age. Ninety-five percent of all Americans have eaten one at some point in their lives; it crosses all cultural boundaries. Nonperishable, portable, tasty, and nourishing, it means something specific to America. It enables mobility and freedom. It can be an indulgence; it can take you back to when you were a kid; or sometimes it's just a convenient way to fuel up if you don't have time, room, or money for anything else.

People often imagine that the peanut is a more pedestrian nut. Superficially, it does seem so. They're cheaper, and they are standard issue in the nut mix you reach for when you are playing cards or watching a ballgame. So that's where they "live" in the mind. But on an ice cream sundae, there's really nothing better. There are lots of peanut varieties out there, but the only one for me is the Spanish Red. We get ours hand roasted and salted from Picosos' in Texas. They are firm, crunchy, and creamy with the perfect balance of salt.

Almonds

Almonds are the most agreeable of all the nuts, very cooperative. Their soft texture, milky flavor, and neutral color, give them great flexibility. They pollinate easily, grow with tremendous abundance, and can be processed into all different types of shapes and forms (whole, slivered, sliced, granulated, blanched, meal, and flour).

In Christianity the almond blossom is a symbol of the virgin birth of Jesus, but these days they are workhorse nuts used to make soda in Greece, Amaretti in Italy, and Turron in Spain. More than half of the world's almonds come from California, where they are regularly blamed for droughts, sucking up one gallon of water in cultivation per almond tree. Their thirsty appetite may spell their demise, but frankly, they won't be missed in ice cream as they are rarely used as more than a garnish.

Walnuts

I'm not a fan of walnuts, because almost all the walnuts we get in America are the Persian or English walnuts. They have a bitter skin that flakes and gets stuck in your teeth but is somehow impossible to remove from the nut itself. My preferred walnut is the black walnut, indigenous to North America with an unfortunately hard shell that makes them labor intensive to process commercially making them pricey. Their flavor is rich and meaty, without the pronounced bitterness of their English cousins. The flavor of this nut balances perfectly with bourbon or Fernet, both delicious in ice cream.

Macadamia Nuts

In the US, these are sometimes known as the Hawaii Nut, but their indigenous homeland of Australia, where they are called the Queensland Nut, should hold the naming rights. Large scale cultivations started 100 years ago in Hawaii and have continued to this day. These are the most delicious nut out there, making them highly sought after, expensive, and worth it. They make an outstanding complement to ice cream when they are roasted, candied, or turned into praline, and stand up very well as a base flavor on their own.

Pecans

These guys are closely related to the walnut but have more mass appeal. Their claim to fame has got to be the pecan pie, though I'd personally like a vote for Butter Pecan (page 174) ice cream. Pecans are less bitter, sweeter than walnuts, and candied or toasted, they make a great topping for ice cream.

Pistachios

These are in the canon as the most important nut for ice cream flavoring. No other nut carries the torch for being a standalone ice cream flavor like pistachio. The balanced herbaceous flavor makes for terrific ice cream, but more common, you'll find pistachio in ice cream's Italian cousin, gelato.

Hazelnuts

The second most popular ice cream nut, most likely due to Nutella, the chocolate and hazelnut spread. Hazelnuts don't have the same widespread appreciation in America as in Europe, where they are found in everything. Despite their lack of popularity, anytime we add a chocolate and hazelnut flavor to our menu, it sells out quickly. My favorite application for this nut is fried.

Pine Nuts

AKA pignolis, these are some of my favorites. They are mostly known in America for their essential role in pesto. They are very well suited to ice cream; their small size makes them bite sized jewels of exploding richness. I have never seen them on an ice cream menu other than ours, probably due to their relative obscurity and high price. Stay away from Chinese Pine Nuts, they have a weak flavor, mealy consistency.

FRIED NUTS

Conventional wisdom that all nuts improve on roasting might be true. This may be primarily dictated by the fact that we do not handle nuts with the care that their sensitive nature requires. Nuts go rancid, quickly, if kept at room temperature and exposed to light. Ideally, they should be stored in a tightly sealed container, preferably vacuum-packed, in the fridge. When was the last time you vacuum-packed your nuts and refrigerated them? Same here.

Roasting nuts helps extend their shelf life a bit. When they are fresh, roasting (and salting) gives them a terrific crunch and more of that buttery nutty flavor we all love. If you really want to go to another level, though, frying is the move. Fried nuts are like a roasted nut in stereo—you can feel them in your eardrums when you crunch them between your molars. They are also very flavorful.

How to fry nuts:
PAY ATTENTION!

Nuts should be fried whole because they are more consistent in size and will cook more evenly. Usually they are too large to add to ice cream this way, though sometimes we add fried hazelnuts whole to Mascarpone (page 172) ice cream. Whole nuts are a bit obscene in a scoop of ice cream a somewhat overly indulgent surprise.

Frying nuts is as dangerous as making caramel. And while a caramel burn is worse, the probability of a frying accident is far greater. The oil becomes less viscous the hotter it gets. It will splash around like water looking to jump out of the pot. Always make sure you have a pot that is large enough to accommodate four times the volume of nuts that you intend to fry at any one time.

Fill the pot half full with grapeseed oil. Heat it on medium heat to 375°F. Measure the temperature of the oil using a candy thermometer. Once the oil reaches temperature, add the nuts carefully. I recommend using a spider if you have one, or you can pour them in carefully. Either way, when you do this, the oil will pop and bubble and splatter, so WATCH OUT. Let the nuts fry for 8 to 12 minutes. They will sink, so stirring regularly to keep them from burning on the bottom of the pot is required. Have a pan with lots of paper towels ready and remove the nuts with a slotted spoon or spider when they are done and drain on the paper towels. Immediately salt them liberally. Once they are cool, store them in an airtight container.

PEANUT BUTTER CUP

IF YOU HAVE AN ICE CREAM SHOP IN AMERICA, you no doubt serve this flavor. It may not be as obvious as cookies 'n' cream, vanilla, or chocolate, but trust me, the timeless, comforting indulgence of peanut butter and chocolate will never ever go out of style.

Makes approximately 1 quart

....

WHOLE MILK	1⅔ CUPS (414G)
HEAVY CREAM	1 CUP (239G)
GLUCOSE SYRUP	2 TABLESPOONS (40G)
GRANULATED SUGAR	½ CUP (100G)
WHOLE MILK POWDER	¼ CUP (30G)
KOSHER SALT	¼ TEASPOON (2G)
POWDERED SUGAR	½ CUP (60G)
CREAMY SKIPPY PEANUT BUTTER	½ CUP (96G)
REESE'S PEANUT BUTTER CUPS, CHOPPED	¼ CUP (45G)

....

In a 4-quart saucepan, heat the milk, cream, and glucose syrup over medium heat, stirring with a rubber spatula or wooden spoon to keep it from burning, until small bubbles appear around the edges and the temperature reaches 180°F.

In a large bowl, whisk together the granulated sugar, milk powder, and salt.

Slowly pour the hot cream mixture into the bowl, stirring constantly.

Pour the mixture back into the pot and cook over medium heat, stirring constantly, until it returns to 180°F.

Using a fork, in a large bowl, whisk together the powdered sugar and peanut butter and pour the hot cream over the top. Stir slowly to incorporate. Strain through a fine-mesh strainer into a clean container.

Fill a large bowl with ice and cold water to make an ice bath.

Put the container into the ice bath and let the base cool to 38°F, stirring occasionally.

Freeze in an ice cream maker according to the manufacturer's instructions. Stir in the chopped peanut butter cups.

HONEY ALMOND CUSTARD

ALMONDS PLAY A SUPPORTING ROLE AS A TOPPING or a mix-in, but almost never as the base of the flavor. Chopped almonds, sliced almonds, and slivered almonds, have their place on a banana split or on ice cream sundaes, adding texture and a little bit of flavor, but basically that's about all the almond is good for. Except here.

We make the flavor as a custard, an egg-based ice cream, steeped with toasted almonds. Then those almonds get strained out and we add a chopped almond honeycomb, creating a bumped-up, elevated honey-almond texture.

Makes approximately 3⅓ cups

SLICED ALMONDS	⅔ CUP (77G)
HEAVY CREAM	2 CUPS (478G)
WHOLE MILK	⅓ CUP (85G)
HONEY	⅓ CUP (110G)
EGG YOLKS	5
GRANULATED SUGAR	1 CUP (200G)
KOSHER SALT	¼ TEASPOON (2G)
LEMON JUICE	¼ TEASPOON (2G)
HONEY ALMOND HONEYCOMB (PAGE 152), FINELY CHOPPED	⅓ CUP (55G)

Preheat your oven to 325°F.

Toast the almonds in a small baking dish for 10 to 15 minutes, until lightly golden. Remove from the oven and keep them in the baking dish to retain their heat.

In a 4-quart saucepan, heat the cream, milk, and honey over medium heat, stirring with a rubber spatula or wooden spoon to keep it from burning, until small bubbles appear around the edges and the temperature reaches 180°F. Add the hot toasted almonds to the pot, cover, and steep for 15 minutes.

In a large bowl, whisk together the egg yolks, sugar, and salt.

Slowly pour the hot cream mixture into the bowl, stirring constantly.

Pour the mixture back into the saucepan and return to medium heat, stirring constantly, until it returns to 180°F.

Remove from the heat and immediately strain through a fine-mesh strainer into a clean container. Fill a large bowl with ice and cold water to make an ice bath.

Put the container into the ice bath and let the base cool to 38°F, stirring occasionally.

Add the lemon juice and freeze in an ice cream maker according to the manufacturer's instructions.

Stir in the honeycomb as soon as the ice cream is frozen, being careful not to overmix.

HONEY ALMOND HONEYCOMB

Makes approximately 1 cup (broken up)

Toasted Sliced Almonds	1 cup (119g)
Granulated Sugar	½ cup (100g)
Glucose Syrup	1½ tablespoons (30g)
Honey	1 tablespoon (22g)
Baking Soda	1 teaspoon (5g)

Sprinkle the toasted almonds evenly on the surface of a nonstick baking sheet. Set aside.

Combine the sugar (spread the sugar to cover the entire bottom of the pan), the glucose syrup, and honey in a 4-quart saucepan, and bring to a boil over medium heat.

Once boiling, let the mixture caramelize for about 5 minutes, or until golden brown.

Add the baking soda to the pot and stir to dissolve.

Allow the mixture to rise for 20 seconds and then carefully pour it over the almonds on the baking sheet, working quickly before it hardens.

Allow the honeycomb to cool completely.

As soon as it's cool, break it up and store it in an airtight container. It will keep for 2 weeks.

PISTACHIO BLACK CURRANT

It was not until 2018 that we decided to make a bona fide entirely pistachio ice cream, so I went all out with a double shot of richness: 100 percent Sicilian pistachios and black currants, the small tart berry packing a powerful punch. These two combined is a super charged PB&J, the dark purple black currant jelly a perfect foil for the rich pistachio. The only way to make this is using the best pistachio paste, with not more than 30 percent sugar.

Makes approximately 1 quart

....

WHOLE MILK	1⅔ CUPS (414G)
HEAVY CREAM	1 CUP (239G)
GLUCOSE SYRUP	2 TABLESPOONS (40G)
GRANULATED SUGAR	1 CUP (200G)
WHOLE MILK POWDER	¼ CUP (30G)
KOSHER SALT	¼ TEASPOON (2G)
PISTACHIO PASTE, WELL-STIRRED	6 TABLESPOONS (96G)
BLACK CURRANT JAM (PAGE 158)	¼ CUP (68G)

....

In a 4-quart saucepan, heat the milk, cream, and glucose syrup over medium heat, stirring with a rubber spatula or wooden spoon to keep it from burning, until small bubbles appear around the edges and the temperature reaches 180°F.

In a large bowl, whisk together the sugar, milk powder, and salt.

Slowly pour the hot cream mixture into the bowl, stirring constantly.

Pour the mixture back into the pot and cook over medium heat, stirring constantly, until it returns to 180°F.

Remove from the heat, stir in the pistachio paste until fully dissolved, and immediately strain through a fine-mesh strainer into a clean container.

Fill a large bowl with ice and cold water to make an ice bath.

Put the container into the ice bath and let the base cool to 38°F, stirring occasionally.

Freeze in an ice cream maker according to the manufacturer's instructions. Swirl in the Black Currant Jam to create ribbons. Do not overmix, you will melt your ice cream.

BLACK CURRANT JAM

Note: The jam will remain loose and pourable.

Makes ⅔ cup

Black Currant Purée	⅓ cup (80g)
Water	¼ cup (60g)
Granulated Sugar	¼ cup (50g) plus 2 tablespoons (30g), divided
Sure-Jell Original Powdered Pectin	½ teaspoon (2g; measured by weight rather than volume, if possible)
Kosher Salt	pinch of
Glucose Syrup	2 teaspoons (13g)
Lemon Juice	1 tablespoon (15g)

In a 2-quart saucepan, heat the black currant purée, water, and the ¼ cup plus 1 tablespoon of sugar over medium heat, stirring until it comes to a light boil.

Thoroughly combine the remaining 1 tablespoon of sugar and the pectin in a small bowl and quickly whisk into the black currant purée. Return to a full boil, then keep at a lively simmer over medium heat until the liquid thickens and the surface is covered with thick, viscous bubbles, 7 to 10 minutes. The liquid should be starting to gel but remain pourable.

Remove from the heat and stir in the salt, glucose syrup, and lemon juice.

Immediately strain through a fine-mesh strainer into a clean container and let cool completely. Keep the jam covered in the refrigerator until ready to use, up to 2 weeks.

HAZELNUT RISBO

My friend Boris (Risbo is a nickname for Boris in French) loves hazelnuts, and this is the flavor I made for him. Making an ice cream for someone is like buying them a very personal gift. Boris is a special person, with an incredible, almost childish generosity and love for life. When he eats bad food, it hurts him, physically. But when he eats good food, he gets a twinkle in his eyes and he has a reason for breathing. The French love hazelnuts and hazelnut praline, and they love hazelnuts in their ice cream. It's one of the flavors that you'll regularly see on the menu in France. For this flavor we use both hazelnut paste, and crushed hazelnuts. We add a touch of Armagnac to both smooth it out and give it a bit of bite at the same time. It is just as tasty with a dark rum that is not to sweet.

Note: Finding delicious pure hazelnut paste can be challenging. At the shop we use paste that is 70 percent hazelnuts, but that's hard to find for most people. I have adapted this recipe for a paste with a little more sugar added. If you can find one with at least 50 percent hazelnut you will be okay, but you may want to cut back the sugar in your recipe by a few percentage points. I do recommend that you steer clear of anything that contains hydrogenated fat for this one. If you can't find good hazelnut paste, you can even make this with gianduja (chocolate hazelnut), but you will need to reduce the sugar by 10 to 20 percent, depending on how sweet it is. If you really want to have the full Risbo experience, eat this scoop with salt fried hazelnuts, a little dab of crème fraiche, and a glass of Armagnac neat.

Makes approximately 3⅔ cups

....

WHOLE MILK	1¾ CUPS (429G)
HEAVY CREAM	1 CUP (239G)
GLUCOSE SYRUP	2 TABLESPOONS (40G)
GRANULATED SUGAR	½ CUP (100G)
WHOLE MILK POWDER	¼ CUP (30G)
KOSHER SALT	¼ TEASPOON (2G)
HAZELNUT PASTE (35% SUGAR)	¼ CUP (70G)
ARMAGNAC OR DARK RUM	1 TABLESPOON (15G)

....

Combine the milk, cream, and glucose syrup in a 4-quart saucepan, and heat the mixture over medium heat, stirring with a rubber spatula or wooden spoon to keep it from burning, until small bubbles appear around the edges and the temperature reaches 180°F.

In a large bowl, whisk together the sugar, milk powder, and salt.

Slowly pour the hot cream mixture into the bowl, stirring constantly.

Pour the mixture back into the pot and cook over medium heat, stirring constantly, until it returns to 180°F.

Remove from the heat, stir in the hazelnut paste until dissolved, add the alcohol and immediately strain through a fine-mesh strainer into a clean container.

Fill a large bowl with ice and cold water to make an ice bath.

Put the container into the ice bath and let the base cool to 38°F, stirring occasionally.

Freeze in an ice cream maker according to the manufacturer's instructions.

"THE KOPPELMAN" *by Brian Koppelman*

Ice cream is like magic in that, if it's done right, the final effect feels like a miracle, and all the work required to produce it is in the background, invisible, hidden from view. And that is as it should be. A treat as good as truly exceptional ice cream should only exist right then, in the present, a rare moment of pure, uncomplicated joy that resets our complicated, complex day.

The thing is, making truly exceptional ice cream is not a miracle at all. It takes focused, disciplined imagining, rigorous planning, relentless testing, and the willingness to completely change course the second you see you are headed down the wrong tributary. It takes, in other words, talent and work. I learned all this by watching Nicholas Morgenstern do his thing up close. We met, Nick and I, in Las Vegas, another land of sleight of hand and misdirection, on a trip with a few chefs, and a few writers, and found that we cared about a bunch of the same things when it came to food, friendship, and the need for a minimum number of hours slept. Somehow, in Vegas, that's a rarity.

When we came back to New York, we began meeting up for weekly breakfasts where the subject always turned to ice cream and memories, and how those two things are often intertwined. I realized, very quickly, that Nick was an obsessive. I had met other ice cream obsessives but never one who was so fascinated by the way ice cream affected people emotionally, tapped into their childhoods, resonated with them the way their favorite freshman year song did.

And that is how the two of us got to talking about peanut butter and jelly sandwiches. Well, that's how we got started on it. Most of the conversations didn't take place between sips of espresso at the Italian pastry shop. Most happened as Nick was building the Morgenstern's flagship store on Lafayette and Houston.

And I mean building it. Finishing it. Once the contractor had framed it out and installed the fixtures, Nicholas did most of the rest himself, with a small skeleton team. I'd stop in after leaving the *Billions* set, late at night, to check on the progress, and I would find him there, atop a counter, paint brush in hand, or on hands and knees double-checking the floor tiles.

It was during these midnight talks that the Koppelman cake came to be. The idea was to re-create that feeling of the perfect PB&J, the one that saved you as a kid from having to eat whatever some grown up wanted you to eat. I suggested the flavor, we debated the merits of Skippy, Jiff, and Peter Pan, and off Nick went into wonderland.

He can tell you how it came together, technically, I can only say that I have had many great jobs in my life, but being the official taster of Peanut Butter ice cream, concord Grape Jelly, and Picosos' peanuts is just about the best one I have ever had.

THE KOPPELMAN

My friend Brian Koppleman carefully suggested making an ice cream flavor out of the classic combination of peanut butter and jelly. He found it odd that we had not at least tried it, but it was a bit too obvious for me. And so, the Koppelman ice cream cake was born: Peanut Daquoise, Peanut Butter ice cream, house-pressed concord grape jelly — a very indulgent slice requiring commitment and resolve.

Concord grapes are available in the northeast for a couple of months at the end of summer and into the early fall, usually September and October. If you have never had one fresh, they can be shockingly artificial tasting. Bright and acidic, the experience of eating one is confounded by the contrast in texture of the interior of the grape (firm jelly) and the slightly gritty astringency of the skin. There are several large bitter seeds in each one making the experience even more challenging. They are very difficult to prep or handle in any way other than to get the juice (if you are a fine dining chef and have decided to have your team peel and remove the seeds, good for you), the answer to this is Grape Jelly. Both the flavor and color are outstanding in their brilliance.

We make our own concord grape juice, which is a worthwhile task. If you can't do it, Welch's will work pretty well. To make the juice, we rinse the grapes thoroughly, removing all of the stems. We put them in a large stock pot and add just enough water to cover, then bring them to a simmer over medium heat, and cook for 10 minutes, allowing the skins to burst. We pour the cooked grapes into a large cheesecloth and tie them up so that they drain into a pan in the refrigerator overnight. We then strain the juice through a chinois and freeze it to be used throughout the year.

The ideal ratio of ice cream for this cake is two parts Peanut Butter ice cream, one part Grape ice cream. If you don't have a scale, try your best to eye ball it. It is best to start with ice cream that has been churned and then fully frozen for at least 24 hours.

Note: This cake was originally conceived as a 10-inch cake that stands over 4 inches tall. The size, flavors, and intensity required that it command space. I realize that if you are making this cake at home, 10 inches is very large, and will not fit in most home freezers easily. The recipe is designed for an 8-inch cake (4 inches tall), which is more manageable. It is still a very intensely flavorful showstopper, great for a special occasion. I recommend cutting into 12 to 16 slices.

Makes one 8-inch cake (Serves 12 to 16)

....

Two 7-inch Dacquoise (page 168)

Peanut Butter (from two batches; page 170)   5 cups (1150g)

Grape Jelly (page 334)   1½ cups (335g), divided

Grape (page 171)   2½ cups (575g)

PB Frosting (page 171)

Chopped Picosos' Peanuts, salted   ½ cup (50g)

Equipment

8-inch stainless steel cake ring

9-inch cardboard cake circle

Pastry bag with a star tip

....

Place the 8-inch cake ring on top of the 9-inch cardboard cake circle.

Place one of the Dacquoise inside the bottom of the cake ring. Quickly fill the ring with the Peanut Butter ice cream, spreading it evenly over the Dacquoise.

Pour 1 cup (225g) of Grape Jelly over the Peanut Butter ice cream.

Put the cake in the freezer to harden for at least 2 hours.

Place the second Dacquoise on top of the jelly and press it flat.

Fill the ring with the Grape ice cream. Smooth the surface and wrap with plastic and freeze for 24 hours.

Using a hair dryer, warm the cake ring gently until it releases from the cake and can be slid off.

Put about ½ cup of PB Frosting into the pastry bag and set aside. Spread the remaining frosting over the top and sides of the cake. Grab the pastry bag and pipe a ribbon of frosting around the edge of the cake.

Pour the remaining ½ cup (110g) of Grape Jelly in the middle of the cake.

Fill the center of the jelly with the peanuts.

Keep in the freezer, covered, for up to 5 days.

To serve this cake, I recommend that it be removed from the freezer 15 to 20 minutes before you plan to cut it. This will allow it to soften a bit, as it can be very dense and difficult to cut.

To cut smooth slices, it is important to have a sharp knife (a chef's knife is best). A large container of very hot water so that the knife can be fully submerged between each slice is very helpful, or at a minimum run the knife under hot water from the tap. Wiping the knife with a clean towel in between each cut will give a clean slice. Have your plates and utensils ready. If you can't serve the cake slices standing up, they will melt quickly as soon as they hit the plate unless you put them in the freezer beforehand.

DACQUOISE

Makes two 7-inch Dacquoise

....

Powdered Sugar 1½ cups (125g)

Picosos' Peanuts, salted ¾ cup (100g)

Egg Whites, at room temperature 4

Granulated Sugar ½ cup (100g), divided

....

Preheat the oven to 325°F. Line a 16 x 13-inch baking sheet with parchment paper.

Grind the powdered sugar and peanuts in a food processor until they resemble a coarse flour.

In a stand mixer, on high speed, whip the egg whites until they have tripled in volume. Add ¼ cup (50g) of granulated sugar, making sure it is fully incorporated.

Whip until the egg whites are a stiff meringue.

Fold in the remaining ¼ cup (50g) of granulated sugar, again making sure it is fully incorporated. Then gently fold in the powdered sugar/peanut mixture in three additions, folding in between, until completely incorporated.

Carefully fill a piping bag with the mixture.

Pipe two 7-inch circles onto the prepared baking sheet.

Bake for 35 to 40 minutes, until dark golden brown. Let cool to room temperature and cover tightly.

The dacquoise be stored tightly wrapped at room temperature for up to 4 days.

PEANUT BUTTER

Makes approximately 1 quart

....

WHOLE MILK	1⅔ CUPS (414G)
HEAVY CREAM	1 CUP (239G)
GLUCOSE SYRUP	2 TABLESPOONS (40G)
GRANULATED SUGAR	½ CUP (100G)
WHOLE MILK POWDER	¼ CUP (30G)
KOSHER SALT	¼ TEASPOON (2G)
POWDERED SUGAR	½ CUP (60G)
CREAMY SKIPPY PEANUT BUTTER	⅓ CUP (96G)

....

Combine the milk, cream, and glucose syrup in a 4-quart saucepan, and heat the mixture over medium heat, stirring with a rubber spatula or wooden spoon to keep it from burning, until small bubbles appear around the edges and the temperature reaches 180°F.

In a large bowl, whisk together the granulated sugar, milk powder, and salt.

Slowly pour the hot cream mixture into the bowl, stirring constantly.

Pour the mixture back into the pot and cook over medium heat, stirring constantly until it returns to 180°F.

In a large bowl, using a fork, combine the powdered sugar and peanut butter. Pour the hot cream mixture over the top slowly, stirring to incorporate. Strain through a fine-mesh strainer into a clean container.

Fill a large bowl with ice and cold water to make an ice bath.

Put the container into the ice bath and let the base cool to 38°F, stirring occasionally.

Freeze in an ice cream maker according to the manufacturer's instructions.

GRAPE

Makes approximately 1 quart

....

Whole Milk	1½ cups (368g)
Heavy Cream	½ cup (100g)
Glucose Syrup	2 tablespoons (40g)
Granulated Sugar	¾ cup plus 1½ tablespoons (170g)
Whole Milk Powder	¼ cup (30g)
Kosher Salt	¼ teaspoon (2g)
Welch's Concord Grape Juice	1⅓ cups (300g)
Lemon Juice	1½ teaspoons (15g)

....

Combine the milk, cream, and glucose syrup in a 4-quart saucepan, and heat the mixture over medium heat, stirring with a rubber spatula or wooden spoon to keep it from burning, until small bubbles appear around the edges and the temperature reaches 180°F.

In a large bowl, whisk together the sugar, milk powder, and salt.

Slowly pour the hot cream mixture into the bowl, stirring constantly.

Pour the mixture back into the pot and cook over medium heat, stirring constantly until it returns to 180°F.

Remove from the heat and immediately strain through a fine-mesh strainer into a clean container. Fill a large bowl with ice and cold water to make an ice bath.

Put the container into the ice bath and let the base cool to 38°F, stirring occasionally.

Add the grape juice and lemon juice and freeze in an ice cream maker according to the manufacturer's instructions.

PB FROSTING

Makes about 2 cups

....

Creamy Peanut Butter	1 cup (250g)
Powdered Sugar	1 cup (120g)
Unsalted Butter, at room temperature	5 tablespoons (75g)
Kosher Salt (fine grain, such as Diamond Crystal)	¼ teaspoon (2g)
Heavy Cream	⅓ cup (75g)

....

Using a stand mixer with the paddle attachment, combine the peanut butter, powdered sugar, butter, and salt on medium speed until smooth and creamy, scraping down the bowl as needed. Add the cream at the end, mix thoroughly, and set aside.

The frosting can be made a few hours in advance and kept at room temperature.

MASCARPONE

The combination of salty fried hazelnuts and rich Italian Mascarpone cheese is extremely indulgent. Mascarpone has a delicate sweet flavor under its plaster thick rich texture, which shines beautifully when it is turned into an ice cream. When I fry the nuts for this flavor, I nearly burn them, rendering some of the fat in them and adding a bite to contrast with the sweet ice cream. But do not actually burn the nuts, they will be bitter and rancid tasting if you do.

Makes approximately 1 quart

Whole Milk	1¼ cups (306g)
Glucose Syrup	2 tablespoons (40g)
Granulated Sugar	1 cup (200g)
Whole Milk Powder	⅓ cup (40g)
Kosher Salt	¼ teaspoon (2g)
Mascarpone	1⅔ cups (375g)
Lemon Juice	1 tablespoon (15g)
Hazelnuts, fried and salted	½ cup (55g)

In a 4-quart saucepan, heat the milk and glucose syrup over medium heat, stirring with a rubber spatula or wooden spoon to keep it from burning, until small bubbles appear around the edges and the temperature reaches 180°F.

In a large bowl, whisk together the sugar, milk powder, and salt.

Slowly pour the hot cream mixture into the bowl, stirring constantly.

Pour the mixture back into the pot and cook over medium heat, stirring constantly, until it returns to 180°F.

Remove from the heat, add the mascarpone, and stir to combine. Immediately strain through a fine-mesh strainer into a clean container.

Fill a large bowl with ice and cold water to make an ice bath.

Put the container into the ice bath and let the base cool to 38°F, stirring occasionally.

Stir in the lemon juice and freeze in an ice cream maker according to the manufacturer's instructions. Add the fried hazelnuts just before scooping.

FINALLY, A NOTE ON PECANS

Pecans were my grandfather's favorite nut, and he was the only person I have ever unequivocally respected. He had a tough life and took it as it came. He tirelessly applied himself to make a better life for his family, and never complained. It is unpopular to say, but he pulled himself up by his bootstraps every day that he was alive. He was serious, and hilarious. He never lied, and never broke his word. If he could help a person he would, and more important, if he could not, he would not shy away from straight talk; he would tell you to your face. He did not suffer fools, but he was never rude or mean.

When he was diagnosed with colon cancer, he found himself in the hospital for the first time in his life. After multiple successful procedures, he decided he was done. He did not give up, he was not beaten, but he was done. He told me that he had lived a great life, and like Popeye, enough was enough, and enough was too much. He was a tough sonofabitch, and I miss him. He never saw Morgenstern's, and this is the only thing in my life that I wish I could change. He would have been very proud. He loved Butter Pecan (page 174) ice cream. So, this one is for you Lew.

BUTTER PECAN

Many butter pecan ice creams are made by adding untoasted pecans to vanilla ice cream where they take on the a rich chewey texture.. While I admit this works, somehow, it is not very good. For this recipe we make a pecan butter to add into the base before it freezes and then add big pieces of buttered pecans after it is frozen.

Makes approximately 1 quart

WHOLE MILK	1¾ CUPS (429G)
HEAVY CREAM	1 CUP (239G)
GLUCOSE SYRUP	2 TABLESPOONS (40G)
GRANULATED SUGAR	1 CUP (200G)
WHOLE MILK POWDER	⅓ CUP (43G)
KOSHER SALT	¼ TEASPOON (2G)
PECAN BUTTER (PAGE 176)	⅓ CUP (88G)
BUTTERED PECANS (PAGE 176)	½ CUP (75G)

In a 4-quart saucepan, heat the milk, cream, and glucose syrup over medium heat, stirring with a rubber spatula or wooden spoon to keep it from burning, until small bubbles appear around the edges and the temperature reaches 180°F.

In a large bowl, whisk together the sugar, milk powder, and salt.

Slowly pour the hot cream mixture into the bowl, stirring constantly.

Pour the mixture back into the pot and cook over medium heat, stirring constantly, until it returns to 180°F.

Remove from the heat and immediately strain through a fine-mesh strainer into a clean container. Stir in the Pecan Butter.

Fill a large bowl with ice and cold water to make an ice bath.

Put the container into the ice bath and let the base cool to 38°F, stirring occasionally.

Freeze in an ice cream maker according to the manufacturer's instructions.

I prefer adding the pecans just before scooping. Their flavor and crunch will be clear and pronounced. However, there is a case to be made for adding them as soon as the ice cream comes out of the machine and letting them set. They add a soft but rich texture to the ice cream that can be a hallmark for many Butter Pecan lovers, including my grandfather who I would have had to convince of my method. I think I would have won, but I can't be sure. Use your discretion, Butter Pecan lovers can be sensitive.

BUTTERED PECANS AND PECAN BUTTER

Makes approximately 1½ cups

LIGHT BROWN SUGAR	3 TABLESPOONS (36G)
UNSALTED BUTTER	2 TABLESPOONS (30G)
VANILLA SUGAR (PAGE 19) OR GRANULATED SUGAR	2 TABLESPOONS (25G)
LIGHT CORN SYRUP	2 TABLESPOONS (40G)
KOSHER SALT	PINCH OF
PECAN PIECES	1¼ CUPS (163G)

To make the buttered pecans: Preheat your oven to 325°F. Prepare a nonstick baking sheet or a baking sheet lined with baking paper sprayed with nonstick baking spray.

Put the brown sugar, butter, Vanilla Sugar, and corn syrup in a 1-quart saucepan and melt over medium heat. Stir until well combined.

Mix the salt and pecan pieces together in a large bowl.

Pour the melted butter mixture over the nuts and mix thoroughly.

Spread the pecan mixture onto the prepared baking sheet in an even layer and toast in the oven for 10 to 15 minutes, until golden.

Remove from the oven and let cool.

To make the pecan butter: take one third of the nuts and blend in a food processor, scraping down the sides of the bowl as needed, into pecan butter.

Chop the other two thirds of the nuts into medium size chunks (pea size).

DRUNKEN MONKEY

BANANA CURRY

CHARRED BANANA

MACADAMIA PRALINE BANANA

BANANA

BANANA PHOBIA IS AN EXTREMELY RARE CONDITION that I first encountered in one of my employees. She found the smell or sight of bananas repulsive. The cause is often trauma-based, from being forced to eat bananas as a child, or the humiliation caused from slipping on a banana peel, or being told that their texture is similar to that of slugs (not necessarily banana slugs though). I love bananas, but this bananaphobia created a tension between the two of us, and I found myself subconsciously limiting bananas on our menu for many years.

Bananas are now the most popular fruit in America, more popular even than apples. They were displayed at the World's Fair in 1876, where they were largely overlooked due to Alexander Graham Bell's introduction of the telephone, and up until the early twentieth century, most Americans had never tasted one. They are a very delicate fruit which must be picked and packed by hand, requiring great care to transport. While they are tropical, their singular identity creates a unique food category encompasing: banana bread, breakfast, and banana ketchup. The hallmark of bananas in America is how consistent they are banana to banana. This is obvious once you know that every banana you have ever eaten is a clone.

I love bananas, but they pose a challenge for ice cream manufacturing. They are best fresh but can be difficult to deal with. They take up space, require even ripening, and produce waste and/or pest issues. If you purchase frozen banana puree, it is stabilized with some sugar and some acid to control the Achilles' heel of all bananas; oxidization. No one likes a brown banana, and I doubt brown banana ice cream would be a top seller, so you must either buy industrialized batches of partially oxidizing sweetened banana puree, or you set up a ripening operation inside your production space. It is a pain in the neck, and probably explains why there are so few ice cream companies dedicated to making banana flavors these days.

Despite all of this, for me bananas are the perfect fruit for ice cream. They have a signature flavor, which is easily recognized, and their unique balance of water, starch, and sugar creates a beautiful texture in ice cream. They are versatile at creating ice cream flavors that can excite and soothe at the same time. And let's not forget that the name sounds great—unless of course you are banana phobic.

CHUNKY MONKEYS

In 1988, when one of my favorite pint of ice cream was created, I was 10 years old. Chunky Monkey. Banana ice cream loaded with giant chocolate fudge chunks and walnuts. Banana ice cream was not popular at the time, and after a lifetime of summers with my grandparents eating the classic butter pecan, vanilla, or rainbow sherbet all served from a half-gallon rectangular box, this was novel. It was only available in a pint, and it was made by a couple of hippies who looked more like my father than my grandfather. These guys were flavor genii! Sadly, things changed in 2000 when Unilever—one of the largest multinational companies on earth, responsible for hits such as I Can't Believe It's Not Butter! and Axe body spray—completed their hostile takeover of Ben & Jerry's. The flavor was discontinued for a period and has returned off and on with limited availability. I have eaten Chunky Monkey a few times since and it is not the same. The ice cream is gummier, with chocolate fudge chunks that are waxier, and with less walnuts and less banana flavor. It's a shame. I have read lots of interviews and official statements about the Ben & Jerry's Unilever transaction, and after filtering PR bullshit I am pretty sure Ben and Jerry would be happier if they had not sold; the product would be better, and they may have had an even larger social impact. I have always been inspired by the success of their independent spirit and see their story as a cautionary tale of what can happen if you lose control of your creation. Just imagine what other Chunky Monkeys they might have created.

DRUNKEN MONKEY

EVEN THOUGH UNILEVER RUINED one of my favorite childhood flavors, I thought we should try to come up with a tongue-in-cheek homage. We start with fresh banana ice cream and add Japanese and American Whiskey. The American whiskey is the backbone with heat and a little sweetness while the Japanese whiskey is less hot, clearer, and more direct. In place of walnuts and chocolate, we use Picassos' peanuts and peanut butter cups. It's nothing like the original, but when I eat it, it is a nostalgic rewire.

Makes approximately 1 quart

....

Heavy Cream	1½ cups (357g)
Whole Milk	1 cup (245g)
Glucose Syrup	2 tablespoons (40g)
Granulated Sugar	½ cup (100g)
Whole Milk Powder	¼ cup (30g)
Kosher Salt	¼ teaspoon (2g)
Large Banana	1 (150g; about 1 cup sliced)
Japanese Whiskey	2 tablespoons (30g)
Old Overholt Whiskey	1 tablespoon (15g)
Chopped Mini Reese's Peanut Butter Cups	4 tablespoons (40g)
Chopped Picosos' Peanuts, salted	3 tablespoon (30g)

....

Heat the cream, milk, and glucose syrup in a 4-quart saucepan, over medium heat, stirring with a rubber spatula or wooden spoon to keep it from burning, until small bubbles appear around the edges and the temperature reaches 180°F.

In a large bowl, whisk together the sugar, milk powder, and salt.

Slowly pour the hot cream mixture into the bowl, stirring constantly.

Pour the mixture back into the pot and cook over medium heat, stirring constantly, until it returns to 180°F.

Remove from the heat and immediately strain through a fine-mesh strainer into a clean container. Add the bananas and both whiskeys and blend with an immersion blender until smooth.

Fill a large bowl with ice and cold water to make an ice bath.

Put the container into the ice bath and let the base cool to 38°F, stirring occasionally.

Freeze in an ice cream maker according to the manufacturer's instructions.

Once the ice cream is done churning, add the peanut butter cups and peanuts and mix them in.

BANANA CURRY

I love to make this ice cream, but I really dislike the final product. Luckily lots of customers disagree. Hopefully, you will, too. Bananas sometimes make a cameo with curries, substituted for the more common chutney as a sort of sweet condiment.

The base for this flavor comes from cooking the bananas in melted butter and unrefined brown sugar. If you can get it, Gula Jawa or jaggery will give the richest flavor. Both are different types of unrefined sugar made from palm sap or boiled dates. Brown sugar will also work, but the flavor will not be as rich or complex. This is an unusual flavor, not for the unadventurous.

Makes approximately 1 quart

Unsalted Butter	2 tablespoons (30g)
Gula Jawa or jaggery, chopped or broken up	½ cup (97g)
Roughly Chopped Bananas	1 cup (about 2 large bananas; 300g)
Yellow Curry Powder	1 teaspoon (3g)
Heavy Cream	1⅔ cups (403g)
Whole Milk	½ cup (123g)
Glucose Syrup	2 tablespoons (40g)
Whole Milk Powder	¼ cup (30g)
Kosher Salt	¼ teaspoon (2g)

In a 4-quart saucepan, melt the butter completely and then add the Gula Jawa.

Once the sugar has melted, add the bananas and curry powder. Cook the bananas until they are soft and broken down, 5 to 8 minutes.

Add the cream, milk, and glucose syrup to the banana mix and heat the mixture over medium heat, stirring with a rubber spatula or wooden spoon to keep it from burning, until small bubbles appear around the edges and the temperature reaches 180°F.

In a large bowl, whisk together the milk powder and salt.

Slowly pour the hot cream mixture into the bowl, stirring constantly.

Pour the mixture back into the pot and cook over medium heat, stirring constantly, until it returns to 180°F.

Remove from the heat and pour into a clean container.

Fill a large bowl with ice and cold water to make an ice bath.

Put the container into the ice bath and let the base cool to 38°F, stirring occasionally.

Freeze in an ice cream maker according to the manufacturer's instructions.

BANANAS FOSTER

BANANAS FOSTER IS A DESSERT DATING BACK TO 1951, invented at Brennan's restaurant in New Orleans. This is not an ice cream recipe, but rather a party trick for making dessert at home, when all you have is ice cream, and you need to produce something more. This concept can be applied to almost any fruit, and even bread or leftover cake. The alcohol needs to be 40 percent by volume to give you a real flambé, which is the point. I like an American bourbon like Barrell Bourbon for this one, but any dark spirit will work.

Serves 2

GRANULATED SUGAR	½ CUP (100G)
BANANAS	2 MEDIUM-SIZE (1 CUP; 300G)
SALTED BUTTER	3 TABLESPOONS (45G)
KOSHER SALT	¼ TEASPOON (2G)
AMERICAN BOURBON OR OTHER DARK SPIRIT (I LIKE BARRELL BOURBON BEST)	¼ CUP (60G)
VANILLA ICE CREAM	(YOUR CHOICE)

As usual, pay attention. This one has hot caramel, which will burn you badly, as well as an uncontrolled open flame, which will also burn you, but not as badly as the caramel. Tie your hair back and watch your eyebrows.

Normally I suggest you have all of your ingredients prepped and in place before you start, however for this recipe, I don't want the bananas to brown and dry out at all, so start by heating a sauté pan before you do anything else. Try to use a pan with enough surface area to hold your chopped fruit in one layer. If you don't there will probably be a little soup of juices from the fruit and the sugar, which you want to cook off quickly so that you don't completely obliterate your fruit. Cook your bananas in a couple of batches if you need to, and adjust how large, small, or thinly you chop them.

Heat a 10-inch sauté pan over medium heat. Once your pan is hot, add half the sugar to the pan and stir until melted. Add the remaining sugar. Chop your bananas quickly while keeping an eye on the color of the sugar, which will caramelize quickly and can burn easily. Stir in the butter and salt and finish chopping your fruit. Add the fruit to the caramel as soon as the butter has melted and is completely incorporated. Quickly toss the fruit in the caramel over medium flame and wait until the liquid has reduced to a saucy consistency. This will take about a minute. Add the alcohol and wait until it is simmering, then tip the pan and let the flame from the cooktop ignite the alcohol in the pan. The flame will jump high. DO NOT PANIC, wait for the flames to calm down as the alcohol burns off, and decide how much further to reduce the sauce. Be ready to immediately spoon this over ice cream. The whole point of this is to eat piping hot alcohol caramel with cold melting ice cream. Don't burn your mouth.

COMMODITY BANANAS

Almost all the imported bananas in the US come through New York City, a holdover bottleneck that started over 100 years ago. They are ripened in a series of giant temperature-controlled rooms to achieve the perfectly ripe banana. This unfortunately unglamorous process has hundreds of thousands of cases of bananas hitting the shelves across the country at just the right ripeness. They are so common that we take them for granted, but when working with bananas, it is important to remember that before they were a commodity, they were special, delicate. For many of us, they were the first food after our mother's milk, naturally soft and sweet, easy to chew and harmless. While most of the bananas you find today are the same Cavendish variety, there are hundreds of others out there. If you find yourself in a hot climate somewhere, try a local banana, I guarantee you will be surprised, and, possibly delighted, to taste the different ways this fruit can express itself.

CHARRED BANANA

I DEVELOPED THIS RECIPE OUT OF DISTASTE for a common technique employed by many of the chefs I've worked for. It involved baking bananas in their skin until they steam and split open. Sometimes the bananas would have aromatic spices like cinnamon bark or star anise scattered over them to add flavor. On paper this sounds good, but bananas steamed in their skin are bland and watery. Fortunately, when the skins split, the bananas would ooze out onto the hot baking tray, the juices creating a natural banana caramel, sometimes charring a bit at the edges. That flavor was delicious, but rarely made it into the recipe. After many attempts, I finally landed on an ice cream that delivered the layers of burnt banana caramel I had scraped off so many baking trays. The key is to caramelize the banana in its skin (this recipe could be called Charred Steamed Banana). The skin traps the moisture as it cooks and steams the banana while the exposed parts of the fruit are given a delicious banana brûlée. The more the banana is charred, the stronger the flavor will be.

Makes approximately 1 quart

FOR THE CHARRED BANANAS

BANANAS	4 (ABOUT 1½ CUPS; 400G)
CANOLA OIL	

FOR THE ICE CREAM BASE

HEAVY CREAM	1⅔ CUPS (403G)
WHOLE MILK	¾ CUP (184G)
GLUCOSE SYRUP	2 TABLESPOONS (40G)
GRANULATED SUGAR	½ CUP (150G)
WHOLE MILK POWDER	¼ CUP (30G)
KOSHER SALT	¼ TEASPOON (2G)

To make the charred bananas: A cast iron skillet works great, but a sauté pan will also do. Heat the pan on medium heat. While the pan is heating, use a sharp knife to filet the bananas lengthwise, keeping the pieces together in their skins so that the cut surfaces do not dry out or oxidize while waiting to go into the pan. Add a little oil to the pan and press the bananas down to make an even seal. Let the bananas cook for a few minutes, checking how soft they are by pressing the skin with your finger. As usual, be careful. The pan is hot, the oil is hot, the bananas are hot.

Scrape them free from the pan using a spatula and place them on a plate or baking tray. Do not stack them, as the banana peel will leave a strong astringent taste which is bad. Once they are cooled enough to handle, scrape the cooked flesh from the peel into a medium bowl, and set it aside.

To make the base: In a 4-quart saucepan, combine the cream, milk, and glucose syrup and heat over medium heat, stirring with a rubber spatula or wooden spoon to keep it from burning, until small bubbles appear around the edges and the temperature reaches 180°F.

In a large bowl, whisk together the sugar, milk powder, and salt.

Slowly pour the hot cream mixture into the bowl, stirring constantly.

Pour the mixture back into the pot and cook over medium heat, stirring constantly, until it returns to 180°F.

Remove from the heat and immediately strain through a fine-mesh strainer into a clean container. Add the charred bananas and using a hand-held or immersion blender, blend until smooth.

Fill a large bowl with ice and cold water to make an ice bath.

Put the container into the ice bath and let the base cool to 38°F, stirring occasionally.

Freeze in an ice cream maker according to the manufacturer's instructions.

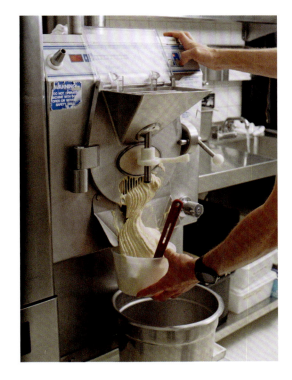

MACADAMIA PRALINE BANANA

THIS IS AN EPIC FLAVOR, combining two of my favorite ingredients, fresh bananas and macadamia nuts. I've always loved both, but this love was only fully crystalized during my time living in Hawaii on a property with banana palms growing wildly. Bananas in tropical places taste different, they are local and have not been harvested green but allowed to ripen on the plant. They also come in lots of different varieties that help you understand the complex subtleties in flavor this fruit is capable of. Raw macadamia nuts are rich and mild. Once they are toasted, they take on the epitome of buttery nuttiness. Combined with the smooth silky sweetness of fresh bananas, this makes for an irresistible combination.

Makes approximately 1 quart

Heavy Cream	1½ cups (357g)
Whole Milk	¾ cup (184g)
Glucose Syrup	2 tablespoons (40g)
Granulated Sugar	¾ cup (150g)
Whole Milk Powder	¼ cup (30g)
Kosher Salt	¼ teaspoon (2g)
Medium Bananas	2 (about 1 cup; 300g)
Macadamia Praline (page 194)	

In a 4-quart saucepan, heat the cream, milk, and glucose syrup over medium heat, stirring with a rubber spatula or wooden spoon to keep it from burning, until small bubbles appear around the edges and the temperature reaches 180°F.

In a large bowl, whisk together the sugar, milk powder, and salt.

Slowly pour the hot cream mixture into the bowl, stirring constantly.

Pour the mixture back into the pot and cook over medium heat, stirring constantly, until it returns to 180°F.

Remove from the heat and immediately strain through a fine-mesh strainer into a clean container. Add the bananas and using a handheld or immersion blender, blend until smooth.

Fill a large bowl with ice and cold water to make an ice bath.

Put the container into the ice bath and let the mixture cool to 38°F, stirring occasionally.

Freeze in an ice cream maker according to the manufacturer's instructions.

Add a healthy drizzle of macadamia praline to the banana ice cream just before it is scooped.

Enjoy.

MACADAMIA PRALINE

Macadamias are the Tiffany's of nuts. Their balanced richness and texture is the platonic ideal of what a nut can be. Typically cultivated in a tropical environment, they're also exotic and expensive, which adds to their appeal. Their flavor is arguably the most crave-able, with a perfectly dense crunch. While I love them toasted and added into an ice cream, they are beautifully suited for a praline paste.

The macadamia praline is made by caramelizing the macadamia nuts. Half the nuts are caramelized in sugar and half are roasted in the oven. And then they're all blended together until they make a paste. It has an outstanding toasted macadamia caramel flavor. The consistency is very similar to peanut butter, and when you add it into a bright, acidic flavor, such as passion fruit ice cream, it's an instant hit.

This recipe takes time. Be patient and follow along, the result is worth it.

Makes a generous ½ cup

MACADAMIA NUTS	1 CUP (97G)
COOKING SPRAY	
GRANULATED SUGAR	¼ CUP (50G)
POWDERED SUGAR	½ CUP PLUS 2 TABLESPOONS (60G)

Preheat your oven to 325°F. Line two baking sheets with parchment paper.

Divide the nuts evenly between the prepared baking sheets and place them in the oven. Remove one baking sheet once the nuts are warm and lightly toasted, about 10 minutes. Remove them from the oven and place them in a small heat proof container, like a coffee cup or small bowl. Do not cover them as they will sweat. Continue cooking the second baking sheet until the nuts are golden brown, 5 to 10 minutes longer. Set aside to cool completely.

Prepare a baking pan with parchment paper and spray it with cooking spray.

Over medium heat, cook the granulated sugar in a 2-quart saucepan large enough to accommodate the lightly toasted macadamia nuts. Once the sugar has melted and is blonde, add the warm batch of macadamia nuts and stir vigorously with a wooden spoon to combine. Continue cooking over medium-low heat stirring constantly. The nuts and the sugar should be loose, and the sugar will continue caramelizing while the nuts toast in their hot caramel bath. Both the caramel and the nuts can burn, so be vigilant. Once you smell the toasting nuts and slightly acrid bitter caramel, about 5 to 7 minutes, you are done. Immediately remove from the heat and pour out onto the prepared baking pan. Cool completely. If it is humid, you will need to keep an eye on these and be prepared to grind them as soon as they are cool, they will absorb moisture and become sticky if you don't.

Place the cooled toasted macadamia nuts and the powdered sugar in a food processor. Grind to a mealy consistency. Transfer to a small bowl and set aside.

Break up the caramelized macadamia nuts and place them in the food processor. Pulse them until you have a coarse meal. Add the powdered sugar macadamia meal and pulse together until you have a smooth paste. This will take time, about 15 minutes, and require scraping down the sides of the food processor with a rubber spatula regularly. The macadamia nuts will slowly release their oils and the praline will become smooth and pourable at which point it is done.

This will keep covered at room temperature for up to 2 weeks.

197

AVOCADO

COCONUT SORBET

PINEAPPLE SALTED EGG YOLK

STRAWBERRY GUAVA SORBET

MANGO PASSION RICE

DURIAN BANANA

TROPICAL FLAVORS

Tropical is a state of mind, often marketed as exotic and healthy—beaches and bikinis and palm trees and drinks and bright colors and relaxation and fun. For a lot of people, a tropical flavor tasted for the first time on vacation transports them back. It's foreign but familiar at the same time—especially if it is an ice cream or sorbet. No matter how cold and barren it may be outside, it's always warm and beautiful somewhere.

We've had a tropical category on our menu for years and the list of fruits we feature is long: It covers the usual suspects—mango, pineapple, and coconut—but also pandan, mangosteen, papaya, and durian. Bananas are technically tropical but have become their own flavor category (see page 179). Coconut is technically a nut, but it belongs in the tropical category, because it is clearly part of the tropical state of mind.

Tropical fruits are seasonless, suggesting perennial flourishing, vitality, and vibrancy. Bright and colorful and fresh, I love how clear and distinctly their flavors land on the palate. They present lots of creative possibilities in ice cream. When combining them with other ingredients they can create compelling colors and tastes, almost like artificial candy, especially in sorbets.

AVOCADO TOAST

A few years into running Morgenstern's, avocado toast became very popular in cafés and restaurants in New York. It was a silly trend, because putting avocado on toast is about as hard as putting on a T-shirt. A friend told me I should make an avocado ice cream toast to thumb my nose at the trend and simultaneously cash in on it. So, I toasted some Japanese white bread, layered it with avocado ice cream, drizzled it with condensed milk and olive oil, and sprinkled it with salt. When you eat it, you recognize it, you understand that you're eating toast, and you understand that you're eating avocado. It's simultaneously familiar and unexpected. It's a sweet version of a savory taste. As the trend settled in, our avocado toast became popular, so we stopped serving it.

AVOCADO

AVOCADO ICE CREAM SOUNDS MORE INTERESTING THAN IT ACTUALLY IS. Once you take a bite, you might say "That's just how I thought it would taste." And you'd be right: it is predictable. Avocado is technically a fruit. It is rich and fatty, and lends itself to making something smooth and creamy—which of course is what ice cream is. The flavor is subtle but also distinctly flexible. Even though we mostly eat it as guacamole, it can easily go sweet or savory.

Behind a banana, nothing browns like an avocado. Once you take it out of the skin and, most important, remove the pit, the clock is ticking, so make sure you get everything together before you start peeling. In fact, if you really want to capture the bright green color, get your base finished first and then start peeling and pitting. As soon as the avocados are cleaned, add them to the base, blend, strain immediately, and freeze as quickly as possible.

Makes approximately 1 quart

....

WHOLE MILK	1¼ CUPS (306G)
HEAVY CREAM	¾ CUP (179G)
GLUCOSE SYRUP	1½ TABLESPOONS (30G)
GRANULATED SUGAR	¾ CUP (150G)
WHOLE MILK POWDER	¼ CUP (30G)
KOSHER SALT	¼ TEASPOON (2G)
AVOCADO, RIPE FLESH	1¾ CUPS (385G)
LEMON JUICE	2 TABLESPOONS (30G)
CITRIC ACID	½ TEASPOON (2 G)

....

In a 4-quart saucepan, heat the milk, cream, and glucose syrup over medium heat, stirring with a rubber spatula or wooden spoon to keep it from burning, until small bubbles appear around the edges and the temperature reaches 180°F.

In a large bowl, whisk together the sugar, milk powder, and salt.

Slowly pour the hot cream mixture into the bowl, stirring constantly.

Pour the mixture back into the pot and cook over medium heat, stirring constantly, until it returns to 180°F.

Remove from the heat and immediately strain through a fine-mesh strainer into a clean container. Add the avocado and using a hand-held or immersion blender, immediately blend until smooth.

Fill a large bowl with ice and cold water to make an ice bath.

Put the container into the ice bath and let the base cool to 38°F stirring occasionally.

Stir together the lemon juice and citric acid in a small bowl and add to the avocado mixture. Freeze in an ice cream maker according to the manufacturer's instructions.

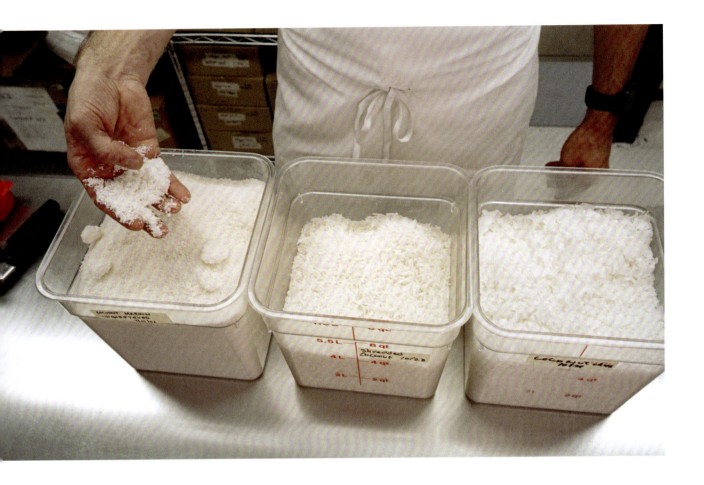

COCONUT

Coconut is very popular as a topping. Toasted coconut flakes add a tropical nutty crunch to ice cream, but choosing between sweetened, unsweetened, and flakes is tricky. Normally I am not a fan of sweetened ingredients, but in this case, there is something very nostalgic about sweetened shredded coconut. It has a specific shape and size which lends itself to being incorporated as a mix in, or as a topping. The other version is a macaroon of finely shredded coconut. This is great for toasting and steeping as you get the most surface area by weight, and therefore the most flavor. If you go the unsweetened route, then large coconut flakes are terrific, either toasted or dried. You cannot go wrong, no matter which of these you choose.

COCONUT SORBET

Coconuts are a good-time ingredient. If you're enjoying coconut in something, you're supposed to be having fun. They provide the foundation for the piña colada and the Mounds bar, and coconut milk and coconut cream are also the basis for some of the best nondairy ice creams.

Real life coconut is much different than coconut in ice cream. A fresh coconut has a shell that is hard like wood, protecting a spongy white flesh that is squeaky between your teeth. Its benignly pleasant flavor has made it popular, the same way that vanilla has become the default for subtle taste. I generally think that coconut should be shredded and toasted and steeped into a coconut ice cream base fortified by coconut milk or coconut cream. My favorite version is coconut sorbet which has milk, so it is technically a sherbet, but here we use coconut milk, making it vegan. It is just as delicious.

Makes approximately 1 quart

....

Unsweetened Shredded Coconut	1 scant cup (70g)
Coconut Milk	2⅔ cups (640g)
Coconut Cream	½ cup (122g)
Agave Syrup	⅓ cup (110g)
Kosher Salt	¼ teaspoon (2g)
Lime Juice	1 teaspoon (5g)

....

Preheat your oven to 325°F.

Line a baking tray with parchment paper and toast the coconut in the oven, 10 to 15 minutes, until golden brown.

Heat the coconut milk, coconut cream, agave, and salt in a 4-quart saucepan, on medium heat, stirring with a rubber spatula or wooden spoon, until it reaches 160°F.

Off heat, add the warm toasted coconut to the coconut mixture and steep for 30 minutes.

Strain through a fine-mesh strainer into a clean container. Using a spatula, press firmly on the strained coconut, to ensure that you've removed all the liquid, then add the lime juice.

Freeze in an ice cream maker according to the manufacturer's instructions.

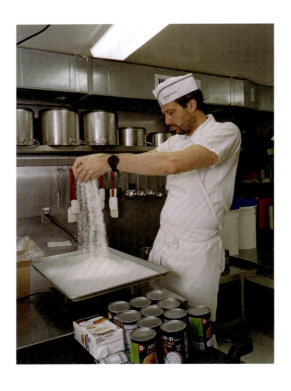

PINEAPPLE

Prized for their beautiful appearance, aroma, and flavor, if it was not for the durian (see page 225), pineapple might be king. Pineapple was brought to Hawaii in the late 1800s where it enjoyed a 60-year run of commercial cultivation, becoming a symbol of the state. And once the US started cultivating it, it was off to the races with the Pineapple Growers Association suggesting that it be served with baked ham and, of course, the ever-classic piña colada. All of these approaches were about marketing, aimed to help promote the consumption of pineapple in circa 1950s industrialized America.

Sadly, that culinary legacy—upside-down cake, fruit salad, and polarizing pizza topping—is what has remained. As far as ice cream goes, pineapple was long considered a mandatory ingredient in the banana split, but that is about it.

It works for sorbet but is actually an outstanding element in an ice cream where it stands alone with its own special acidity, completely unlike citrus acids; a lemon or a lime just can't do the same job as the pineapple. I have paired it with more predictable flavors like pandan and coconut, but I was shocked by the popularity of salted egg yolk pineapple. Salted eggs are egg yolks that are cured in salt for about 30 days until they are firm like a piece of cheddar cheese. They have an extra rich yolk and butter flavor which turns out to be perfect for balancing the acidity of pineapple. Don't underestimate pineapples' capability to create bright contrasting excitement to balance a mellow or rich flavor.

PICKLED PINEAPPLE

THIS IS NOT A TRULY PICKLED PINEAPPLE, more of a quick pickle. The vinegar and the honey both amplify and mellow the condiment out. Over the years customers have figured out this is a great addition to other flavors, such as Raw Milk (page 320) or Green Tea Pistachio (page 338). It's always good to have a little pickle on hand.

Makes about 2 cups

PINEAPPLE, CUT INTO ½-INCH CUBES	1¾ CUPS (330G)
KOSHER SALT	PINCH OF
LEMON JUICE	1 TABLESPOON (15G)
SIMPLE SYRUP	⅓ CUP (100G)
HONEY	2 TABLESPOONS (43G)
WHITE BALSAMIC VINEGAR	1 TABLESPOON (15G)

Toss the pineapple with the salt and lemon juice in a medium bowl.

In a 1-quart saucepan, bring the Simple Syrup, honey, and balsamic vinegar to a boil.

Pour the hot liquid over the pineapple to cover completely. Let cool completely and refrigerate.

The pickled pineapple will keep for 4 weeks covered and refrigerated.

Note: To make Simple Syrup, combine equal parts sugar (1 cup) and water (1 cup) in a saucepan and boil together for 5 minutes. Remove from the heat. Cool and keep in the fridge in an airtight container for up to 2 weeks. This yields 1½ cups.

PINEAPPLE SALTED EGG YOLK

SALTING EGG YOLKS IS AN ANCIENT METHOD FOR PRESERVING THEM. Their place of origin seems to be Malaysia, where eggs are buried in the sandy clay of caves near the ocean. The salt water permeates the clay, soaking through the shells and preserving the egg inside and making the yolk dense and rich. The eggs are then often dried out in an oven and crumbled on dishes, as if they were cheese. In Singapore, they are served as a bar snack, and have jumped directly to packaged chips that are now popular in the US. I have become a fan of the chips, and the flavor, which is at once umami, sweet, and salty. For this flavor, pineapple is a necessary foil. The richness of the egg needs acidity. Lemons or limes are too harsh, but the tropical punch of the pineapple is perfect. By the time this flavor had been on our menu for three months, it was consistently out selling strawberry and chocolate.

Makes approximately 1 quart

....

HEAVY CREAM	1½ CUPS (357G)
WHOLE MILK	¼ CUP (61G)
GLUCOSE SYRUP	1½ TABLESPOONS (30G)
LARGE EGG YOLKS	7
GRANULATED SUGAR	¾ CUP (150G)
KOSHER SALT	1 SCANT TEASPOON (4G)
PINEAPPLE PURÉE	1¼ CUPS (306G)
SALTED EGG YOLK STREUSEL (PAGE 212)	1 CUP (171G)

....

Combine the cream, milk, and glucose syrup in a 4-quart saucepan, and heat over medium heat, stirring with a rubber spatula or wooden spoon to keep it from burning, until small bubbles appear around the edges and the temperature reaches 180°F.

In a large bowl, whisk together the egg yolks, sugar, and salt.

Slowly pour the hot cream mixture into the bowl, stirring constantly.

Pour the mixture back into the pot and cook over medium heat, stirring constantly, until it returns to 180°F.

Remove from the heat and immediately strain through a fine-mesh strainer into a clean container. Fill a large bowl with ice and cold water to make an ice bath.

Put the container into the ice bath and let the base cool to 38°F, stirring occasionally.

Add the pineapple purée and freeze in an ice cream maker according to the manufacturer's instructions. Stir in the Salted Egg Yolk Streusel.

SALTED EGG YOLK STREUSEL

SALTED EGG YOLKS CAN BE PURCHASED FROZEN from stores that specialize in Asian ingredients, or online. They have the texture of semi-firm cheddar cheese.

Makes about 1⅓ cups

WHOLE SALTED EGG YOLKS	1 CUP (171G)
COARSE CORNMEAL	¼ CUP (30G)
KOSHER SALT	½ TEASPOON (4G)
UNSALTED BUTTER, MELTED	2 TABLESPOONS (30G)

Preheat your oven to 325°F.

Line a sheet pan with parchment paper and place the salted egg yolks on the pan. Bake for 15 minutes until they sweat.

Remove from the oven and let the yolks cool completely. Leave the oven on.

In a food processor, grind the egg yolks, cornmeal, and salt to a fine meal texture.

Add the butter and pulse to combine.

Spread the mixture back over the parchment-lined sheet pan and toast in the oven for about 10 minutes until golden brown.

Remove from the oven and cool completely. The streusel be stored in an airtight container in the refrigerator for 2 weeks.

PASSIONFRUIT

Passionfruit is one of the best tart ingredients available. Better than lemon, better than lime, better than even cranberries or green apples. Its tartness is punctuated by a subtle tropical perfume. It is easy to find, relatively inexpensive, and as a sorbet it is always a winner—far better than lemon or lime sorbet. Somehow, although it has been part of plated dessert culture in America for at least three decades, it has not yet jumped over to the mainstream and isn't widely found in candy, soda, or ice cream foods. Passionfruit Skittles? Passionfruit Magic Shell? At Morgenstern's, we typically use passionfruit for sorbet, mixing it in with mango or something similar, however it is also excellent with milk chocolate, delicious in the same way that raspberry and dark chocolate are a perfect pair. If you really want to take it to another level, order the seeds or pulp separate from the purée and make a caramel with them.

GUAVA

Guava is the sexier, more complex cousin of passion fruit. Also bright and tart, it is vibrant in color with a pure aromatic, tropical flavor. The fruit stands up very well in both sorbet and ice cream and also makes delicious marshmallows and jellies. It is a fruit to watch in the twenty-first century. In countries where it grows wild, it can seem like a scourge, littering the streets and highways, smashed and creating guava jam all over the roads. While passion fruit seeds are a part of its identity, most people associate guava with the purée only. The fruit is loaded with small round seeds hard as stones which is probably why fresh guava is not a household item.

STRAWBERRY GUAVA SORBET

THIS FLAVOR IS GREATER THAN THE SUM OF ITS PARTS. Strawberry and guava complement each other in a way that creates an exciting and delightful new flavor. They were made for each other.

Makes about 3½ cups

GUAVA PURÉE	2¼ CUPS (555G)
STRAWBERRY PURÉE	1 CUP (245G)
SIMPLE SYRUP (PAGE 209)	⅓ CUP (108G)
KOSHER SALT	¼ TEASPOON (2G)
LEMON JUICE	1 TABLESPOON (15G)

In a large bowl, thoroughly combine the guava and strawberry purées, the Simple Syrup, salt, and lemon juice.

Strain through a fine-mesh strainer into a clean container.

Fill a large bowl with ice and cold water to make an ice bath.

Put the container into the ice bath and let the base cool to 38°F, stirring occasionally.

Freeze in an ice cream maker according to the manufacturer's instructions.

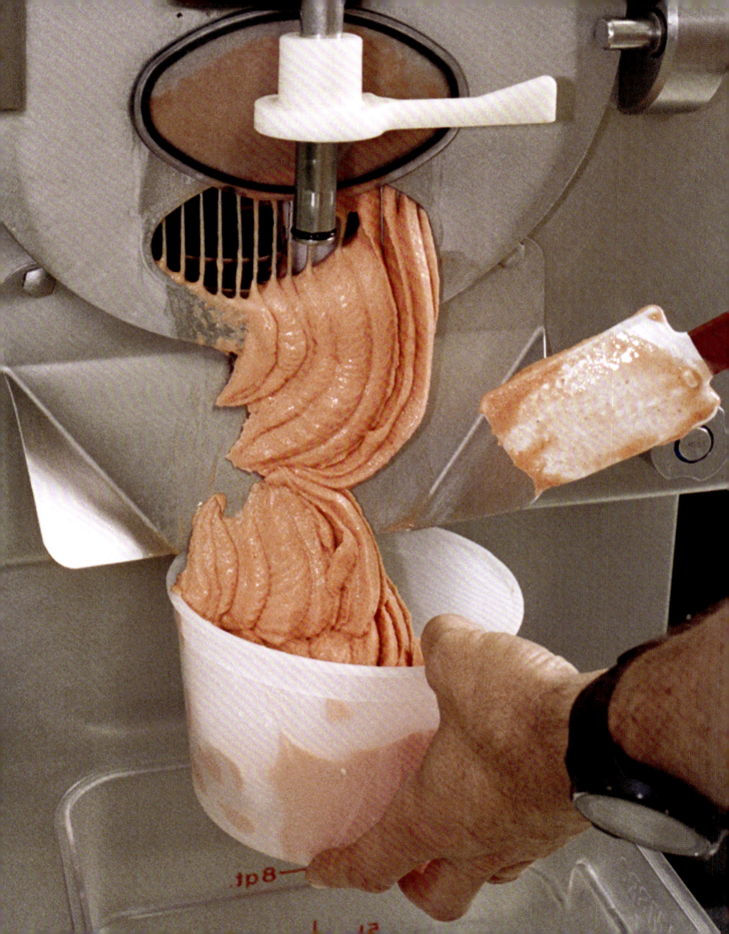

MANGO PASSION RICE

VEGAN IS ANNOYING. It is an unnecessary obstacle on the road to deliciousness. When I started cooking, this obstacle was not taken seriously, and often ignored. That is no longer the case. We are leaps and bounds from tofu over rice, but most vegan food still tastes bad, and a lot of it is terrible for your health—and the health of our ecosystems. That's another story. Occasionally, though, you stumble upon a vegan version that is far better than the original; this is the case with Mango Passion Rice. Mango lends itself beautifully to a nondairy ice cream, adding richness in texture and flavor. We add passionfruit to pump up the flavor, and in the shop we make our own rice milk using sushi rice. Making rice milk is great, but a lot of work, so I recommend getting the best you can from the store, which means the lowest amount of oil and sugar you can find.

Makes approximately 1 quart

Rice Milk	½ cup (123g)
Coconut Milk	1¼ cups (305g)
Light Agave Syrup	2 tablespoons (42g)
Granulated Sugar	1 cup (200g)
Kosher Salt	¼ teaspoon (2g)
Glucose Syrup	2 tablespoons (40g)
Passionfruit Purée	¼ cup (60g)
Mango Purée	1 cup (245g)
Lime Juice	1 tablespoon (15g)

In a 4-quart saucepan, combine the rice milk, coconut milk, agave, sugar, salt, and glucose syrup and heat over medium heat, stirring with a rubber spatula or wooden spoon to keep it from burning, until the sugar has dissolved.

Remove from the heat and immediately strain through a fine-mesh strainer into a clean container. Fill a large bowl with ice and cold water to make an ice bath.

Put the container into the ice bath and let the base cool to 38°F, stirring occasionally.

Add the passionfruit and mango purées, and the lime juice.

Freeze in an ice cream maker according to the manufacturer's instructions.

VEGAN MANGO SUNDAE

This is an extension of the Mango Passion Rice (page 218) flavor. I like to add lots of fresh fruit, in layers, to surprise and delight. The sundae should be assembled in tall clear glasses.

A Note on Supremes: This is a method for separating the flesh of citrus from any zest or pith. It can be time-consuming but is worth it for capturing the essence of the citrus. A sharp chef's knife or paring knife work best. Start by cutting the top and the bottom off the fruit. Carefully cut the zest and pith away from the fruit from top to bottom, working your way around the fruit. Once all of the pith is removed, hold the fruit in the palm of your hand and cut out the center of each segment, making sure none of the inner membrane comes with it. Remove any seeds and store refrigerated in a sealed container of their own juices..

Makes 4 sundaes

....

Ripe Champagne Mangoes, peeled and cut into ¼ inch pieces	2
Mango Passionfruit Caramel (page 222)	½ cup (151g)
Coconut Whipped Cream (page 222)	3 cups (480)
Navel Orange, supremed, cut into ¼ inch pieces	1
Lemon, supremed, cut into ¼ inch pieces	1
Lime, supremed, cut into ¼ inch pieces	1
Crushed Pineapple (page 92)	1 cup (250g)
Coconut Sorbet (page 205)	1 pint (455g)
Mango Chips (page 223)	1 sheet

....

To assemble the sundae

Distribute half the mango among four glasses.

Cover the mango with the Mango Passionfruit Caramel, enough to completely submerge it.

Add a layer of Coconut Whipped Cream.

Distribute the remaining mango and cover with more Mango Passionfruit Caramel.

Add a layer of the navel orange pieces.

Add a layer of the lemon and lime pieces.

Distribute the pineapple evenly among the glasses and smooth the surface.

Add one small scoop of Coconut Sorbet to each glass

Make a rosette of Coconut Whipped Cream and drizzle with the Mango Passionfruit Caramel.

Add the Mango Chips.

Enjoy.

COCONUT WHIPPED CREAM

Whipped cream is the most difficult thing to make for a vegan sundae. I have tried all kinds of alternatives and landed on this one. I only serve this on a sundae that will benefit from the flavor of coconut. The best way to make it is in a charger, which forces CO2 into the liquid. The best ones are made by iSi, come in small sizes, and are not that expensive. The coconut cream can be whipped by hand, but it will never get stiff enough to hold a peak without stabilizers, which I don't like to use. The coconut cream needs to be very cold (38°F) to hold a nice peak, so put the cream in the fridge for a few hours before you make it, and plan to hold the canister in an ice bath while making the sundaes.

Makes 2 cups

| Canned Coconut Cream | 2 cups (480g) |
| Powdered Sugar | 1 tablespoon (7g) |

Put the coconut cream and sugar into the canister, seal and shake it to dissolve the sugar. Load the cartridge and hold in an ice bath.

MANGO PASSIONFRUIT CARAMEL

Caramel is candy, so get your shit together before you start.

Makes about 1¼ cups

Granulated Sugar	1 cup (200g)
Water	3 tablespoons (40g)
Mango Purée, at room temperature	½ cup plus 2 tablespoons (145g)
Passionfruit Purée at room temperature	¼ cup (61g)

In a 4-quart saucepan, combine the sugar and water. Carefully rinse the inside edges of the pot with cold water on your hands to get any stray sugar granules off the edges.

Put the pot on high heat and cook until the caramel is light amber. Turn off the heat and gently swirl until the caramel is dark brown and the color of coffee (no milk). Gently pour a third of the mango purée into the caramel. BE CAREFUL! It will boil over and steam violently and can burn your hands or face. Gently swirl the pot until the mango purée is combined and then add another third. Continue until all the mango purée is incorporated. Stir in the passionfruit purée. Strain into a jar using a fine-mesh strainer and cool to room temperature. The caramel can be stored in the refrigerator for up to 2 weeks.

MANGO CHIPS

These are a garnish, and can be excluded, but a sundae is not a sundae without a flourish. These are basically crispy fruit rollups, and a delicious snack all on their own.

Makes 8 to 12 chips

Mango Purée	2 cups (490g)
Granulated Sugar	2 tablespoons (25g)
Lemon Juice	1 teaspoon (5g)

Preheat your oven to 200°F.

Combine the purée, sugar, and lemon juice in a medium bowl and whisk until the sugar has dissolved.

Pour the contents onto a nonstick baking sheet and spread into a thin layer.

Place the baking sheet in the oven and allow to dry out for 8 to 12 hours.

Remove from the oven and peel off large pieces while they are warm. They will cool quickly and should become crispy immediately. If they are still soft, put them back on the baking sheet and return them to the oven to continue drying until they are crisp. The chips can be stored in an airtight container for up to 1 week.

DURIAN BANANA

Durian are called the King of Fruit, with good reason. They are large and imposing, with flavor and aroma to match. In *Time for a Tiger*, author Anthony Burgess describes durians as "like eating a sweet raspberry blancmange in a lavatory." They remind me of a combination of white onion, banana, and ripe brie, but his sentiment is accurate; they aren't for everyone. Despite their horrific odor, the fruits are considered a delicacy in most of Southeast Asia. They are an aphrodisiac and one of nature's most nutritious fruits. These fruits are charged with controversy, one of the most polarizing ingredients I have ever encountered. I was introduced to them years ago, on the streets of Chinatown. I grew to love them for their outsize identity; no other fruit commands the space it occupies quite like the King of Fruit.

My feelings for durian were crystallized during the opening of my first store. It had been a very rough year leading up to the opening on Memorial Day weekend, 2014. A friend committed suicide in the summer of 2013 days after I signed the lease. I was sad and confused, unable to work. I came to my senses months later having lost crucial time for designing, planning, and building, with an exceptionally tough winter season settling in. Days were well below freezing for months. Working with no doors or windows on freezing steel plate floors, I installed plumbing, painted, and wrote the menu, freezing all day long. As spring approached, I was out of cash. I hired three people to help open the store and made all the ice cream for the holiday weekend myself. With the freezers stocked, I ran around installing the light fixtures and screwing in the coat hooks under the counter. When I pulled myself from under the counter there were 50 or 60 people waiting outside. We opened late that day and scooped nonstop all weekend. On Sunday evening when we were restocking the freezers, I could not find any Durian Banana. Impossible! I had made 5 gallons. I checked the freezers again and found it was true, we had nothing left. Monday was a holiday, and I could not get any Durian. We would eighty-six a flavor, my worst nightmare. The next day, I worked the register again, and to my surprise, many large groups, mostly families, had come from the outer boroughs and New Jersey for the Durian Banana flavor. We had been open for three days, and somehow word had spread. I spent the rest of the day enduring the looks of disappointment, frustration, and sadness as I told people we were out of Durian Banana. It has been on the menu since, and we have never run out.

Makes approximately 1 quart

Heavy Cream	1⅔ cups (403g)
Whole Milk	⅔ cup (170g)
Glucose Syrup	2 tablespoons (40g)
Granulated Sugar	⅔ cup (130g)
Whole Milk Powder	¼ cup (30g)
Kosher Salt	¼ teaspoon (2g)
Durian Fruit, cleaned and pitted (or frozen and defrosted)	½ cup packed (140g)
Banana (one large banana), peeled	¾ cup (150g)

Heat the cream, milk, and the glucose syrup in a 4-quart saucepan, over medium heat, stirring with a rubber spatula or wooden spoon to keep it from burning, until small bubbles appear around the edges and the temperature reaches 180°F.

In a large bowl, whisk together the sugar, milk powder, and salt.

Slowly pour the hot cream mixture into the bowl, stirring constantly.

Pour the mixture back into the pot and cook over medium heat, stirring constantly, until it returns to 180°F.

Remove from the heat and immediately strain through a fine-mesh strainer into a clean container.

In a medium bowl, blend the durian and banana with an immersion or tabletop blender until smooth.

Fill a large bowl with ice and cold water to make an ice bath.

Put the container into the ice bath and let the base cool to 38°F, stirring occasionally.

Freeze in an ice cream maker according to the manufacturer's instructions.

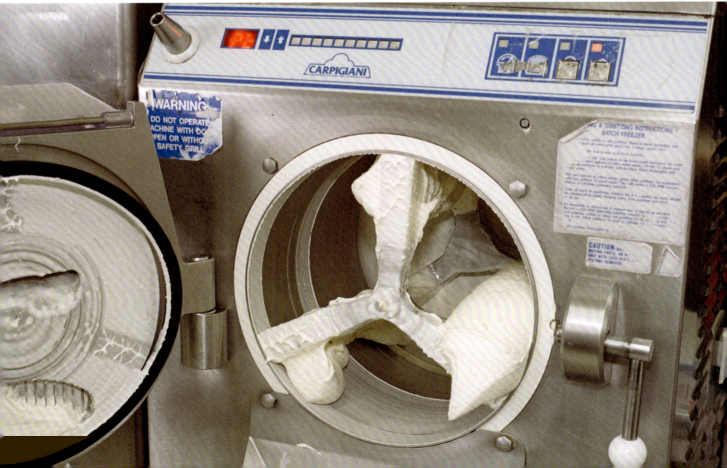

CARDAMOM LEMON JAM

LEMON CURD POPPYSEED

MANGO SATSUMA

YUZU TOASTED RICE

CITRUS

With its balance of expressive acidity and oily aromatic sweetness, citrus is (almost) always exciting. Getting the citrus of your imagination into a cup or cone, though, can be challenging. Because citrus juices are almost exclusively water, with no starch and very little pulp, they require lots of sugar to keep them from freezing, which makes them too sweet and separated. When dairy is in the mix curdling also becomes a factor. These challenges have forced innovation and yielded some unexpected citrus flavors; however, it is very common for citrus to act in a supporting role in its own flavor—as with our Cardamom Lemon Jam (page 232) or Blueberry Milk Chocolate (page 52).

In desserts, pairing dairy with citrus is generally relegated to curds and custards like lemon meringue pie or lemon bars, but at Morgenstern's, we use lots of lemon and/or lime juice in many of our ice creams and sorbets. Adding citrus can really change the flavor in unexpected ways; if something is too sweet, or the flavor is flat, lemon juice is probably the antidote. If you want a flavor that will turn up the volume, citrus is the answer.

CITRUS FAVORITES

Unlike the Minotaur or Sphinx, citrus hybrids are real. Citrus's ability to cross pollinate and reproduce—especially when grafting to create new fruits—has created many more varieties than the 10 or so original species. This includes lots of exotic varieties like the calamansi and yuzu but also covers most of the basics we eat everyday like grapefruit, tangelo, blood orange, clementine, Meyer lemon, and tangerine. Through hybridization and cultivation, hundreds of species and varieties have been created with many more surely to come. Distinguishing genetically pure citrus strains from hybrids has still not been fully accomplished, further complicating our understanding of the fruit, and more important, its characteristics.

Unfortunately, in the US we have an extremely restrictive policy on fruits and vegetables, which limits the variety of citrus and tropical fruits we can access. The diversity of citrus available throughout Asia is staggering when compared to what we have here, not just the variety, but the dramatic range of flavors. The industrialization of food has hurt few fruits (maybe the strawberry) more than the orange in America, creating an extraordinarily consistent if boring crop.

There are tons of other varieties of citrus out there, most of them best enjoyed fresh, but some of them make terrific options for ice cream, sorbet, or sherbet, and more citrus is on the way. Pay attention to the details in anything you are eating and be cautious and curious. Like other complex ingredients, it can be tough to know what to do with these different citrus flavors. I break some citrus varieties down into basic categories here. This is not comprehensive, but it can help guide tasting and working with different types of citruses. In general, trust your palate, and be patient.

SUPER SOUR

Citrus is known for nothing if not being sour, but there's a lot of variety in the tartness levels of their juices. Sometimes you need the most sour, and for that these are the best.

Lemon and **Lime** are as common in America as apples and bananas. They make a terrific sorbet or sherbet, but are best used as fresh juice to balance everything from Blueberry Milk Chocolate Ice Cream (page 52) to Raspberry Papaya Sorbet (page 268).

Sudachi is a Japanese citrus with powerful tart juice and a peppery aroma. It is a necessary ingredient in ponzu sauce. Sudachi are small, with a tight green peel that has loads of flavor and tons of seeds. The juice is similarly powerful to yuzu, but with a less subtle aromatic profile, and is terrific added to a lime sorbet popsicle to pump up the intensity of the tartness.

Calamansi is a hybrid of the kumquat and mandarin, unusual as kumquats have not historically cross-bred due to differences in their flowering cycle compared to other citruses. Small, and loaded with large seeds, calamansi are tough to deal with, like their parent the kumquat. Also like the kumquat, the skin is edible, with a sweet, fragrant balanced acidity. I love calamansi for sorbet, especially popsicles, given its puckering, refreshing acidity. It can also be made into a delicious marmalade, but you have to pick out all of those seeds.

SWEET AND SUBTLE

While tartness and sourness are the main features of citrus, these fruits are also known for their aromatics. The examples below are some of my favorite options for adding unexpected citrus flavor to a recipe.

Etrog lemon is most well-known for its use in the Jewish ceremony of Sukkot holiday rituals. It is a specific variety of citron (basically a prehistoric lemon) with an extraordinarily thick pith, lots of seeds, and very little pulp or juice. What makes this fruit special is its aromatic peel, and spongy pith. When candied and frozen into an ice cream, they take on a marshmallow like texture.

Pomelo is the largest citrus fruit. This is the original grapefruit, with bittersweet pulp and juice, and a very thick outer pith. The flavor is more subtle than grapefruit, and they typically have a neutral color similar to a lemon. The skin and juice of this fruit makes a terrific jam to be poured over a scoop of ice cream like a sauce, but when candied and frozen the peel takes on a great chew.

Meyer lemon is pretty well known by now for its subtle aromatic sweetness. The smooth skin and sweet juice makes it an ideal fruit to be added to ice cream whole (without the seeds). Inspired by limeade in Brazil, I love to blend these whole with condensed milk and ice for a delicious beverage. You can also do the same for a frozen yogurt, with the whole lemon blended and added after the base is strained.

"ARTIFICIALLY" DELICIOUS

There are a few citrus that have such perfectly balanced acidity and sweetness, that they almost taste artificial—in a good way. These can be used on their own, or with support from a neutral ingredient like Mascarpone cheese, banana or coconut.

Yuzu is incredible, and gets more attention by the day. Originally from central China, yuzus now feature prominently in Japanese cuisine. While it has been grown in the US for over 100 years, yuzu has only started to become readily available in the last 25 or so. The fresh yuzu I have found in the US can be very inconsistent, and pales in comparison to the (pasteurized) juice that is imported from Japan. The flavor is very bright and aromatic with a specific, bitter zing. Once you have tried one, the flavor is unmistakable, shining through when even a small amount is added. I find this fruit very strong when used on its own, even as a sorbet with sugar and water added. I prefer combining it with something more mellow, like toasted rice (see page 245) or combined with orange or mandarin juice. If you find yourself with a fresh yuzu, use it in place of lime juice in a Margarita.

Satsuma citrus has a perfect pucker to sweetness ratio, especially the juice. They are popular in the southern states as they were brought to Louisiana by Jesuit priests in the eighteenth century, and towns named after the fruit can be found in Texas, Florida, and Alabama. For me, this is the absolute platonic ideal of a creamsicle citrus, perfect for balancing with vanilla ice cream, ideally in a popsicle, or for pairing with the mellow sweetness of fresh mangos.

CARDAMOM LEMON JAM

THIS HAS BEEN ON OUR MENU FROM THE FIRST DAY WE OPENED. An instant classic that remains popular, it was created out of necessity. When we were testing all of the flavors for the shop, I found that we were using a lot of lemon juice. Piles and piles of lemon peels going in the trash was wasteful; we needed to do something with them. I worked out a lemon jam recipe based on an old orange marmalade recipe which was mostly orange peels and sugar. We keep the sugar to a minimum, cooking the lemon peels until they are translucent and then fortifying them with fresh lemon juice at the end. This creates a toothsome jam with a tart citrus pop, a perfect complement to the mellow and herbaceous green cardamom, which has a strong, pungent aroma, totally distinct, and unforgettable.

Makes approximately 1 quart

HEAVY CREAM	1⅔ CUPS (402G)
WHOLE MILK	1½ CUPS (367G)
GLUCOSE SYRUP	1½ TABLESPOONS (30G)
GRANULATED SUGAR	¾ CUP (150)
GREEN CARDAMOM PODS	1 TABLESPOON (5G)
WHOLE MILK POWDER	¼ CUP (30G)
KOSHER SALT	¼ TEAPOON (2G)
LEMON JAM (PAGE 233)	¼ CUP (68G)

In a 4-quart saucepan, heat the cream, milk, and glucose syrup over medium heat, stirring with a rubber spatula or wooden spoon to keep it from burning, until small bubbles appear around the edges and the temperature reaches 180°F.

In a food processor, grind the sugar and cardamom for about 5 minutes, pulsing until the pods are broken up into the sugar.

In a large bowl, whisk together the cardamom sugar, milk powder, and salt.

Slowly pour the hot cream mixture into the bowl, stirring constantly.

Pour the mixture back into the pot and cook over medium heat, stirring constantly, until it returns to 180°F.

Remove from the heat and immediately strain through a fine-mesh strainer into a clean container.

Fill a large bowl with ice and cold water to make an ice bath. Put the container into the ice bath and let the base cool to 38°F, stirring occasionally.

Freeze in an ice cream maker according to the manufacturer's instructions. Add a teaspoon of Lemon Jam to each scoop when serving.

LEMON JAM

I was tired of throwing out lemon peels, so I made lemon jam. Lemon peel jam is not new. Lots of different cultures use it as a condiment with fish, cheese, or desserts. Like chicken stock or Bolognese, everyone has their own style. Ours is about the peel, with the pith (the bitter white stuff) included. This is a recipe where you can fudge some of the measurements, and the results will still be good. It works for oranges, yuzu, and grapefruit. I prefer Oro Blanco grapefruit over Ruby Red or pink grapefruit because it is less bitter, and its zest is more aromatic. If using a fruit other than lemon, the sugar and acid will need to be adjusted. This jam has tremendous lemon flavor and texture, perfect for our Cardamom Lemon Jam (page 232), or frozen in a popsicle or ice cream cake.

Makes about 1¼ cups

Lemons	2
Granulated Sugar	½ cup (100g) plus ¼ cup (50g), divided
Water	⅔ cup (163g)
Sure-Jell Original Powdered Pectin	½ teaspoon (2g; measured by weight rather than volume, if possible)
Lemon Juice	3 tablespoons (45g)
Glucose Syrup	1½ tablespoons (30g)
Kosher Salt	pinch of

Juice the lemons thoroughly by hand. Do not use a motorized juicer, which may be more convenient but will shred the interiors of the lemon, making the juice bitter. Remove any seeds and reserve the juice in the refrigerator.

Soak the peels in cold water for 24 hours.

Drain and rinse the peels, removing any remaining seeds. Dice the peels. You should have 1 to 1¼ cups of diced peel (144g). The pieces need to be roughly the same size, but don't kill yourself.

In a 2-quart saucepan, combine the lemon peel with the ½ cup of sugar and the water. Cook at a low simmer over low heat, stirring occasionally, until the lemon is translucent and cooked through, 30 to 40 minutes. The liquid in the pan should remain at a pourable consistency. Keep the heat low, and stir in an additional tablespoon or so of water if needed to keep it saucy.

Stir together the remaining ¼ cup of sugar and the pectin in a small bowl. Slowly whisk it into the jam and return to a boil. Reduce to a gentle simmer for 20 minutes, stirring constantly.

Remove from the heat and add the lemon juice, glucose syrup, and salt.

Cool completely before using. Store in an airtight container in the refrigerator for up to 1 month.

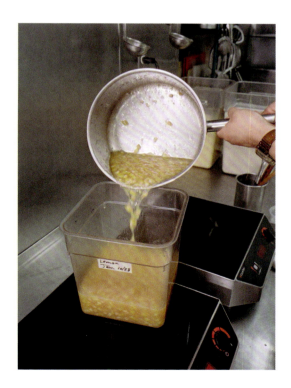

ZESTY

Citrus zest is superpowered. The essential oils in the peel add citrus flavor to so many things. Any chocolate orange candy is flavored with orange peel, not juice.

Fresh zest should be zested as close to the time you are going to use it as possible. I prefer to use a micro plane when zesting, being careful not to zest any of the white pith which is bitter. This method works well for giving a very clear and nonacidic version of whatever citrus you are using. Most of the time I strain the zest out of the ice cream base, but on occasion I will grind it with sugar, and leave it in for color and a little texture. Remember, zest can be very pungent, like freshly diced onions. Warming, grinding, and even burning the peels adds dimension to the flavor. Use a vegetable peeler to peel the citrus, and then caramelize the peel with a blowtorch before steeping it in your base. This will give an elevated caramelized orange peel flavor, reminiscent of a Sazerac.

Candied Zest

Properly candied zest is outstanding when frozen, giving it a chewy toothsome texture that is better than candy; gummy with a citrus flavor. In order to achieve this chewy texture, the zest and the pith (the spongey white interior) must remain intact. There are several ways to candy citrus zest. I prefer to soak the zest in cold water and cook it slowly over low heat in sugar and water until the zest is cooked through and translucent. I then store the zest in a light syrup to be added to ice creams either before scooping or just after they are frozen.

Marmalade

One of my favorite inclusions in ice cream is marmalade. Let me be clear, I don't love marmalade itself, but I love the technique, and I use it often with other citrus fruits. Marmalade as we know it today is a cultural mutation that started with quince paste, or something like Membrillo in Spain some thousand years ago. Sour oranges replaced quince in England sometime in the 1400s and it became a part of the breakfast and tea culture, popular to this day. It is not nearly as popular here in America where we prefer sweeter strawberry or apricot jams, but it is never difficult to find a jar of marmalade on the shelf of your chain grocery store. The traditional recipes are loaded with sugar, often too sweet to taste the citrus. I prefer a version where the fruit remains somewhat intact, thickened with pectin. Pectin-free jam purists please sit down; I would rather eat pectin than jam or marmalade loaded with sugar. We also add lots of fresh citrus juice at the end, so our marmalade or jam is very tart, sweet, and chewy with zest. It is a great addition, and once you get the hang of it you can mix it up with lots of other zests and fruit.

JUICY

Oranges first landed on US soil by way of Brazil sometime in the late 1800s, and we have been starting our day with a glass of orange juice since then. For me, fresh orange juice is the perfect morning beverage before coffee. I love that sweet, tart zing first thing. Citrus juice is amazing in all cooking, adding electricity wherever it goes. When it comes to cooking, the king of all citrus juices, though, is lemon, with its fresh, bright aroma and acidic zip that the color of the peel suggests. Lime and orange juice sit equally on either side of lemon juice. Limes are the most acidic, less sweet, with a slightly bitter finish. Orange juice is usually sweet first, with balanced acidity backing it up. Orange juice can be a great balance for something that needs light acidity and a little sweetness. All three can be used together. However, they need to be balanced to create harmony among them.

As for grapefruit, I have not found success with it in ice cream, or sorbet. Its watery bitterness is pronounced when it is frozen, and it does not play well with others.

It is important to keep citrus juice as fresh as possible. We use it a lot at the shop, so we always keep it on hand, juicing every other day. If you leave the juice in the fridge for more than three days, the flavor will lose its bite and become dull. If you are making small recipes, squeeze the juice fresh and strain out any seeds or pulp.

LEMON CURD POPPYSEED

Is it necessary to cook eggs and lemon juice in a water bath just to add them to a custard which is going to be frozen? I think so, as it ensures that the flavor and texture of the curd added to the ice cream base is rich, creamy, and lux. Poppyseeds are silly and pointless, with the exception of this flavor (and maybe muffins that people don't eat). They do add that characteristic pop, which for some reason has been paired with lemon, and lemon curd. In this ice cream the novelty of the poppyseed crunch set against the smooth lemon curd ice cream creates a unique yet familiar flavor.

Makes approximately 1 quart

Whole Milk	1⅓ cups (330g)
Heavy Cream	½ cup (119g)
Glucose Syrup	1½ tablespoons (30g)
Granulated Sugar	¾ cup (150g)
Whole Milk Powder	2 tablespoons (15g)
Kosher Salt	¼ teaspoon (2g)
Lemon Curd (page 240)	1 cup (275g)
Lemon Juice	1 tablespoon (15g)
Poppy Seeds (a lot!)	¼ cup (40g)

In a 4-quart saucepan, heat the milk, cream, and glucose syrup over medium heat, stirring with a rubber spatula or wooden spoon to keep it from burning, until small bubbles appear around the edges and the temperature reaches 180°F.

In a large bowl, whisk together the sugar, milk powder, and salt.

Slowly pour the hot cream mixture into the bowl, stirring constantly.

Pour the mixture back into the pot and cook over medium heat, stirring constantly, until it returns to 180°F.

Remove from the heat and immediately strain through a fine-mesh strainer into a clean container.

Fill a large bowl with ice and cold water to make an ice bath. Put the container into the ice bath and let the base cool to 38°F, stirring occasionally.

Using an immersion blender, fully incorporate the Lemon Curd and lemon juice.

Freeze in an ice cream maker according to the manufacturer's instructions. The poppyseeds can be stirred in at this time, or just before scooping.

LEMON CURD

Makes 1 cup

Egg Yolks	2
Egg	1
Lemon Juice	⅓ cup (88g)
Granulated Sugar	¼ cup (50g)
Kosher Salt	¼ teaspoon (2g)
Greek Yogurt	½ cup (113g)
Unsalted Butter	¼ cup (60g)

Fill an 8-quart stock pot with 1 quart of water, and bring to a simmer over medium heat.

In a large bowl, whisk together the egg yolks, egg, lemon juice, sugar, and salt. Whisk thoroughly.

Place the bowl over the simmering water, not actually touching the water, and turn down to low heat.

Cook over the simmering water, whisking regularly, for 10 to 15 minutes, until the curd begins to thicken.

Remove from the heat and, using a spatula, stir in the yogurt and butter.

Fill a large bowl with ice and cold water to make an ice bath.

Put the container into the ice bath stirring occasionally and let the curd cool to 38°F.

The curd can be stored, refrigerated, in a tightly sealed container for up to 7 days.

MANGO SATSUMA

Mango is one of the perfect fruits for making sorbet. It has the unique quality of being very fruit forward with lots of identity and plenty of starch to create a smooth and creamy texture when it is frozen. The tuned up sweet acidity of tangerine juice is an outstanding foil to the mellow sweetness of the mango and this sorbet tastes like candy, almost artificial, but in a good way.

Makes approximately 1 quart

Mango Purée 1¾ cups (428g)

Satsuma Juice (can be substituted with tangerine juice) 1⅓ cups (325g)

Simple Syrup (page 209) ½ cup (157g)

Kosher Salt ¼ teaspoon (2g)

Lemon Juice 2 tablespoons (30g)

Thoroughly combine the purée, satsuma juice, Simple Syrup, salt, and lemon juice in a large bowl.

Strain through a fine-mesh strainer into a clean container.

Fill a large bowl with ice and cold water to make an ice bath.

Put the container into the ice bath and let the base cool to 38°F, stirring occasionally.

Freeze in an ice cream maker according to the manufacturer's instructions.

ORANGES AND PINEAPPLE AND HOWARD JOHNSON'S

I've never been to a Howard Johnson's, Hojo's as it was once known. At its height it was the largest food service operation in America, long before McDonald's. Howard Johnson's were essentially giant diners, with huge menus served throughout the day. Popular with motorists, they were often positioned on the side of the highway.

In the beginning, the founder and owner, Howard Johnson, famously added ice cream to the menu to standout. It worked. They were known for serving 28 flavors which rarely changed (those 28 flavors are probably what led to Baskin-Robbins serving 31). The list is somewhat predictable, with vanilla in the number 1 slot, and you guessed it, chocolate in the number 2 position. But HoJo must have been a man after my own heart, because he also included grape nut and ginger flavors on the menu. Even the mythical black raspberry had a spot. These are interesting enough, but what stands out to me is pineapple orange. This flavor never left the mix and seems odd next to all the rich and creamy buttercrunch, butter pecan, and butterscotch flavors. Ice cream was at the foundation of the chain from the beginning, and the pineapple orange combination was a welcome novelty. It is also a terrific combo, and the inspiration for me to combine a tropical flavor with a conventional one in many of our sorbets. It works every time.

YUZU

Popular momentum around yuzu has been growing in the US for decades. Today it is available on grocery store shelves as soda, candy, and even face scrubs. What's so special about this stuff?

Less tart and more subtle than a lemon, with mythic flavor properties, the self-assured superhero of the citrus family with concentrated clarity and light aromatics. Sadly, yuzu fruit and trees are still banned by the USDA, and cannot be brought into the United States. However, pasteurized yuzu juice is readily available from Japan in both salted and unsalted versions. While I love the way that salt enhances oranges and limes, Yuzu does not need it, coming fresh with its own boosters built in. It is available in 1.8 liter bottles, and it is very strong, so not too much is needed. Fresh yuzu has recently become more widely available in the US, and while it is not the same as anything you might get in Japan, it is a good start, more interesting than lemons or limes.

YUZU TOASTED RICE

For us at Morgenstern's, highlighting the flavor of yuzu is key. Since the fruit is expensive, and availability can be an issue, I prefer making jam, jelly, or candy with it. Yuzu jelly is simple, and it allows the yuzu flavor to punch up. It can be used with a lot of flavors, from vanilla to chocolate.

Toasted Rice is used in a lot of different cuisines and dishes. It adds a background flavor and texture, and it tastes like what you might guess—roasty toasty nutty rice. We use it here to flavor our ice cream base and then strain it out. It gives a beautiful nutty vanilla flavor that rounds the electric acidity of the yuzu jelly.

Note: The jam should ideally be made at least 24 hours before the ice cream is going to be frozen to allow it to cool and set. You can add it the same day if you have no choice, but don't add it hot.

Makes approximately 3½ cups

Short-Grain Sushi Rice	½ cup (108g)
Whole Milk	1½ cups (367g)
Heavy Cream	1½ cups (357g)
Glucose Syrup	2 tablespoons (40g)
Granulated Sugar	⅔ cup (138g)
Whole Milk Powder	¼ cup (30g)
Kosher Salt	¼ teaspoon (2g)
Yuzu Jelly (page 248)	⅓ cup (94g)

Preheat your oven to 400°F

Toast the rice on a baking sheet for about 15 minutes, or until golden brown.

While the rice is toasting, heat the milk, cream, and glucose syrup in a 4-quart saucepan, over medium heat, stirring with a rubber spatula or wooden spoon to keep it from burning, until small bubbles appear around the edges and the temperature reaches 180°F.

In a large bowl, whisk together the sugar, milk powder, and salt.

Slowly pour the hot cream mixture into the bowl, stirring constantly.

Pour the mixture back into the pot and cook over medium heat, stirring constantly, until it returns to 180°F.

Remove from the heat, add the hot toasted rice to the mix, and steep for 15 minutes.

Strain through a fine-mesh strainer into a clean container.

Fill a large bowl with ice and cold water to make an ice bath.

Put the container into the ice bath and let the base cool to 38°F, stirring occasionally.

Freeze in an ice cream maker according to the manufacturer's instructions. Swirl in the Yuzu Jelly, it should not be fully incorporated.

YUZU JELLY

NOTE: The jelly will remain loose and pourable.

Makes ½ cup

Yuzu Juice	⅓ cup (88g)
Water	⅓ cup (81g)
Granulated Sugar	¼ cup (50g) plus 2 tablespoons (25g)
Sure-Jell Original Powdered Pectin	1 teaspoon (4g; measured by weight rather than volume, if possible)
Glucose Syrup	1 tablespoon (20g)
Lemon Juice	1 tablespoon (15g)
Kosher Salt	¼ teaspoon (2g)

In a 2-quart saucepan, bring the yuzu juice, water, and ¼ cup (50g) of sugar to a boil over medium heat.

Thoroughly combine the remaining 2 tablespoon of sugar and the pectin in a small bowl and quickly whisk into the yuzu juice. Return to a full boil, then keep at a lively simmer over medium heat for 7 to 10 minutes, until the liquid thickens and the surface is covered with thick, viscous bubbles. The liquid should be starting to gel but remain pourable.

Remove from the heat and stir in the glucose syrup, lemon juice, salt, and butter.

Strain through a fine-mesh strainer. Cool completely and keep covered in the refrigerator until ready to use, up to 2 weeks.

SALTY CITRUS

When I was five, my Chinese babysitter handed me a plate of orange slices coated with table salt. The effect was alarming, the flavor of the orange turned up by magnitudes. I love salt on or in everything but use caution; too much salt makes food . . . salty. Adding citrus and salt to many of our recipes unlocks a layer of amplified flavor unlike anything else. Especially when we make a flavor which is a little sweeter, a little richer, or a just a little mellow. The default is lemon juice + salt, which works particularly well for fruit flavored ice creams or sorbets. Occasionally we will add these two to a cheese base such as mascarpone or cream cheese, which is not intuitive but really works. After you're comfortable with lemon juice, try combining different citrus juices with salt and play with the balance of flavor. Use caution and be patient, as this can take multiple revisions to get right. If you are adding lemon juice and/or citric acid to a base, you will need to do it right before you put it in the freezer, to prevent curdling.

POPSICLES

I think of frozen fruit juice when I hear the word popsicle, but the definition is a frozen dessert on a stick. The creamsicle was always one of my favorites, and while I was bummed to learn that Häagen-Dazs had discontinued their line of "Sorbet & Cream" bars, but I'm sure it was not worth the effort. They are a real hassle, so I can relate, but I love pops, so we keep making them. For us, the best version of this classic treat is made using a silicone mold with an opening for a popsicle stick in the side, as opposed to the more traditional style of freezing them standing up. This allows us to put different flavors and textures inside, which make them more compelling. We have also found that for a fruit flavor, it is best to freeze the pop without churning it as a sorbet, and then dip it in a fruit syrup exterior to add a punch of flavor on the outside with the added benefit of making them shiny.

KATHY'S KALAMANSI GIN POP

IN THE HEART OF THE PANDEMIC, we were approached by the tourism board for Singapore, which was interested in working together to develop a line of ice creams that would highlight the flavors of that country. With the help of Max Ng, a Singaporean chef in New York, we developed different flavors for ice cream pints using flavors like salted egg yolk, pandan, and candied black ginger. All of the package design and flavor names were created by Singaporean tattoo artist and illustrator moo.inks, who beautifully captured the playful spirit of the food and culture of Singapore. My personal favorite of the group was the only non-pint, a popsicle, Kathy's Kalamansi Gin Pop, which was inspired by the robust cocktail culture in Singapore. Calamansi is a citrus indigenous to Southeast Asia, probably a hybrid of a Kumquat and a mandarin. It has a very sour flavor punctuated by a tight bitter finish, the perfect foil for gin and its smooth herbaceous flavor.

Makes approximately 12 (4-ounce) pops

FOR THE POPSICLES

WATER	2 CUPS (470G)
SIMPLE SYRUP (PAGE 209)	1 CUP (315G)
CALAMANSI JUICE	⅔ CUP (176G)
SINGAPORE GIN	½ CUP (118G)
ORANGE JUICE	1 TABLESPOON (15G)
LEMON JUICE	1 TABLESPOON (15G)
CONDENSED MILK FLUFF (RECIPE FOLLOWS)	

FOR THE PINEAPPLE DIP

PINEAPPLE JUICE	2¾ CUPS (675G)
WATER	1 CUP (250G)
GRANULATED SUGAR	¼ CUP (50G)

EQUIPMENT

POPSICLE MOLDS

POPSICLE STICKS

To make the popsicles: Mix the water, Simple Syrup, calamansi juice, gin, and orange and lemon juices together.

Fill the molds halfway with the popsicle mixture. Reserve the remaining mixture. Spoon a thin layer (about 1 tablespoon per popsicle) of the Condensed Milk Fluff into each popsicle mold; it will likely sink to the bottom. Insert the popsicle sticks into each mold and place in the freezer to set for 2 hours.

Fill the molds just below the surface with the remaining popsicle mixture, and freeze for 24 hours, until solid.

To make the pineapple dip: Mix the pineapple juice, water, and sugar together. Stir to dissolve the sugar.

Remove the popsicles from the molds, place them on a parchment lined baking sheet, and put them back in the freezer.

One at a time, dip each popsicle individually into the pineapple dip.

Repeat the dipping process twice more to achieve a shell around the popsicle. Return to the freezer until ready to eat.

The popsicles can be kept, laying flat on parchment paper, in an airtight container in the freezer for up to 2 weeks.

CONDENSED MILK FLUFF

This recipe will make considerably more fluff than you need. It's a commitment. Any leftovers can be used as a topping for most ice creams.

Makes approximately 1 quart

Granulated Sugar	1 cup (200g)
Light Corn Syrup	¾ cup (246g)
Water	⅓ cup (81g)
Egg Whites, at room temperature	3 (96g)
Sweetened Condensed Milk	4 tablespoons (75g)

Place the sugar, corn syrup, and water into a 1-quart saucepan.

Start mixing the egg whites in a stand mixer on medium speed.

While the whites are mixing, cook the syrup mixture over high heat to 240°F.

Slowly pour the hot sugar syrup down the side of the bowl, over the whipping egg whites. Turn the mixer to high speed and whip, 5 to 10 minutes, until the mixing bowl is room temperature.

Once cool, lower the speed, and mix in the condensed milk until incorporated. Place the fluff in a piping bag. It will hold at room temperature for up to 4 hours.

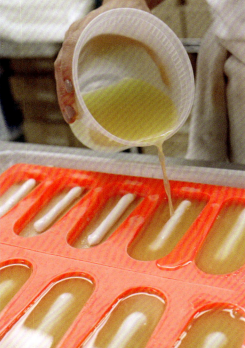

RASPBERRY DARK CHOCOLATE

RASPBERRY CHEESECAKE

RASPBERRY GREEN TEA JELLY

RASPBERRY PAPAYA SORBET

RASPBERRY

In this, the shortest chapter in the book, I want to make the case for raspberry. Perhaps blueberry seems more obvious? Or cherry? But neither packs the same punch as raspberry, which—for a fruit with such a strong identity—is oddly uncommon in American ice cream. The benign ubiquity of the strawberry overshadows any other berry ice cream the same way that vanilla is so much more popular than chocolate. And while I scratch my head at their ice cream obscurity, the truth is, we have made very few flavors with raspberry at Morgenstern's over the years.

Raspberries are an enigma; delicate and shy, hiding their bright, clear flavor behind thorn-covered branches. The physical structure of the fruit is extraordinary, with dozens of drupelets containing hundreds of seeds surrounding a hollow core. If people did not find it too tart, too strong, too pronounced, or often times, just too much, we'd have a lot more raspberry ice cream out there. It's a commitment to order two scoops of raspberry on a cone. It is best enjoyed as a well-balanced pairing, but there are not that many dance partners that can keep up. But once you taste it, you will see why it deserves a category of its own.

RASPBERRY DARK CHOCOLATE

Raspberry and dark chocolate are a tried-and-true pairing, with the acidity of the raspberry balancing the acidity of the chocolate. It's that rare instance where acid on acid elevates the qualities of each. Even though it is, no pun intended, low-hanging fruit in the ice cream lexicon, this flavor was on our menu for many years, becoming a cult favorite. It's an obvious ice cream, not to be overlooked.

Makes approximately 3½ cups

Heavy Cream	1½ cups (357g)
Whole Milk	½ cup (123g)
Glucose Syrup	1½ tablespoons (30g)
Granulated Sugar	⅔ cup (138g)
Whole Milk Powder	2 tablespoons (15g)
Kosher Salt	¼ teaspoon (2g)
Chopped Dark Chocolate (64% cocoa)	⅔ cup (115g)
Raspberry Purée	¾ cup (183g)
Lemon Juice	2 teaspoons (10g)

In a 4-quart saucepan, heat the cream, milk, and glucose syrup over medium heat, stirring with a rubber spatula or wooden spoon to keep it from burning, until small bubbles appear around the edges and the temperature reaches 180°F.

In a large bowl, whisk together the sugar, milk powder, and salt.

Slowly pour the hot cream mixture into the bowl, stirring constantly.

Pour the mixture back into the pot and cook over medium heat, stirring constantly, until it returns to 180°F.

Remove from the heat, add the chocolate, and blend with an immersion blender until smooth. Strain through a fine-mesh strainer into a clean container.

Fill a large bowl with ice and cold water to make an ice bath.

Put the container into the ice bath and let the base cool to 38°F. Stir in the raspberry purée and lemon juice and freeze in an ice cream maker according to the manufacturer's instructions.

RASPBERRY CHEESECAKE

Cheesecake was probably first made in Greece, and then throughout Europe, using different types of soft cheese. Cream cheese, however, was invented in Chester, New York, about 150 years ago. You've probably never heard of the soft French cheese that was the inspiration, but Philadelphia Cream Cheese is known all over the world and it is the basis for New York–style cheesecake, the best version of that dessert. It has a very rich unctuous cheese flavor that's delicious on its own but is elevated and amplified with the addition of fruit. Sometimes that fruit is strawberry, or strawberry jam. But more commonly it's raspberry. The concentrated punch of raspberry, with its bright acidity, adds a more pronounced balance to the cheesecake and its graham cracker crust. And the color of the fruit contrasts perfectly against the creamy white of the cheese. When we make Raspberry Cream Cheese ice cream, we stay true to the traditional cheesecake, with graham cracker crust sprinkled in, as well as ribbons of raspberry jam.

Makes approximately 1 quart

....

WHOLE MILK	1⅔ CUPS (414G)
HEAVY CREAM	¼ CUP (60G)
GLUCOSE SYRUP	2 TABLESPOONS (30G)
GRANULATED SUGAR	1 CUP (200G)
WHOLE MILK POWDER	2 TABLESPOONS (15G)
KOSHER SALT	¼ TEASPOON (2G)
CREAM CHEESE, AT ROOM TEMPERATURE, CUT INTO 1-INCH CUBES	1⅓ CUPS (307G)
LEMON JUICE	2 TABLESPOONS (30G)
GRAHAM CRACKER CRUMB (PAGE 262)	½ CUP (65G)
RASPBERRY SWIRL (PAGE 262)	½ CUP (137G)

....

In a 4-quart saucepan, heat the milk, cream, and glucose syrup over medium heat, stirring with a rubber spatula or wooden spoon to keep it from burning, until small bubbles appear around the edges and the temperature reaches 180°F.

In a large bowl, whisk together the sugar, milk powder, and salt.

Slowly pour the hot milk mixture into the bowl, stirring constantly.

Pour the mixture back into the pot and cook over medium heat, stirring constantly, until it returns to 180°F.

Remove from the heat, add the cream cheese, stir to combine, and blend with an immersion blender until smooth.

Immediately strain through a fine-mesh strainer into a clean container.

Fill a large bowl with ice and cold water to make an ice bath.

Put the container into the ice bath and let the base cool to 38°F, stirring occasionally.

Add the lemon juice and freeze in an ice cream maker according to the manufacturer's instructions. Stir in the Graham Cracker Crumb, and the Raspberry Swirl to create ribbons (do not overmix, you will melt your ice cream!).

GRAHAM CRACKER CRUMB

Graham Crackers were inspired by the teachings of pastor Sylvester Graham, who preached against meat and masturbation. He baked crackers of coarsely ground wheat which became a symbol of this austere lifestyle, gaining popularity during the cholera epidemic of the mid-nineteenth century. His teachings have slipped away, but the graham cracker is as popular as ever, largely due to its use in one of the most popular pie crusts in American, the Graham Cracker crust. The Raspberry Cheesecake ice cream would not be complete without it, masturbation be damned.

Makes ½ cup

....

Graham Cracker Crumbs (about 3 whole graham crackers)	⅓ cup (39g)
Unsalted Butter, melted	1 tablespoon (15g)
Granulated Sugar	2 teaspoons (8g)
Kosher Salt	pinch of

....

Preheat your oven to 325°F. Line a baking sheet with parchment paper.

In a large bowl, thoroughly mix together the graham cracker crumbs, butter, sugar, and salt and spread on the prepared baking sheet.

Bake for 10 to 12 minutes, until golden brown.

Cool and store in the refrigerator in a covered container for up to 2 weeks.

RASPBERRY SWIRL

Makes approximately ¾ cup

....

Raspberry Purée	½ cup (122g)
Granulated Sugar	2 teaspoons (8g) plus ½ cup (100g)
Sure-Jell Original Powdered Pectin	½ teaspoon (2g; measured by weight rather than volume, if possible)
Glucose Syrup	2 tablespoons (30g)
Lemon Juice	½ teaspoon (2.5g)

....

In a 2-quart saucepan, bring the raspberry purée and 2 teaspoons of sugar to a boil over medium heat.

Thoroughly combine the remaining ½ cup of sugar and the pectin in a small bowl and quickly whisk into the raspberry purée. Return to a full boil, then keep at a lively simmer over medium heat, 7 to 10 minutes, until the liquid thickens and the surface is covered with thick, viscous bubbles. The liquid should be starting to gel but remain pourable.

Remove from the heat and stir in the glucose syrup and lemon juice.

Cool completely and keep in a covered container in the refrigerator until ready to use, up to 2 weeks, giving it a quick stir, to loosen it before using, if needed.

RASPBERRY GREEN TEA JELLY

GREEN TEA HAS AN ALKALINE ASTRINGENCY that creates a specific type of pucker in the mouth when paired with the bright acidity of the raspberry. Perhaps just reading about this flavor, it sounds odd. Raspberry ice cream is more fun than strawberry, but it needs to be balanced or cut. The acidity will tweak your jaw, the same way a Sour Patch Kid will.

The jam should ideally be made at least 24 hours before the ice cream is going to be frozen to allow it to cool and set. You can add it the same day if you have no choice, but don't add it hot.

Follow the directions for the ice cream base and skip the green tea jelly and you'll have yourself a first-class plain raspberry ice cream.

Makes approximately 1 quart

....

WHOLE MILK	1½ CUPS (367G)
HEAVY CREAM	⅔ CUP (164G)
GLUCOSE SYRUP	1½ TABLESPOONS (30G)
GRANULATED SUGAR	¾ CUP (150G)
WHOLE MILK POWDER	¼ CUP (30G)
KOSHER SALT	¼ TEASPOON (2G)
RASPBERRY PURÉE	1 CUP PLUS 2 TEASPOONS (280G)
LEMON JUICE	2 TEASPOONS (10G)
GREEN TEA JELLY (PAGE 266)	⅓ CUP (94G)

....

In a 4-quart saucepan, heat the milk, cream, and glucose syrup over medium heat, stirring with a rubber spatula or wooden spoon to keep it from burning, until small bubbles appear around the edges and the temperature reaches 180°F.

In a large bowl, whisk together the sugar, milk powder, and salt.

Slowly pour the hot cream mixture into the bowl, stirring constantly.

Pour the mixture back into the pot and cook over medium heat, stirring constantly, until it returns to 180°F.

Remove from the heat and immediately strain through a fine-mesh strainer into a clean container.

Fill a large bowl with ice and cold water to make an ice bath. Put the container into the ice bath and let the base cool to 38°F, stirring occasionally.

Add the raspberry purée and lemon juice and freeze in an ice cream maker according to the manufacturer's instructions.

Stir in the Green Tea Jelly to create ribbons (do not overmix, you will melt your ice cream!).

GREEN TEA JELLY

NOTE: The jelly will remain loose and pourable.

Makes approximately ⅓ cup

Water	½ cup (118g)
Matcha Powder	1 tablespoon (5g)
Granulated Sugar	1 tablespoon (13g) plus ¼ cup (50g)
Sure-Jell Original Powdered Pectin	1 teaspoon (4g; measured by weight rather than volume, if possible)
Glucose Syrup	1 tablespoon (20g)

In a 2-quart saucepan, bring the water, matcha powder, and the 1 tablespoon of sugar to a boil over high heat.

Thoroughly combine the remaining ¼ cup of sugar and the pectin in a small bowl and quickly whisk into the matcha syrup. Return to a full boil, then keep at a lively simmer over medium heat until the liquid thickens and the surface is covered with thick, viscous bubbles, 7 to 10 minutes.

Remove from the heat and stir in the glucose syrup.

Strain through a fine-mesh strainer. Cool completely and keep covered in the refrigerator until ready to use, up to 2 weeks.

BLACK RASPBERRY

Black raspberries are delicious, beautiful, and rare. They are a white whale in the ice cream world; occasional sightings feed an obsession for the many Americans who can't find the flavor anywhere, but order it anytime they can. For them, black raspberry tastes like the freedom found in small waterfront ice cream shops, where the menu never changes and those first few licks spell pure summer bliss. Even the fruit's nickname—bear's eye blackberry—conjures up a taste adventure.

Black raspberry embeds itself in the memory, which is how nostalgic appetites are created. While they grow anywhere that raspberries are cultivated, most commonly in the Pacific Northwest and the northern parts of the United States, black raspberries limited availability—they're only around for about three weeks out of the year—and their high perishability and low yield makes them a luxury. We do get them at the farmers' market in New York City, but they're extremely expensive and, again, limited in their availability. If we relied solely on what we could purchase via the farmers' market, we would only be able to make ice cream for a few days. If I could find an abundant, reliable source, I would keep black raspberry ice cream on our menu permanently.

If you are able to find black raspberries, blend them into a purée, strain them, and use the base recipe for the Raspberry Green Tea Jelly (page 264), skipping the jelly, to make them into ice cream. Adjust the sugar to taste, as black raspberries have a much lower acidity than red ones.

RASPBERRY PAPAYA SORBET

RASPBERRY PAPAYA IS ALMOST A COP OUT—not because it's obvious, but because it's easy. The papaya adds a rich texture making this a creamy sorbet and the two fruits create a new flavor when they are properly balanced together. This is a good example of how raspberry shines best with a partner: its punchy acidity offset and enhanced by papaya's subtle aromatic sweetness.

Makes approximately 1 quart

PAPAYA PURÉE	2½ CUPS (672G)
RASPBERRY PURÉE	½ CUP (122G)
SIMPLE SYRUP (PAGE 209)	½ CUP (157G)
LEMON JUICE	2 TABLESPOONS (30G)
KOSHER SALT	¼ TEASPOON (2G)

In a large bowl, thoroughly combine the papaya and raspberry purées, the Simple Syrup, lemon juice, and salt.

Strain through a fine-mesh strainer into a clean container.

Fill a large bowl with ice and cold water to make an ice bath.

Put the container into the ice bath and let the base cool to 38°F, stirring occasionally.

Freeze in an ice cream maker according to the manufacturer's instructions.

RASPBERRY MILKSHAKE

We sell lots of Bourbon Vanilla, Cookies N' Cream, and Salted Chocolate milkshakes, but I'm always excited when I see someone order something more unusual—black licorice, durian, or chocolate eggplant. I was delighted the first time I saw someone order raspberry. The directions below will work for any kind of milkshake, but raspberry is an unexpected treat—give it a try.

Milk shakes should be rich and use the least amount of milk possible. We use about 1 part milk for every 4 parts ice cream. This makes for a very thick milkshake when the ice cream is cold, but not too cold. If your ice cream is soft, use less milk, and if it is hard, stick with the 1:4 ratio, but blend it a little longer to soften up the ice cream and emulsify it. Our ice cream does not have any stabilizers, starches, or gums, so it is important to mix it thoroughly to get the milkshake smooth and creamy. We prefer a milkshake machine for this, however a blender will work. Just remember that a blender is more powerful than a milkshake machine, so pulse it if you can, and scrape down the sides of the pitcher periodically to keep it smooth.

PEACHES N' CLOTTED CREAM

SOUR CREAM CANNED PEACH

PEACH SWEET TEA

HONEY LAVENDER PEACH

PEACHES

Genetically, peaches and nectarines are virtually the same. The flavors are slightly different, with the peach a little sweeter, more aromatic and nuanced compared to the nectarines' punchy authority, but the real difference is the skin; that peach fuzz is what sets a peach apart. That's why, personally, I have always preferred nectarines. To this day, just the idea of that fuzz hitting my teeth gives me the chills, but I've had to get over it. Because, unfortunately, my preference for nectarines does not translate into ice cream.

The peach provides a perfect foil for ice cream, and on many ice cream shop's menu occupies the coveted fruit slot, oftentimes in place of strawberry ice cream. If you had to choose between the two, peach sounds a little more special, a little more exotic, and that is because it is. There are lots of varieties of peaches, but just two types: Freestones and Clingstones. Freestones release from their pit easily, while Clingstones do not. The Clingstone has better potential for flavor, in my opinion, but are difficult to eat, and require more work to prepare, but either will work, as long as they are ripe.

There is a much-perpetuated myth in the US that peaches come from the South; Georgia, specifically. Georgia has delicious peaches, sure, however, most of the peaches found here come from California, or China. Peaches are very fickle. A good peach should come off the tree ripe, or semi ripe, but this is not possible when they are going to be loaded in cases stacked, in the back of a semitrailer, and hauled across the country. A great peach, or nectarine, is a wonderful thing, but sadly most of them are bad, mealy, and flavorless. The best peaches are juicy, with bracing acidity to balance the sweet perfume.

When I think about making a fruit ice cream, I have to consider whether we will be able to consistently get the fruit. It's not possible, so usually, I'm confined to fruit puree and while fresh peaches are one thing, canned peaches occupy a special place in food history in America because they were one of the rations given to soldiers on duty overseas. Food memories are powerful, and many soldiers returned from WWII and Vietnam with a strong nostalgia for the peaches they ate in the field which reminded them of home. Ham and peas and corned beef hash were the staples of field rations, but canned peaches (and maybe a canned pound cake) were considered the ultimate treat. The canned peach offers the option to use canned fruit, which is often times better than fresh because of that nostalgic component. Their texture and flavor make them delicious in ice cream as a jam or jelly.

PEACHES 'N' CREAM

There are no less than TEN songs titled "Peaches 'n' Cream." Most of them written in the early 1900s, when the dish became popular. The simple appeal of peaches plus cream is so universal that you'll find it everywhere, from a side at BBQ restaurants, to flavored rum, to Lifesavers candies. More than a recipe, it's almost a state of mind.

The basic premise that is a bowl of sliced ripe peaches with cream poured on top of them sounds good enough, but personally, I don't think that's where the appeal comes from. Instead, I believe that the ice box cake is probably the inspiration for the version of peaches 'n' cream that has become ubiquitous today. Favored for its ease and ability to be assembled well ahead, with the majority of the "work" done in the refrigerator (in the 1940s and 1950s, a novel idea—a no-bake dessert), the peaches 'n' cream ice box cake is made with layers of fruit and lightly whipped cream, set in a dish for a few hours or even overnight. While the cream dries out a bit, it also soaks up some of the juices of the peaches, which have been peeled and sweetened with sugar. Assembled in advance for a longer refrigeration time for the fullest possible melding of flavors, it is delicious. As you can guess, I prefer this dish with canned peaches.

PEACHES N' CLOTTED CREAM

PEACHES 'N' CREAM ICE CREAM IS TOO OBVIOUS. Which is why we tweaked it to become Peaches N' Clotted Cream. Clotted cream is the table butter of England, slathered on scones and biscuits with jam or preserves. This stuff is special and in the southern part of the UK, where it originated, clotted cream has elevated status by law under its protected Designation of Origin. The combination of dairy from cows who graze on the mellow pastures of Cornwall or Devon and a centuries-old tradition of using nothing but cream and patience gives it a signature nutty sweet cream flavor. Do not substitute with something else.

Makes 1 quart

WHOLE MILK	1⅓ CUPS (330G)
GLUCOSE SYRUP	2 TABLESPOONS (40G)
GRANULATED SUGAR	¾ CUP (150G)
WHOLE MILK POWDER	⅓ CUP (40G)
KOSHER SALT	¼ TABLESPOON (2G)
CLOTTED CREAM	⅔ CUP (150G)
PEACH PURÉE	1½ CUPS (320G)
LEMON JUICE	2 TEASPOONS (10G)

In a 4-quart saucepan, heat the milk and glucose syrup over medium heat, stirring with a rubber spatula or wooden spoon to keep it from burning, until small bubbles appear around the edges and the temperature reaches 180°F.

In a large bowl, whisk together the sugar, milk powder, and salt.

Slowly pour the hot cream mixture into the bowl, stirring constantly.

Pour the mixture back into the pot and cook over medium heat, stirring constantly, until it returns to 180°F.

Remove from the heat, add the clotted cream, and stir to combine. Immediately strain through a fine-mesh strainer into a clean container.

Fill a large bowl with ice and cold water to make an ice bath.

Put the container into the ice bath and let the base cool to 38°F, stirring occasionally.

Stir in the peach purée and lemon juice.

Freeze in an ice cream maker according to the manufacturer's instructions.

SOUR CREAM CANNED PEACH

THIS FLAVOR IS INSPIRED BY PEACH ICE BOX CAKE, which I think is the secret to peaches 'n' cream's incredible popularity. The key to this ice cream is the canned peaches. If you can, order some from an orchard. They will be pricier, but worth it as they will have been canned as close to peak ripeness as possible.

Note: The jam should ideally be made at least 24 hours before the ice cream is going to be frozen to allow it to cool and set. You can add it the same day if you have no choice, but don't add it hot.

Makes approximately 1 quart

Whole Milk	1⅔ cups (414g)
Heavy Cream	⅔ cup (165g)
Glucose Syrup	1½ tablespoons (30g)
Granulated Sugar	¾ cup (150g)
Whole Milk Powder	¼ cup (30g)
Kosher Salt	¼ teaspoon (2g)
Sour Cream	⅓ cup (80g)
Plain Yogurt	⅓ cup (80g)
Canned Peach Purée	3 tablespoons (45g)
Lemon Juice	3 teaspoons (15g)
Peach Jam (page 281)	

In a 4-quart saucepan, heat the milk, heavy cream, and glucose syrup over medium heat, stirring with a rubber spatula or wooden spoon to keep it from burning, until small bubbles appear around the edges and the temperature reaches 180°F.

In a large bowl, whisk together the sugar, milk powder, and salt.

Slowly pour the hot cream mixture into the bowl, stirring constantly.

Pour the mixture back into the pot and cook over medium heat, stirring constantly, until it returns to 180°F.

Remove from the heat, add the sour cream and yogurt, and immediately strain through a fine-mesh strainer into a clean container.

Fill a large bowl with ice and cold water to make an ice bath.

Place the container into the ice bath and let the base cool to 38°F, stirring occasionally.

Add the peach purée and lemon juice and freeze in an ice cream machine according to the manufacturer's instructions. Mix in the peach jam, to create ribbons, once the ice cream is frozen.

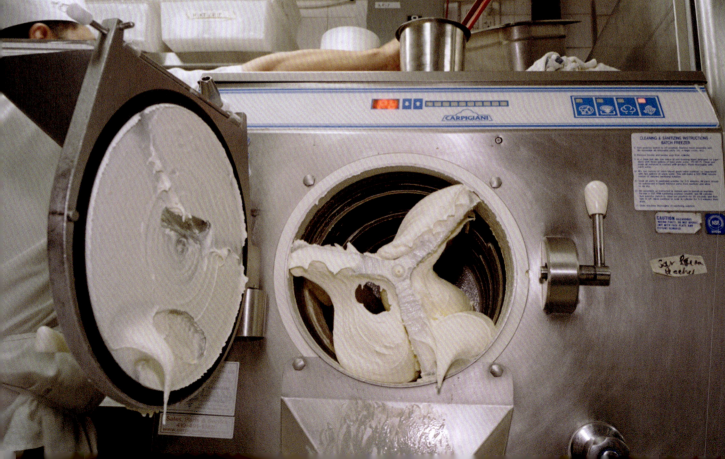

PEACH JAM

Makes approximately ½ cup

....

CANNED PEACHES, DRAINED
                               ½ CUP (120G)

GRANULATED SUGAR   1 TABLESPOON (12G)

SURE-JELL ORIGINAL POWDERED PECTIN
      ¼ TEASPOON (2G; MEASURED BY WEIGHT RATHER THAN VOLUME, IF POSSIBLE)

GLUCOSE SYRUP   1½ TABLESPOONS (30G)

LEMON JUICE   1 TEASPOON (5G)

KOSHER SALT   PINCH OF

....

Chop the peaches until they are a little smaller than pea-size, add them to a 2 quart sauce pot, and bring them to a simmer over medium heat.

Whisk in the sugar and pectin and simmer for another 7 to 10 minutes.

Add the glucose syrup, bring back to a simmer, and then remove from the heat.

Stir in the lemon juice, and salt.

Pour into a container, cool and refrigerate. The jam will keep for 2 weeks covered and refrigerated.

PEACH SWEET TEA

Peach sweet tea, already a known and loved beverage in the US, has the kind of mass recognition that translates to ice cream. As sweet tea is almost exclusively enjoyed on ice, it makes for a natural choice for an ice cream flavor. Black tea creates a sturdy foil for the gentle aromatics of the peaches, while the peach flavor uplifts and enlivens otherwise staid black tea. I use PG Tips, the stalwart tea of cupboards all across England, known for its consistent if generic smooth strong taste.

Makes 1 quart

HEAVY CREAM	1⅔ CUPS (414G)
WHOLE MILK	2 TABLESPOONS (32G)
GLUCOSE SYRUP	2 TABLESPOONS (40G)
GRANULATED SUGAR	¾ CUP (150G)
WHOLE MILK POWDER	2 TABLESPOONS (15G)
KOSHER SALT	¼ TEASPOON (2G)
WHITE PEACH PURÉE	⅔ CUP (168G)
BREWED PG TIPS (OR OTHER BLACK TEABAGS; SEE NOTE)	⅔ CUP (160G)
LEMON JUICE	2 TEASPOONS (10G)

In a 4-quart saucepan, combine the cream, milk, and glucose syrup and heat over medium heat, stirring with a rubber spatula or wooden spoon to keep it from burning, until small bubbles appear around the edges and the temperature reaches 180°F.

In a large bowl, whisk together the sugar, milk powder, and salt.

Slowly pour the hot cream mixture into the bowl, stirring constantly.

Pour the mixture back into the pot and cook over medium heat, stirring constantly, until it returns to 180°F.

Remove from the heat and immediately strain through a fine-mesh strainer into a clean container.

Fill a large bowl with ice and cold water to make an ice bath. Put the container into the ice bath and let the base cool to 38°F, stirring occasionally.

Add the peach purée, tea, and lemon juice and freeze in an ice cream machine according to the manufacturer's instructions.

Note: To make the tea, steep 4 teabags (preferably PG Tips) in 2 cups (450g) scalding water for 2 minutes.

HONEY LAVENDER PEACH

I DON'T LIKE LAVENDER. It tastes like soap, which is a primary use for the herb. But people like it in food, specifically in dessert, so give the people what they want, I guess. Occasionally I will have a flavor on the menu that I do not like. We don't make any bad flavors, so my dislike is purely personal. The original lavender ice cream on our menu was a vegan lavender vanilla. It was regularly a top seller, despite my personal distain for lavender. When we changed the menu, I avoided restoring lavender until the bitter end. But after peaches n' pecorino didn't make the cut, lavender was there to pick up the slack in the peach category. This combination of honey, lavender, and peach is at once simple but complex. The three different flavors complement and balance one another, also succeeding in hiding any soapiness.

Makes 1 quart

Whole Milk	1¼ cups (306g)
Heavy Cream	⅔ cup (164g)
Honey	½ cup (173g)
Dried Lavender	2¼ teaspoons (1.5g)
Whole Milk Powder	¼ cup (40g)
Granulated Sugar	2 tablespoons (25g)
Kosher Salt	¼ teaspoon (2g)
Blood Peach Purée	1⅓ cups (320g)
Lemon Juice	2 teaspoons (10g)

Combine the milk, cream, honey, and lavender in a 4-quart saucepan and heat the mixture over medium heat, stirring with a rubber spatula or wooden spoon to keep it from burning, until small bubbles appear around the edges and the temperature reaches 180°F.

In a large bowl, whisk together the milk powder, sugar, and salt.

Slowly pour the hot cream mixture into the bowl, stirring constantly.

Pour the mixture back into the pot and cook over medium heat, stirring constantly, until it returns to 180°F.

Remove from the heat and immediately strain through a fine-mesh strainer into a clean container.

Fill a large bowl with ice and cold water to make an ice bath.

Put the container into the ice bath and let the base cool to 38°F, stirring occasionally.

Add the peach purée and lemon juice and freeze in an ice cream machine according to the manufacturer's instructions.

COOKIES N' CREAM

BUBBLE GUM

S'MORES

RUM RAISIN

SCHOOLYARD MINT CHIP

CLASSICS

There is a long history of ice cream fads and trends in America, from rainbow sherbet to cake batter to key lime pie, lots of flavors come and go. Just like car colors, certain flavors seem to mark an era. The flavors in this chapter have stood the test of time, and if they fall out of favor for a bit, they always make their way back in. I have also included some ice cream cakes in this chapter, as it is always a good idea to make a cake out of a flavor that everyone will like, and classics are a good place to look. There are too many iconic American flavors for me to include here, but these are a handful that we have found meet our standard for excellence and popularity.

COOKIES IN ICE CREAM

A terrific idea that should be explored. When added to ice cream, baked chocolate chip cookies don't offer the same softened chew as the more wafer-like Oreo or Nutter Butter cookie. A simple rule of thumb—if the cookie disintegrates when dunked in milk, it will probably make a great cookie ice cream. You may want to argue that a chocolate chip cookie fits those criteria, but not true. They get hard and chewy when they freeze. Other cookies that absorb the dairy soften and become part of the ice cream.

COOKIES N' CREAM

OREOS ARE EXPENSIVE. I did not find this out until we started checking the price on very large packs of Oreo "seconds" (broken Oreo's). They cost nearly as much as the whole Oreo, which are barely discounted for bulk wholesale purchase from the retail grocery store price. This matters because Cookies N' Cream is one of the most popular flavors in the shop. We could try to substitute with a generic, or make our own, but neither of these options will satisfy the true nostalgic flavor, which was created sometime in the late '70s, or early '80s, with several companies laying claim to creating what is basically a frozen Oreo ice box cake. While not that original, it is very satisfying. It is often made using vanilla ice cream, but in my opinion, it is much better with a plain milk base ice cream to complement the cookies.

Makes approximately 1 quart

Heavy Cream	1⅔ cups (403g)
Whole Milk	1½ cups (367g)
Glucose Syrup	1½ tablespoons (30g)
Granulated Sugar	¾ cup (150g)
Whole Milk Powder	¼ cup (30g)
Kosher Salt	¼ teaspoon (2g)
Oreo Cookie Crumbs	⅓ cup (40g)

In a 4-quart saucepan, heat the cream, milk, and glucose syrup over medium heat, stirring with a rubber spatula or wooden spoon to keep it from burning, until small bubbles appear around the edges and the temperature reaches 180°F.

In a large bowl, whisk together the sugar, milk powder, and salt.

Slowly pour the hot cream mixture into the bowl, stirring constantly.

Pour the mixture back into the pot and cook over medium heat, stirring constantly, until it returns to 180°F.

Remove from the heat and immediately strain through a fine-mesh strainer into a clean container. Fill a large bowl with ice and cold water to make an ice bath.

Put the container into the ice bath and let the base cool to 38°F, stirring occasionally.

Freeze in an ice cream maker according to the manufacturer's instructions. Stir in the Oreo crumbs before transferring to the freezer.

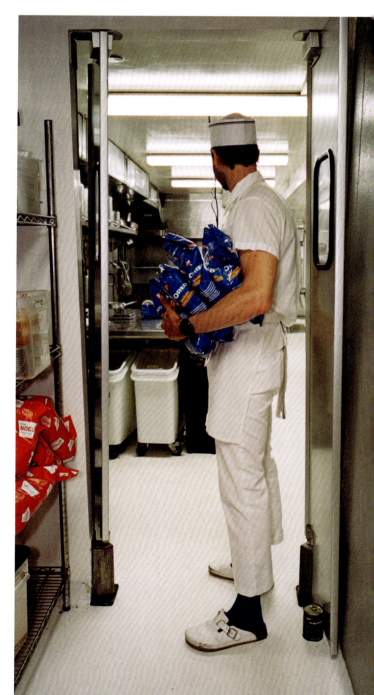

BUBBLE GUM

The world record for the largest bubble gum bubble ever blown is almost 2 feet across. I was never a big bubble gum bubble blower, but I do enjoy the flavor occasionally. It finds itself in a very narrow category of flavors that have enjoyed extreme popularity, but yet cannot be properly identified. What does bubble gum taste like? A little sweet, and a little fruity? The flavor releases quite easily into dairy for making ice cream, and surprise, was quite popular when I put it on the menu.

No surprise, though, bubble gum is a mess once you start heating it up and steeping it. We use Big League Chew to achieve this childhood classic, which comes in pouches in a shredded format meant to resemble "dip," the tobacco that was, and maybe still is, popular among baseball players. I'm not a fan of "dip," but I always loved the over-the-top bubble gum flavor from Big League Chew, no doubt aided by the fact that there was no portion control.

Makes approximately 1 quart

Heavy Cream	1⅔ cups (403g)
Whole Milk	1½ cups (367g)
Glucose Syrup	1 tablespoon (20g)
Granulated Sugar	⅔ cup (138g)
Whole Milk Powder	¼ cup (30g)
Kosher Salt	¼ teaspoon (2g)
Big League Chew	½ cup packed (50g)

In a 4-quart saucepan, heat the cream, milk, and glucose syrup over medium heat, stirring with a rubber spatula or wooden spoon to keep it from burning, until small bubbles appear around the edges and the temperature reaches 180°F.

In a large bowl, whisk together the sugar, milk powder, and salt.

Slowly pour the hot cream mixture into the bowl, stirring constantly.

Pour the mixture back into the pot and cook over medium heat, stirring constantly, until it returns to 180°F.

Remove from the heat and, using a silicone spatula, stir in the Big League Chew. Immediately strain through a fine-mesh strainer into a clean container.

Fill a large bowl with ice and cold water to make an ice bath.

Put the container into the ice bath and let the base cool to 38°F, stirring occasionally.

Freeze in an ice cream maker according to the manufacturer's instructions.

BUBBLE GUM ICE CREAM CAKE

Bubble Gum ice cream is perfect for ice cream cakes. Bubble gum is a terrific flavor for fun and celebration, with a bright pink color, to boot.

S'MORES

THIS CAMPFIRE CLASSIC turned into an ice cream has become quite popular these days. We don't usually follow trends, or even pay attention, but this one has been pointed out to me. The key is, obviously, the toasted marshmallow flavor, which requires burned Jet-Puffed Marshmallows. They do not need to be burned to a crisp, but the exterior must be well charred.

Makes approximately 1 quart

....

WHOLE MILK	1½ CUPS (367G)
HEAVY CREAM	1½ CUPS (357G)
GLUCOSE SYRUP	1½ TABLESPOONS (30G)
GRANULATED SUGAR	½ CUP (100G)
WHOLE MILK POWDER	¼ CUP (30G)
KOSHER SALT	¼ TEASPOON (2G)
JET-PUFFED MARSHMALLOWS	8 LARGE
GRAHAM CRACKERS, CRUSHED	⅓ CUP (35G)
DARK CHOCOLATE CHUNKS (58% COCOA)	½ CUP (40G)

....

Preheat your oven to 325°F.

In a 4-quart saucepan, heat the milk, cream, and glucose syrup over medium heat, stirring with a rubber spatula or wooden spoon to keep it from burning, until small bubbles appear around the edges and the temperature reaches 180°F.

In a large bowl, whisk together the sugar, milk powder, and salt.

Slowly pour the hot cream mixture into the bowl, stirring constantly.

Pour the mixture back into the pot and cook over medium heat, stirring constantly until it returns to 180°F.

Remove from the heat and immediately strain through a fine-mesh strainer into a clean container.

Place the marshmallows on a baking sheet sprayed with nonstick spray and bake for about 10 minutes, or until puffy. Set the oven to low broil, place the baking sheet on the middle rack, and broil until the marshmallows are very dark and burnt in some places.

Add the toasted marshmallows to the hot base and blend with an immersion blender until smooth.

Fill a large bowl with ice and cold water to make an ice bath.

Put the container into the ice bath and let the base cool to 38°F, stirring occasionally.

Freeze in an ice cream maker according to the manufacturer's instructions. Stir the graham cracker pieces and chocolate chunks into the soft ice cream and freeze.

RUM RAISIN

Raisins? Sultanas are great, but sometimes I think they are a little large, so I use the darker, smaller raisin, which allows me to incorporate more of them into the base. I could tell you to choose any rum that you like, but in my opinion, the best option for this ice cream is going to be a smooth dark one with a little spice. Dark rum is usually made by caramelizing the sugar in the recipe (a booze after my own heart). Unfortunately, these rums tend to be a little sweet and lack the necessary kick.

If you can find a Thai style rum, these offer the most delicious combination of spice and kick. Sugar cane is native to Thailand, and smaller distillers have been finding ways to turn this crop into some of the best rum in the world. Combine that with a palette of aromatic spices native to Thailand (kafir lime leaf, coconut, nutmeg, and lemongrass); typically aged in oak barrels and you have something special. They are delicious for sipping and adding to this recipe.

Makes approximately 1 quart

For the rum raisins

Thai Rum (or use Goslings or Meyers)	2 tablespoons (30g)
Simple Syrup (page 209)	1 tablespoon (20g)
Kosher Salt	pinch of
Dark Raisins	¼ cup (50g)

For the ice cream base

Whole Milk	1⅔ cups (414g)
Heavy Cream	1⅔ cups (403g)
Glucose Syrup	1½ tablespoons (30g)
Granulated Sugar	½ cup (100g)
Whole Milk Powder	¼ cup (30g)
Kosher Salt	¼ teaspoon (2g)
Thai Rum (or use Goslings or Meyers)	2 tablespoons (30g)

To make the rum raisins: Begin by soaking the raisins. These will be better if allowed to soak for at least 24 hours, if not more. To do so, in a 1-quart saucepan, stir together the rum, Simple Syrup, and salt and bring to a simmer over medium heat. Place the raisins in a small bowl, and pour the rum syrup over the raisins and cover immediately. Store in the refrigerator until ready to use.

To make the base: In a 4-quart saucepan, heat the milk, cream, and glucose syrup over medium heat, stirring with a rubber spatula or wooden spoon to keep it from burning, until small bubbles appear around the edges and the temperature reaches 180°F.

In a large bowl, whisk together the sugar, milk powder, and salt.

Slowly pour the hot cream mixture into the bowl, stirring constantly.

Pour the mixture back into the pot and cook over medium heat, stirring constantly, until it returns to 180°F.

Remove from the heat and immediately strain through a fine-mesh strainer into a clean container.

Fill a large bowl with ice and cold water to make an ice bath. Put the container into the ice bath and let the base cool to 38°F, stirring occasionally.

Stir in the rum and freeze in an ice cream maker according to the manufacturer's instructions.

Stir in the raisins and their soaking liquid before transferring to the freezer.

SCHOOLYARD MINT CHIP

One of the most popular—and perfect—ice cream flavors of all time; both Baskin-Robbins and Howard Johnson's had mint chip on the menu from the beginning and it has gained popularity to find its way to the top 10 most consumed flavors so far this century. Unfortunately, most of them are made with artificial flavor and if the color matches your grandmother's bathroom, that's artificial, too. There are two factors that separate our mint chip from the rest. Number one, the mint is always fresh and green. Number two, we use two different mints, peppermint and Vietnamese mint.

Makes approximately 1 quart

Peppermint Leaves, fresh, stems removed	½ cup (8g)	Glucose Syrup	1 tablespoon (20g)
Vietnamese Mint Leaves, fresh, stems removed	½ cup (8g)	Whole Milk Powder	¼ cup (30g)
Granulated Sugar	¾ cup (150g)	Kosher Salt	¼ teaspoon (2g)
Whole Milk	1⅔ cups (414g)	Dark Chocolate Chunks (58% cocoa)	¼ cup (45g)
Heavy Cream	1½ cups (367g)		

Rinse the peppermint and Vietnamese mint leaves in cold water. Dry thoroughly with paper towels, try not to bruise the leaves. Grind the mint and the sugar in a food processor until the leaves are completely incorporated and the sugar is bright green.

Heat the milk, cream, and glucose syrup in a 4-quart saucepan over medium heat, stirring with a rubber spatula or wooden spoon to keep it from burning, until small bubbles appear around the edges and the temperature reaches 180°F.

In a large bowl, whisk together the mint sugar, milk powder, and salt.

Slowly pour the hot cream mixture into the bowl, stirring constantly.

Pour the mixture back into the pot and cook over medium heat, stirring constantly, until it returns to 180°F.

Remove from the heat and immediately strain through a fine-mesh strainer into a clean container.

Fill a large bowl with ice and cold water to make an ice bath. Put the container into the ice bath and let the base cool to 38°F, stirring occasionally.

Freeze in an ice cream maker according to the manufacturer's instructions.

Add the chocolate chunks just before scooping.

GRASSHOPPER SUNDAE

To me a grasshopper sundae is a hybrid mint chip/cookies 'n' cream creation. I love it with fudge, Oreo cookie crumbs, brownie bits, chocolate chunks, and, of course, mint ice cream.

Makes 1 sundae (Serves 2)

Sundae Brownies (page 60), about one third of a pan, cut into 1-inch cubes

Morgenstern's Hot Fudge (page 32)   3 to 4 tablespoons

Oreo Cookie Crumbs   2 tablespoons

Schoolyard Mint Chip (page 305)   1 cup

Whipped Cream (page 33; in a piping bag with a star tip)

Dark Chocolate Chunks (58% cocoa)   2 tablespoons

Mint Leaf for garnish (optional)

Chocolate Lace (page 310) for garnish (optional)   2 to 3 large pieces

This sundae should be made on a special sundae dish. The style we use at the shop is vintage and was probably an old candy dish. If you don't have one of those hanging around it should be made on a plate or a bowl with a very wide flat bottom.

In a glass sundae dish, start by placing the brownie bites spaced out with room to fit a scoop of ice cream in between them.

Drizzle the hot fudge over the brownie bites and on the bottom of the glass dish.

Sprinkle the Oreo cookie crumbs over the fudge in between the brownies.

Place one large 5-ounce scoop of Schoolyard Mint Chip in the middle, followed by two smaller scoops directly on top.

Pipe a ribbon of Whipped Cream from the top of the brownie up to the middle of the top scoop of ice cream. Scoop the chocolate chunks over the top.

Using a spoon or ladle, pour a small amount of fudge from the top down the Whipped Cream.

Place a mint leaf at the top, if using, and add the chocolate lace if you made it.

CHOCOLATE LACE

This is made with tempered chocolate, which can be a challenge. For the Grasshopper Sundae, it adds the flourish, and wow factor, but is not required if this step seems like too much work. Any dark chocolate will work, but I prefer 64% cocoa.

Although there are lots of methods for tempering chocolate, which are involved and complex, for this application, I think the seeding method works best.

Makes approximately 6 to 8 large pieces

Chopped Dark Chocolate
1 cup (180g), plus more as needed

Simmer 2 cups of water in a 2-quart saucepan over medium heat.

Making sure that the bottom of the bowl does not touch the water, melt ¾ cup (135g) of chopped dark chocolate in a medium bowl over the simmering water, stirring constantly, with a rubber spatula or spoon.

Once the chocolate reaches 115°F, turn off the heat and remove the bowl from the saucepan of simmering water.

Stir in the remaining ¼ cup (45g) of chopped dark chocolate. Stir constantly until the chocolate reaches 88°F. Add more chocolate if the chocolate is too warm. Any unmelted chocolate pieces should be removed before piping.

Fill a piping bag with the tempered chocolate, cut a small hole in the tip and pipe the chocolate in tight circles on a piece of parchment paper.

Allow the chocolate to solidify, then break off large pieces.

Store in an airtight container at room temperature for up to 7 days.

ICE CREAM CAKES

Ice cream cakes are regionally popular. Growing up in California, I never tasted one, but on the East Coast, Fuggie the Whale—a cake from Carvel—is legendary, and just about every child from every background seems to have had one. This may explain why I did not understand all of the requests we received for ice cream cakes in the early days of Morgenstern's.

When it comes to making them, the idea is great. The reality is tough. For many years I ignored these requests as a nuisance and kept scooping.

It is important to have appropriate freezer space to store the cake during the process of building it, and the time to allow it to set in-between layers as needed. The importance of having ingredients and equipment organized cannot be overstated. I will keep the required tools' list for this job to the absolute minimum.

Stainless steel cake ring—this is nonnegotiable. Yes, you can assemble in a cake pan or spring form, but I do not endorse it.

Cardboard cake circle—Unless you plan on cutting on a plate, this will be the service surface that the cake will be cut on, so I wouldn't cut up the cardboard you were using to catch oil leaks from under the Corvair.

Hair dryer—this makes a terrific tool for unmolding the cake gently. Remember to return it to the bathroom.

Piping bag and star tip—décor is important with a cake. You can cut the tip off a resealable plastic bag for the piping bag, but you will need the star tip to finish it.

Squeeze bottle—I like this for adding the fudge layer at the side of the Cookie Monster Cake to keep the decorating from getting too messy.

Metal cake scraper—this is not a requirement but will significantly improve the speed of frosting the cake to make smooth and straight sides.

Offset spatula—this is required for frosting the cake. I prefer a medium size, about 8 inches long.

You can make an ice cream cake out of just about any ice cream flavor, including sorbet, but there are some things you want to keep in mind. The cake should be thin, like very thin. A thick piece of frozen sponge is not really what you want, trust me. The flourless chocolate cake in the Cookie Monster Cake (page 313) is a great option for anything that goes with chocolate. It is soft when frozen and gets a little gooey as it warms up on the plate.

ICE CREAM CAKE CUTTING

To serve an ice cream cake, I recommend that it be removed from the freezer before you plan to cut it. This will allow it to soften a bit, as it can be very dense. The length of time will depend on how large the cake is, and how cold the freezer is. For an 8-inch cake that has been stored for 24 hours at 0°F, I would recommend 10 to 15 minutes before cutting.

To cut smooth slices, it is important to have a sharp knife (a chef's knife is best). A large container of very hot water so that the knife can be fully submerged between each slice, is very helpful, or at a minimum run the knife under hot water from the tap. Wiping the knife with a clean towel in between each cut will give a clean slice. Have your plates and utensils ready. If you can't serve the cake slices standing up, they will melt quickly as soon as they hit the plate unless you put them in the freezer beforehand.

COOKIE MONSTER CAKE

According to the Cookie Monster, cookies are a "sometimes food." This cake is a "cookie all the time" cake. And while chocolate chip cookies are his favorite, they don't work well in ice cream.

If there was ever a cake to satisfy the Cookie Monster in every kid and adult, this is it, with Oreos and Nutter Butter cookies and a thick layer of fudge inside. My favorite variation on this recipe is to swap out the M&M's for Reese's Pieces. These are the less popular candy-coated peanut butter chocolate, younger siblings to the peanut butter cup. They are bite-size and practically made for inclusion in my opinion.

Note: It is best to start with ice cream that has been churned in the ice cream machine, and then fully frozen for at least 24 hours.

For the Cookie Monster Ice Cream

Raw Milk (Page 320)   2 batches, freshly churned

Oreos, crushed   ⅓ cup (40g)

Nutter Butter Cookies, crushed   ⅓ cup (35g)

M&M's, crushed   ¼ cup (40g)

For constructing the cake

Chocolate Cake (page 316)

Cookie Monster Ice Cream (recipe above)   5 cups

Morgenstern's Hot Fudge (page 32)   ¼ cup, plus more for drizzling

M&M's Frosting (page 315)

Chopped Dark Chocolate, 55% cocoa (optional)   2 tablespoons (22g)

Oreo Cookie, carefully cut in half (optional)   1

Nutter Butter Cookie, carefully cut in half (optional)   1

Equipment

8-inch Stainless Steel Cake Ring

9-inch Cardboard Cake Circle

Offset Spatula

Pastry bag with a medium Star Tip

Hair Dryer

Squeeze Bottle

To make the Cookie Monster Ice Cream: As soon as the Raw Milk ice cream has finished churning, transfer 5 cups to a large bowl and stir in the Oreos, Nutter Butters, and M&M's. Freeze in an airtight container for 24 hours. Freeze the remaining Raw Milk ice cream separately for another use.

To construct the cake: Place the 8-inch cake ring on top of the 9-inch cardboard cake circle.

Fit one round of chocolate cake in the bottom of the ring.

Quickly fill the ring with 2½ cups (1150g) of Cookie Monster ice cream, spreading it evenly over the cake with an offset spatula.

Spoon the fudge over the ice cream.

Put the cake in the freezer to harden for at least 2 hours.

Fill the ring with the remaining 2½ cups Cookie Monster ice cream. With an offset spatula, smooth the surface and wrap with plastic. Freeze for 24 hours.

Place ½ cup of M&M's Frosting into a pastry bag with a medium star tip. Keep the remaining frosting in the bowl.

Remove the cake from the freezer, and using a hair dryer, warm the cake ring gently until it releases from the cake and can be slid off.

Using an offset spatula, frost the top and sides of the cake using the M&M's Frosting in the bowl.

Using a squeeze bottle, drizzle fudge around the top edge of the cake, letting some run down the sides.

Pipe a long continuous spiral of frosting from the pastry bag over the fudge at the edge of the cake.

If you are up for it, melt an ounce of chocolate and pipe the eyes and the word "Monster" on the top of the cake. We use blue M&M's to fill in the eyes and rest a cut Nutter Butter and Oreo on top, against the edge of the frosting.

Keep in the freezer, covered with a cake cover, for up to 5 days.

M&M'S FROSTING

Makes 1 quart

M&M's	¼ cup (45g)
Heavy Cream	2 cups (476g)
Powdered Sugar	1 teaspoon (2.5g)

In a spice grinder or a mini food processor, grind your M&M's into a somewhat fine powder.

Combine the cream, M&M's powder, and powdered sugar in the bowl of a stand mixer, and using the whisk attachment, whip to medium peaks.

Hold in the refrigerator covered up to 20 minutes until ready to frost the cake.

CHOCOLATE CAKE

Leftover cake can be used to make ice cream sandwiches.

Makes one 16 x 13-inch cake

Dark Chocolate (61% cocoa)	1½ cups (225g)	Eggs, large, at room temperature	4
Unsalted Butter	⅔ cup (165g), cut into pieces	Granulated Sugar	1 cup (200g)
Cocoa Powder	⅔ cup (60g)	Kosher Salt	scant teaspoon (4g)

Preheat your oven to 325°F. Prepare a 16 x 13-inch baking sheet (half-sheet pan) with parchment paper and spray with nonstick spray.

In a 4-quart saucepan, bring 1 quart of water to a simmer over medium heat.

In a large bowl, melt the chocolate, butter, and cocoa powder over the simmering water. Make sure the bowl does not touch the water.

Remove from the heat and stir until combined.

In another large bowl whisk the eggs, sugar, and salt until combined.

Whisk the egg mixture into the chocolate mixture.

Spread on the prepared baking sheet and bake for about 15 minutes or until just pulled away from the edges of the pan.

Cool and cut out a round to fit the cake ring.

RAW MILK

CINNAMON RAISIN TOAST

BLACK ASS LICORICE

BURNT SAGE

TAHINI AND JELLY

LABNEH SORBET

FRENCH FRY

GREEN TEA PISTACHIO

MISCELLANEOUS

The ice cream menu categories for Morgenstern's were always clear to me. Vanilla and chocolate led the way, followed by coffee and caramel. But there were other flavors that belonged on the menu but didn't fit any specific group. These flavors are there to intrigue and excite, and usually grab your attention. They are not classic, or predictable, but might be nostalgic, or maybe nostalgic adjacent, such as salt and vinegar or pickles 'n' mayo. It is good to be provocative, but the flavors must always be delicious. It can be tricky to come up with something weird for the sake of weirdness; think about things that are unexpected, it is worth it—people do not forget French Fry ice cream on the menu of a scoop shop.

RAW MILK

SOME PEOPLE DESCRIBE THIS AS VANILLA ICE CREAM without the vanilla, but it is so much more than that. This was the first flavor I made using the recipe and ratios we use for all of the ice creams we make today. If you are trying to develop something new, it is best to start with the most simplified and basic version. In this case, raw unpasteurized milk. The milk originally came from a farm that was run by a husband and wife known for their lamb. They had one cow that they milked daily for their own consumption. In the spring and summer, I don't think they could consume all the milk the cow produced, so if they liked you, they would bring a gallon with your meat order once a week or so. I could not make the ice cream with just the milk, there was not enough fat, and a sherbet's icy texture would not have done the rich raw milk justice, so I started playing with leaving the milk in the fridge for a week, and then two and then four. The flavor developed into a nutty, grassy richness, not sour at all, and I used the least possible amount of all the other ingredients to let the milk flavor shine through. The result is beautiful, and it is where our ethos of low sugar, low butter fat, and low overrun first came from. Some people say this is better than vanilla.

Makes approximately 1 quart

Heavy Cream	1⅔ cups (403g)
Whole Milk	1½ cups (367g)
Glucose Syrup	2 tablespoons (40g)
Granulated Sugar	¾ cup (150g)
Whole Milk Powder	¼ cup (30g)
Kosher Salt	¼ teaspoon (2g)

In a 4-quart saucepan, heat the cream, milk, and glucose syrup over medium heat, stirring with a rubber spatula or wooden spoon to keep it from burning, until small bubbles appear around the edges and the temperature reaches 180°F.

In a large bowl, whisk together the sugar, milk powder, and salt.

Slowly pour the hot cream mixture into the bowl, stirring constantly.

Pour the mixture back into the pot and cook over medium heat, stirring constantly, until it returns to 180°F.

Remove from the heat and immediately strain through a fine-mesh strainer into a clean container.

Fill a large bowl with ice and cold water to make an ice bath.

Put the container into the ice bath and let the mixture cool to 38°F, stirring occasionally.

Freeze in an ice cream maker according to the manufacturer's instructions.

CINNAMON RAISIN TOAST

Bread in ice cream is delicious and cinnamon raisin bread goes way back, before America, but somehow has lodged itself in the cupboards of grandmas from Oklahoma to Ohio. A toasted slice with melted butter conjures childhood for many people. And so we decided to add it to ice cream. I prefer using a generic brand like Pepperidge Farm or Martin's, either will give a terrifically nostalgic flavor. We add extra cinnamon and raisins to bump it up and bring it home, and, of course, there is butter in there for good measure.

Makes approximately 3¾ cups

Cinnamon Raisin Bread	2 slices (72 g)	Granulated Sugar	¾ cup (150g)
Whole Milk	1½ cups (367g)	Whole Milk Powder	¼ cup (30g)
Heavy Cream	1¼ cups (298g)	Ground Cinnamon	1 teaspoon (3g)
Unsalted Butter	1 teaspoon (5g)	Kosher Salt	¼ teaspoon (2g)
Dark Raisins	3 tablespoons (25g)		
Glucose Syrup	1½ tablespoons (30g)		

Toast the bread in a toaster oven until golden brown. Chop into ½-inch cubes and set aside.

In a 4-quart saucepan, combine the milk, cream, butter, raisins, and glucose syrup and heat over medium heat, stirring with a rubber spatula or wooden spoon to keep it from burning, until small bubbles appear around the edges and the temperature reaches 180°F.

In a large bowl, whisk together the sugar, milk powder, cinnamon, and salt.

Slowly pour the hot cream mixture into the bowl, stirring constantly.

Pour the mixture back into the pot and cook over medium heat, stirring constantly, until it returns to 180°F.

Remove from the heat and add the toast. Soak for 15 minutes and then blend until smooth. Strain through a fine-mesh strainer into a clean container.

Fill a large bowl with ice and cold water to make an ice bath.

Put the container into the ice bath and let the base cool to 38°F, stirring occasionally.

Freeze in an ice cream maker according to the manufacturer's instructions.

BLACK ASS LICORICE

I EMBARKED ON MY BLACK LICORICE JOURNEY long before I opened the shop, seeking the cleanest strongest black licorice flavor in all the land. It's an acquired taste. It was found to calm seasickness in weary seamen and maybe this is why most of the varieties in Norway and Finland are heavily salted. I love salt in my sweets, but here is where I had to draw the line; the salty licorice gave me a seawater nausea that I could not stomach. Luckily, I found something from Australia that was outstanding, not too sweet, not too strong, chewy, and clean, the perfect balance. I placed an order for 100 pounds and when we opened the box and unwrapped the bag, it was pitch-black inside. Julie Farias was standing beside me and said "holy shit that's some black ass licorice Nicholas!" And so, a star was born. Well not exactly. The flavor was tested and tweaked and then put in the archive for several years until I was writing the menu for the new shop. It was going to make the cut, but would we call it Black Ass Licorice on the menu? Yes, we would.

It makes an excellent milkshake.

Note: For this flavor, the licorice needs to be well blended with the hot dairy to melt it. Be patient, and thorough, as you want all the licorice melted for the real flavor.

Makes approximately 1 quart

WHOLE MILK	1⅔ CUPS (414G)
HEAVY CREAM	1⅔ CUPS (403G)
GLUCOSE SYRUP	1½ TABLESPOONS (30G)
GRANULATED SUGAR	⅔ CUP (138G)
WHOLE MILK POWDER	¼ CUP (30G)
KOSHER SALT	¼ TEASPOON (2G)
BLACK LICORICE	⅓ CUP (65G)

Heat the milk, cream, and glucose syrup in a 4-quart saucepan over medium heat, stirring with a rubber spatula or wooden spoon to keep it from burning, until small bubbles appear around the edges and the temperature reaches 180°F.

In a large bowl, whisk together the sugar, milk powder, and salt.

Slowly pour the hot cream mixture into the bowl, stirring constantly.

Pour the mixture back into the pot and cook over medium heat, stirring constantly, until it returns to 180°F.

Place the black licorice in a blender, remove the pot from the heat and immediately pour the contents over the black licorice. Blend until smooth, then strain through a fine-mesh strainer into a clean container.

Fill a large bowl with ice and cold water to make an ice bath.

Put the container into the ice bath and let the base cool to 38°F, stirring occasionally.

Freeze in an ice cream maker according to the manufacturer's instructions.

BURNT SAGE

THIS FLAVOR WAS INSPIRED BY A HIPPY MUSICIAN AND CHEF from deep in the woods of Northern California I cooked with years ago. One morning, early in the life of Morgenstern's, he recounted a clandestine visit with a young lady the night before, and how she was burning sage in the morning. Burning sage is nothing new, it's meant to expunge a space of bad juju, or generally create a vibe of wellness. Also, it smells great. He strongly suggested a hot smudge sundae for our menu. Unfortunately, this was when we only had the small store, and a sundae would be too difficult, so I settled on this flavor being available only as a chocolate dip. We make the dip with fresh olive oil, giving it a slightly grassy flavor to complement the smokiness of the burnt sage. This flavor makes a terrific ice cream pie around the holidays, FYI.

Note: The sage should be pungent and fresh, no bruised or black leaves. It is best if the leaves are charred just before they are blended into the sugar and added to the base. They require less charring than you think, as they release their oil as soon as they are singed, easily creating a smokey flavor.

Makes approximately 1 quart

SAGE LEAVES, STEMS REMOVED	¼ CUP (7.5G)
GRANULATED SUGAR	¾ CUP (150G)
WHOLE MILK	1⅔ CUPS (414G)
HEAVY CREAM	1⅔ CUPS (403G)
GLUCOSE SYRUP	1½ TABLESPOONS (30G)
WHOLE MILK POWDER	¼ CUP (30G)
KOSHER SALT	¼ TEASPOON (2G)
SAGE DIP (PAGE 331)	

Lay the sage leaves out on a baking sheet, and lightly burn them using a blow torch. You can also put them under the broiler for 5 to 10 minutes, but you will need to watch them closely. The leaves should be blackened and singed at the edges, but still green in the middle. Once they are cool, combine them with the sugar in a food processor and grind until fine. Set aside.

In a 4-quart saucepan, heat the milk, cream, and glucose syrup over medium heat, stirring with a rubber spatula or wooden spoon to keep it from burning, until small bubbles appear around the edges and the temperature reaches 180°F.

In a large bowl, whisk together the sage sugar, milk powder, and salt.

Slowly pour the hot cream mixture into the bowl, stirring constantly.

Pour the mixture back into the pot and cook over medium heat, stirring constantly, until it returns to 180°F.

Remove from the heat and immediately strain through a fine-mesh strainer into a clean container.

Fill a large bowl with ice and cold water to make an ice bath.

Put the container into the ice bath and let the base cool to 38°F, stirring occasionally.

Freeze in an ice cream maker according to the manufacturer's instructions. Drizzle with the warm Sage Dip just before scooping.

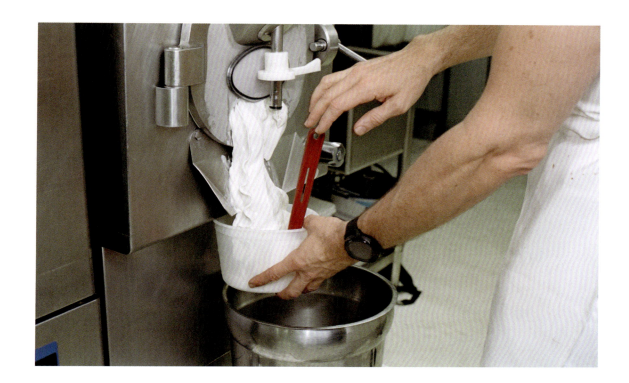

SAGE DIP

Makes 1¼ cups

Dark Chocolate (62% cocoa) 1 cup (180g)

Bitter Chocolate (100% cocoa) ¼ cup (45g)

Olive Oil ⅓ cup (65g)

Fill an 8-quart stock pot with 1 quart water, and bring to a simmer over medium heat. Turn the heat down to low and in a large bowl (make sure the bowl is not actually touching the water), over the simmering water, melt the dark and bitter chocolates and olive oil. Stir constantly to combine.

When the chocolate has melted strain with a fine-mesh strainer into a covered container, and store in the refrigerator for up to 4 weeks. Reheat to room temperature over simmering water or in the microwave before serving.

TAHINI AND JELLY

This flavor makes an attempt at the classic peanut butter and jelly. Tahini is a paste made from sesame seeds; it has a smooth texture and is looser than peanut butter, largely due to the absence of hydrogenated fat. It is more bland and bitter, with no sugar, unlike peanut butter. I love this ice cream made with Concord grape jelly, but it is equally delicious with lemon jam or chocolate fudge swirled in.

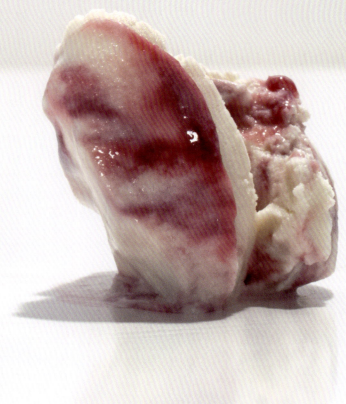

Note: The jam should ideally be made at least 24 hours before the ice cream is going to be frozen to allow it to cool and set. You can add it the same day if you have no choice, but don't add it hot.

Makes approximately 1 quart

....

Whole Milk	2 cups (490g)
Heavy Cream	1 cup (239g)
Glucose Syrup	1½ tablespoons (30g)
Granulated Sugar	1 cup (200g)
Whole Milk Powder	¼ cup (30g)
Kosher Salt	¼ teaspoon (2g)
Tahini, well-stirred	⅓ cup (90g)
Lemon Juice	½ teaspoon (2.5g)
Grape Jelly (recipe follows), depending on how much you like jelly	¼ to ⅓ cup (100g)

....

In a 4-quart saucepan, combine the milk, cream, and glucose syrup over medium heat, stirring with a rubber spatula or wooden spoon to keep it from burning, until small bubbles appear around the edges and the temperature reaches 180°F.

In a large bowl, whisk together the sugar, milk powder, and salt.

Slowly pour the hot cream mixture into the bowl, stirring constantly.

Pour the mixture back into the pot and cook over medium heat, stirring constantly, until it returns to 180°F.

Remove from the heat and stir in the tahini, and immediately strain through a fine-mesh strainer into a clean container.

Fill a large bowl with ice and cold water to make an ice bath.

Put the container into the ice bath and let the base cool to 38°F, stirring occasionally.

Add the lemon juice and freeze in an ice cream maker according to the manufacturer's instructions. Swirl in the Grape Jelly to create ribbons.

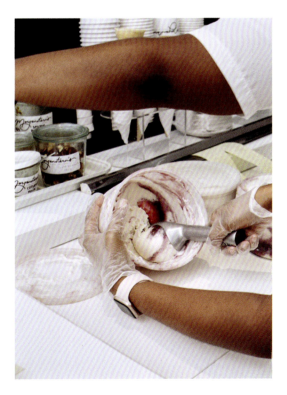

GRAPE JELLY

Note: The jelly will remain pourable. After countless tests, this recipe has been illusive in small quantities. I have increased the pectin to create a jelly that holds when added to an ice cream, or a cake like The Koppelman (page 163). It is a good idea to test the consistency of this jelly after the pectin has been boiled and see if it is thick by checking that it does not run when cooled on a plate and tipped vertically. If it does, allow it to cook over medium heat, stirring consistently, until it sets. Allow the jelly to cool completely in the refrigerator for at least 4 hours before using it. If it seems to stiff, you can loosen it in a bowl using a whisk or a fork.

Makes approximately ⅓ cup

Welch's Concorde Grape Juice
⅔ cup (155g)

Granulated Sugar
4 tablespoons (50g), divided

Sure-Jell Original Powdered Pectin
1 teaspoon (4g; measured by weight rather than volume, if possible)

Glucose Syrup   1 tablespoon (20g)

Lemon Juice   2 teaspoons (10g)

Kosher Salt   ¼ teaspoon (2g)

In a 2-quart saucepan, bring the grape juice and 2 tablespoons (25g) of sugar to a boil over high heat.

Thoroughly combine the remaining 2 tablespoons of sugar and the pectin in a small bowl and quickly whisk into the grape juice. Return to a full boil, then keep at a lively simmer over medium heat until the liquid thickens and the surface is covered with thick, viscous bubbles, 7 to 10 minutes. The liquid should start to gel but remain pourable.

Remove from the heat and stir in the glucose syrup, lemon juice, and salt.

Strain through a fine-mesh strainer into a clean container. Cool completely and keep covered in the refrigerator until ready to use, up to 2 weeks.

LABNEH SORBET

This is made with dairy, so not technically a sorbet, but with no milk or cream it's not an ice cream, or a sherbet, either. Labneh is a strained yogurt from the Middle East. It has a nuttiness and a less acidic flavor than yogurt with a tremendously rich and creamy texture that is closer to sour cream. It is traditionally served in a bowl beneath a pool of olive oil and herbs with pita bread, or as a breakfast with fruit and nuts. Both of those approaches are great, but my favorite way to eat it is as a sorbet. It makes a great complement to a rich flourless chocolate cake, bright acidic fruit, or with nuts and maple syrup drizzled over it.

Makes approximately 3¾ cups

Glucose Syrup	⅓ cup (110g)
Granulated Sugar	⅓ cup (69g)
Simple Syrup (page 209)	⅓ cup (107g)
Labneh	2¾ cups (630g)
Olive Oil	¼ cup (50g)
Lemon Juice	3 tablespoons (45g)
Kosher Salt	¼ teaspoon (2g)

In a 2-quart saucepan, warm the glucose syrup, sugar, and Simple Syrup until the sugar has dissolved.

In a large bowl, whisk together the labneh and the warm sugar syrup.

Add the olive oil, lemon juice, and salt to the bowl and whisk together.

Strain through a fine-mesh strainer into a clean container.

Fill a large bowl with ice and cold water to make an ice bath.

Put the container into the ice bath and let the base cool to 38°F, stirring occasionally.

Freeze in an ice cream maker according to the manufacturer's instructions.

FRENCH FRY

THIS IS A GOOD ONE. It is unusual, it grabs your attention, and it is unexpectedly delicious. If you have ever dipped a starchy, salty French fry into your sweet vanilla milkshake you already know what this is about. French Fry ice cream is great with a scoop of vanilla or chocolate, and of course it makes a terrific milkshake. The fries don't need to be crispy, so if you don't have a fryer, you can buy some and bring them home.

Makes approximately 1 pint

FOR THE FRENCH FRY MILK

WHOLE MILK	1¼ CUPS (306G)
FRENCH FRIES, SUCH AS MCDONALD'S, WARM, ¼-INCH-THICK	1⅓ CUPS (90G)

FOR THE ICE CREAM BASE

HEAVY CREAM	1 CUP (239G)
GLUCOSE SYRUP	1 TABLESPOON (20G)
GRANULATED SUGAR	½ CUP (100G)
WHOLE MILK POWDER	¼ CUP (30G)
KOSHER SALT	¼ TEASPOON (2G)

To make the French fry milk: Heat the milk in a 2-quart saucepan over medium heat to 180°F.

Add the French fries and cover. Soak the fries in the milk for 20 minutes.

Strain through a fine-mesh strainer, pressing down on the fries firmly with the bottom of a ladle to extract all the milk, and reserve.

To make the ice cream base: In a 4-quart saucepan, combine 1 cup of the French fry milk, the cream, and glucose syrup over medium heat, stirring with a rubber spatula or wooden spoon to keep it from burning, until small bubbles appear around the edges and the temperature reaches 180°F.

In a large bowl, whisk together the sugar, milk powder, and salt.

Slowly pour the hot cream mixture into the bowl, stirring constantly.

Pour the mixture back into the pot and cook over medium heat, stirring constantly, until it returns to 180°F.

Remove from the heat and immediately strain through a fine-mesh strainer into a clean container.

Fill a large bowl with ice and cold water to make an ice bath. Put the container into the ice bath and let the base cool to 38°F, stirring occasionally.

Freeze in an ice cream maker according to the manufacturer's instructions.

GREEN TEA PISTACHIO

THE GENESIS OF THIS RECIPE WAS THE PISTACHIO FLAVOR at Emack & Bolio's, which tasted like vanilla ice cream with pistachios in it. The pistachios were frozen, which mutes an already subtle flavor. The vanilla ice cream did nothing to accentuate them. Rather than make a pistachio ice cream, I thought of how tasty freshly toasted chopped pistachios are, and how good they would be added into an ice cream right before it is scooped. I had been introduced to matcha as an ingredient a few years earlier and served it as a panna cotta. Matcha was not very common at the time, but most people were aware of green tea ice cream, and seemed to like it, so that's what we called it.

Makes approximately 1 quart

Heavy Cream	1⅔ cups (403g)
Whole Milk	1½ cups (367g)
Glucose Syrup	1½ tablespoons (30g)
Granulated Sugar	⅔ cup (138g)
Whole Milk Powder	¼ cup (30g)
Matcha Powder	1 tablespoon (5g)
Kosher Salt	¼ teaspoon (2g)
Chopped Toasted Pistachios	½ cup (80g)

In a 4-quart saucepan, combine the cream, milk, and glucose syrup over medium heat, stirring with a rubber spatula or wooden spoon to keep it from burning, until small bubbles appear around the edges and the temperature reaches 180°F.

In a large bowl, whisk together the sugar, milk powder, matcha powder, and salt.

Slowly pour the hot cream mixture into the bowl, stirring constantly.

Pour the mixture back into the pot and cook over medium heat, stirring constantly, until it returns to 180°F.

Remove from the heat and immediately strain through a fine-mesh strainer into a clean container.

Fill a large bowl with ice and cold water to make an ice bath. Put the container into the ice bath and let the base cool to 38°F, stirring occasionally.

Freeze in an ice cream maker according to the manufacturer's instructions.

Stir in the pistachios just before scooping.

IT'S-IT

It's-It is an ice cream sandwich from San Francisco, my hometown. They are terrific; delicious and surprisingly inexpensive. The company has been family owned and operated for over 100 years.

Unfortunately, the It's-It is not widely available in New York, and the name was lost on most. I still love it, and obviously this is an homage to my favorite ice cream treat of all time. The key to the It's-It is the semisoft oatmeal raisin cookie that is short on raisins and cinnamon flavor. When frozen, a chocolate chip cookie becomes hard and brittle, but the oatmeal cookie stays somewhat soft and pliable. This keeps the cookie from shattering and allows for the sandwich to be constructed with a slightly softer ice cream. I must have eaten hundreds of these as a teenager, blindly enjoying their perfectly balanced textures, until I thought about making my own ice cream sandwich years later. I remembered how the cookie was soft and chewy and did not make the ice cream squish out the sides too much. The chocolate shell on the outside was light and crisp. We decided to make our own line of ice cream sandwiches with different flavors, from vanilla and Chocolate (page 42) to Vietnamese Coffee (page 101) and banana.

NICK'S IT

THESE ARE A GREAT ITEM TO MAKE IN ADVANCE for a party or event. There is no service needed, just napkins. At the shop we make a few hundred at a time, to sell over the course of a week or two, and this recipe makes enough cookies for 10 to 12 sandwiches. The dough should be baked all at once but can then be stored in the freezer until it is time to make the sandwiches. The Chocolate Dip can be made well in advance and kept in the fridge. Make sure you use a deep container to dunk the sandwiches in. You can put just about any flavor of ice cream in here, but classics seem to work best.

Makes 10 to 12 sandwiches

....

FOR THE COOKIES

OLD-FASHIONED ROLLED OATS	1½ CUPS (165G)
UNSALTED BUTTER, AT ROOM TEMPERATURE	¾ CUP (180G)
DARK BROWN SUGAR	¾ CUP PACKED (109G)
GRANULATED SUGAR	½ CUP (100G)
EGG	1 LARGE
VANILLA EXTRACT	½ TEASPOON (3G)
ALL-PURPOSE FLOUR	1¼ CUPS (170G)
BAKING SODA	¼ TEASPOON (1G)
CINNAMON	PINCH OF
KOSHER SALT (FINE GRAIN, SUCH AS DIAMOND CRYSTAL)	PINCH OF

TO ASSEMBLE

ICE CREAM

CHOCOLATE DIP (PAGE 347)

SEA SALT

....

Preheat your oven to 300°F. Line two large baking sheets with parchment paper.

To make the cookies: Put the oats in a food processor and pulse until coarsely ground. Set aside.

Using a stand mixer fitted with the paddle attachment, cream the butter and both sugars together at medium speed until they are light and fluffy.

Add the egg and vanilla, and continue to mix until smooth. Scrape down the bowl and cream again.

In a medium bowl, sift together the flour, baking soda, cinnamon, and salt and add to the mixer. Add the oats and mix on low speed until everything is well incorporated.

Use a mechanical scoop to make balls about the size of a golf ball. Space them evenly on one of the prepared baking sheets. Press them down until they are about ½ inch tall.

Bake for 5 minutes and then turn the pan. Bake for about another 5 minutes, or until lightly golden brown at the edges. Allow the cookies tp cool completely and store in an airtight container in the freezer for up to 4 weeks.

To assemble the Nick's It: Line a large baking sheet with parchment paper and set aside. It is best to have someone helping. Lay out all of the cookies "bottoms up" on a tray. Place a scoop of ice cream onto each and immediately place a second cookie on top. Press until the ice cream comes out the sides of the cookies. Freeze for 1 to 2 hours.

Ideally the dip should be between 80° to 90°F. Submerge each sandwich into the dip completely and, using a spatula, remove and allow any excess chocolate to drain back into the dip pan.

Carefully place the chocolate dipped sandwich onto the prepared baking sheet. After 30 seconds sprinkle with sea salt. They can be frozen in an airtight container for up to 2 weeks.

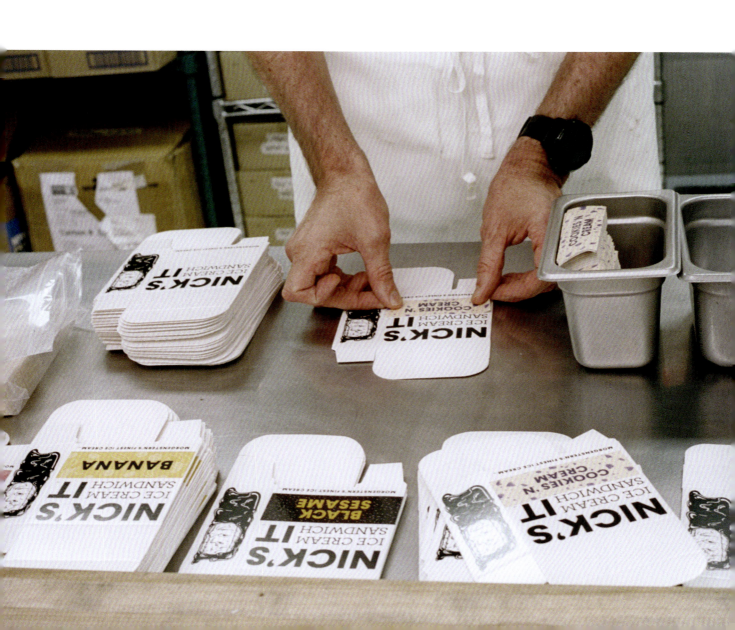

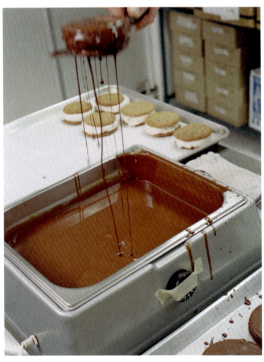

CHOCOLATE DIP

Makes approximately 2 cups

....

Chopped Chocolate (65% cocoa)
                                        1¼ cups (225g)

Chopped Bitter Chocolate (100% cocoa)
                                          ¼ cup (45g)

Olive Oil   ½ cup (100g)

....

Melt the chocolates and olive oil in a mixing bowl over simmering water or in the microwave.

To melt over simmering water: Fill an 8-quart stock pot with 1 quart water, and bring to a simmer over medium heat. Turn the heat down to low, and in a large bowl, over the simmering water, melt the chocolates and olive oil. Make sure that the bottom of the bowl is not touching the water.

To melt in the microwave: Melt the chocolates and olive oil in a microwave safe bowl in 30 second increments, stirring between each increment.

Using a rubber spatula or spoon, combine completely.

Strain through a fine-mesh strainer into a clean container.

Use the dip at a temperature of 80° to 90°F.

The dip can be stored, covered, at room temperature for up to 6 weeks.

THANKS

For most of the lifespan of Morgenstern's, it has been a singular experience. I built the store against some odds, by myself. Sometimes I still feel like I am running it alone. I have certainly fired people along the way who did not meet my expectations for getting things done. There are a handful of people who were integral along the way, without whom it would not have been possible.

Jessica Che: Jess has been a friend and collaborator for 15 years. Without her, there would be no Morgenstern's logo, website, or illustrations. Her attitude and design align with an eye toward restraint.

Thank you for being you Jess. Increase the font size please.

Jack Dakin: Jack and I went to high school together, and then reconnected years later when I needed assistance with Morgenstern's. He has the unique ability to allow irrationality and nonsense to roll off his back and show up with a smile and a solution the next day. The store and its design would not exist without him.

Thank you, Jack.

Jen Driscol: Jen was the opening GM of Morgenstern's. She dove into a complete shit show headfirst and helped hold it all together with happiness and grace.

Tad Barnes: Tad was on the opening counter team at Morgenstern's. He taught me about patience and a positive attitude. He was way overqualified to scoop ice cream, and always looked good doing it.

Gerard Renaud: The best of both worlds, an old-school French beast in the kitchen and a tender heart. I would kill a man to have you back.

Manuel Rodriguez: Manuel Rodriguez started with me in 2008, and has never left my side. Thank you for showing up every day Manuel.

SPECIAL THANKS

Priyaporn Pichitpongchai: It would have been difficult to predict what an impact Pri would have on Morgenstern's when I met her. Humble and unassuming, she has the will to do anything she sets her mind to. Thank you for helping execute the vision of Morgenstern's.

WITH THE BOOK

Writing a book about ice cream is entirely different from making ice cream, or eating it, or selling it. I have never done anything like this before, and I am not sure I would do it again. As you may have guessed, there has been support along the way. Without the people below, this project would not have been possible.

Lucia Bell-Epstein, for shooting this book with patience, commitment, and enthusiasm.

Kim Witherspoon, for seeing the vision and helping me sell it.

Abbey Aronson, for keeping my writing on track and sticking with me through the headache that I presented weekly.

Laura Russell, for attention to detail in getting these recipes tested to our standards.

Tom Pold and **Knopf,** for believing in this project.

INDEX

A

Affogato, ...113
Almond(s), ...144
    Honey Almond Custard,....150
    Honey Almond
        Honeycomb, ...152
    Rockiest Road, ...69
Avocado, ...201
Avocado Toast, ...200

B

Baked Crème Caramel, ...128
Banana(s), ...179
    Banana Curry, ...183
    Bananas Foster, ...186
    Banana Split, ...91
    Charred Banana, ...188
    commodity, ...187
    Drunken Monkey, ...181
    Durian Banana, ...225
    King Kong Banana Split, ...34
    Macadamia Praline
        Banana, ...192
Banana Split, ...91
    King Kong, ...34
Bitter Chocolate, ...54
Black Ass Licorice, ...326
Black Currant
    Black Currant Jam, ...158
    Pistachio Black Currant, ...154
Black raspberry, ...267
Blueberry Milk Chocolate, .. 52

Bourbon
    Bourbon Caramel, ...121
    Bourbon Vanilla, ...26
Brownies, ...58
    Brownie Sundae, ...59
    Sundae Brownies, ...60
Bubble Gum, ...296
Burnt Honey Vanilla, ...28
Burnt Sage, ...328
Butter Pecan, ...174
Butter Pecans and Pecan
    Butter, ...176
Butterscotch, ...129

C

Cake, Chocolate, ...316
Caramel, ...115
    Baked Crème Caramel, ...128
    Bourbon Caramel, ...121
    Butterscotch, ...129
    Caramel Sauce, ...118
    Crème Caramel, ...124
    Dulce de Leche, ...122
    Mango Passionfruit
        Caramel, ...222
    Peanut Butter Caramel, ...73
    Salted Caramel Pretzel, ...138
    Sesame Caramel, ...121
    Water Caramel, ...120
Cardamom Lemon Jam, ...232
Charred Banana, ...188
Cheesecake, Raspberry, ...258

Chocolate, ...37
    Bitter Chocolate, ...54
    Blueberry Milk Chocolate, .. 52
    brownies, ...58
    Brownie Sundae, ...59
    candies, ...62
    Chocolate (ice cream), ...42
    Chocolate Cake, ...316
    Chocolate Dip, ...347
    Chocolate Lace, ...310
    Grasshopper Sundae, ...308
    The Hot Fudge Sundae:
        The Most Important
        Sundae in America, ...31
    Hotter Fudge, ...61
    Morgenstern's Hot Fudge,...32
    Olive Oil Charred
        Eggplant, ...47
    Raspberry and Chocolate, 256
    Ricky Road, ...71
    Rockiest Road, ...69
    Salted Chocolate, ...50
    Schoolyard Mint Chip, ...305
    Sundae Brownies, ...60
Chunky Monkey, ...180
Chunky Strawberry, ...81
Cinnamon Raisin Toast, ...323
Citrus, ...229
    See also individual fruits
    juice, ...237
    oranges, ...244
    salty, ...249
    yuzu, ...244
    zest, ...236

Coconut, ... 204
   Coconut Espresso, ... 110
   Coconut Sorbet, ... 205
   Coconut Whipped
      Cream, ... 222
Coffee, ... 97, 104
   Affogato, ... 113
   brews, ... 98
   Coconut Espresso, ... 110
   Coffee Crisp, ... 106
   creamers, ... 112
   espresso, ... 112
   Espresso Honeycomb, ... 108
   Häagen-Dazs ice cream, ... 105
   Vietnamese Coffee, ... 101
Condensed Milk Fluff, ... 253
Containers, ... 9
Cookie Monster Cake, ... 313
Cookies N' Cream, ... 294
Cream
   Coconut Whipped
      Cream, ... 222
   coffee creamers, ... 112
   Cookies N' Cream, ... 294
   Peaches N' Clotted
      Cream, ... 275
   Strawberries N' Cream, ... 88
   Whipped Cream, ... 33
Crème Caramel, ... 124
   Baked Crème Caramel, ... 128
Crushed Pineapple, ... 92

D

Dacquoise, ... 168
Dairy, ... 6
Digital scale, ... 8
Digital timer and
   thermometer, ... 9
Dip
   Chocolate Dip, ... 347
   Sage Dip, ... 331
Drunken Monkey, ... 181
Dulce de Leche, ... 122
Durian Banana, ... 225

E

Eggplant, Olive Oil Charred, 47
Equipment, ... 7
Espresso, ... 112
   Affogato, ... 113
   Coconut Espresso, ... 110
   Espresso Honeycomb, ... 108

F

Fluff
   Condensed Milk Fluff, ... 253
   Marshmallow Fluff, ... 73
Freezer, ... 8
French Fry, ... 336
French Vanilla, ... 22
Frosting
   M&M's Frosting, ... 315
   PB, ... 171

G

Glucose syrup, ... 6
Graham Cracker Crumb, .. 262
Grape, ... 171
   Grape Jelly, ... 334
Grasshopper Sundae, ... 303
Grater, ... 9
Green Tea
   Green Tea Jelly, ... 266
   Green Tea Pistachio, ... 338
   Raspberry Green Tea
      Jelly, ... 264
Guava, ... 214
   Strawberry Guava Sorbet, .. 216

H

Hazelnut(s), ... 145
   Hazelnut Risbo, ... 160
   Mascarpone, ... 172
Honey
   Honey Almond Custard, ... 150
   Honey Almond
      Honeycomb, ... 152
   Honey Lavender Peach, ... 285
Hot Fudge
   The Hot Fudge Sundae:
      The Most Important
      Sundae in America, ... 31
   Morgenstern's, ... 32
Hotter Fudge, ... 61
Howard Johnson's, ... 244

I

Ice bath, ...9
Ice cream cakes, ...311
   Bubble Gum, ...298
   Cookie Monster Cake, ...313
Ice cream carts, ...137
Ice cream machine, ...7
Ice cream scoops, ...9
Ingredients, ...6
   See also specific ingredients
It's-It, ...342

J

Jam
   Black Currant, ...158
   Cardamom Lemon Jam, ...232
   Lemon Jam, ...233
   Peach Jam, ...281
   Strawberry, ...83
Jelly
   Grape Jelly, ...334
   Green Tea Jelly, ...266
   Raspberry Green Tea Jelly, ...264
   Tahini and Jelly, ...332
   Yuzu Jelly, ...248

K

Kathy's Kalamansi Gin Pop, ...251
King Kong Banana Split, ...34
The Koppelman, ...163
"The Koppelman" by Brian Koppelman, ...162

L

Labneh Sorbet, ...335
Lavender, Honey Lavender Peach, ...285
Lemon
   Cardamom Lemon Jam, ...232
   Lemon Curd, ...240
   Lemon Curd Poppyseed, ...238
   Lemon Jam, ...233
Licorice, Black Ass, ...326

M

Macadamia nuts, ...145
   Macadamia Praline, ...194
   Macadamia Praline Banana, ...192
Madagascar, ...12
Madagascar Vanilla, ...20
Mango
   Mango Chips, ...223
   Mango Passionfruit Caramel, ...222
   Mango Passion Rice, ...218
   Mango Satsuma, ...242
   Vegan Mango Sundae, ...221
Marshmallow(s)
   Marshmallow Fluff, ...73
   Rockiest Road, ...69
Mascarpone, ...172
Measuring cups and spoons, ...8
Mesh strainers, ...9
Milkshake, Raspberry, ...270
Mint Chip, Schoolyard, ...305
Mixing bowls, ...8
M&M's Frosting, ...315
Morgenstern's Difference, The, ...4
Morgenstern's Hot Fudge, ...32
Mulie Fajitas Picoso' Classic Sundae, ...66

N

Neapolitan, ...94
Nick's It, ...343
Nuts, ...143, 146
   See also specific nuts

O

Olive Oil Charred Eggplant, ...47
"The Origins of the Mulie Fajitas Picoso' Classic Sundae" by Julie Farias, ...64

P

Papaya Raspberry Sorbet, ...268
Passionfruit, ...214
   Mango Passionfruit Caramel, ...222
   Mango Passion Rice, ...218
PB Frosting, ...171
Peach(es), ...273
   Honey Lavender Peach, ...285
   Peaches N' Clotted Cream, ...275
   peaches 'n' cream, ...274
   Peach Jam, ...281
   Peach Sweet Tea, ...282
   Sour Cream Canned Peach, ...278

Peanut Butter, ... 170
    PB Frosting, ...171
    Peanut Butter Caramel, ...73
    Peanut Butter Cup, ...148
Peanuts, ... 144
    Dacquoise, ...168
    Picosos' peanuts, ...33
    Ricky Road, ...71
Pecans, ...145, 173
    Butter Pecan, ...174
    Butter Pecans and
        Pecan Butter, ...176
Pectin, ...6
Pickled Pineapple, ... 209
Picosos' peanuts, ... 33
Pineapple, ...208
    Crushed Pineapple, ...92
    Pickled Pineapple, ...209
    Pineapple Salted
        Egg Yolk, ...210
Pine nuts, ... 145
Pistachio(s), ... 145
    Green Tea Pistachio, ... 338
    Pistachio Black Currant, ...154
    Strawberry Pistachio
        Pesto, ...86
Poppyseed, Lemon Curd, ...238
Popsicles, ... 250, 260
    Kathy's Kalamansi
        Gin Pop, ... 251
Pretzel, Salted Caramel, ... 138

R

Raisin
    Cinnamon Raisin Toast, ... 323
    Rum Raisin, ...302

Raspberry, ... 255
    Raspberry Dark
        Chocolate, ... 256
    Raspberry Cheesecake, ...258
    Raspberry Green
        Tea Jelly, ... 264
    Raspberry Milkshake, ... 270
    Raspberry Papaya Sorbet, 268
    Raspberry Swirl, ... 262
Raw Milk, ...320
Ricky Road, ...71
Rockiest Road, ... 69
Rocky Road, ... 68
Rum Raisin, ...302

S

Sage
    Burnt Sage, ... 328
    Sage Dip, ...331
Salt, ...6
Salted Caramel Pretzel, ... 138
Salted Chocolate, ... 50
Salted Egg Yolk Streusel, ... 212
Sauce
    Caramel Sauce, ... 118
    Hotter Fudge, ...61
    Morgenstern's Hot Fudge, .. 32
    Strawberry Sauce, ...94
Schoolyard Mint Chip, ...305
Sesame Caramel, ...121
Smooth and Delicious
    Strawberry, ... 78
S'Mores, ...299
Sorbet
    Coconut Sorbet, ... 205
    Labneh Sorbet, ... 335
    Raspberry Papaya Sorbet, 268

    Strawberry Guava Sorbet, .. 216
Sour Cream Canned
    Peach, ... 278
Spatulas, ...8
Strawberry, ...75
    Chunky Strawberry, ...31
    Smooth and Delicious
        Strawberry, ... 78
    Strawberries N' Cream, ...88
    Strawberry Guava Sorbet .. 213
    Strawberry Jam, ...83
    Strawberry Pistachio
        Pesto, ...86
    Strawberry Sauce, ... 94
Streusel, Salted Egg Yolk, .. 212
Sugar, ...6
    caramel, ... 116
    Vanilla Sugar, ...19
Sundae
    Brownie Sundae, ...59
    Grasshopper Sundae, ...308
    The Hot Fudge Sundae:
        The Most Important
        Sundae in America, ...31
    Mulie Fajitas Picoso'
        Classic Sundae, ...63
    Vegan Mango Sundae, ... 221
Sundae Brownies, ... 60

T

Tahini and Jelly, ...332
Tea
    Green Tea Jelly, ... 266
    Green Tea Pistachio, ... 338
    Peach Sweet Tea, ... 282
    Raspberry Green
        Tea Jelly, ... 264

Toast, Avocado, ... 200
Tropical fruits, ... 199
   See also individual fruits
   coconut, ...204
   guava, ...214
   passionfruit, ...214
   pineapple, ...208

V

Vanilla, ... 11
   Bourbon Vanilla, ...26
   Burnt Honey Vanilla, ...28
   buying, ...13
   French Vanilla, ...22
   Madagascar, ...12
   Madagascar Vanilla, ...20
   processing, ...14
   Vanilla Brûlée, ...25
   Vanilla Sugar, ...19
Vegan Mango Sundae, ... 221
Vietnamese Coffee, ...101

W

Waffle House, ... 132
Walnuts, ... 144
Water Caramel, ... 120
Whipped Cream, ... 33
   Coconut Whipped
     Cream, ...222
Whisks, ...8

Y

Yuzu, ...244
   Yuzu Jelly, ...248
   Yuzu Toasted Rice, ...245

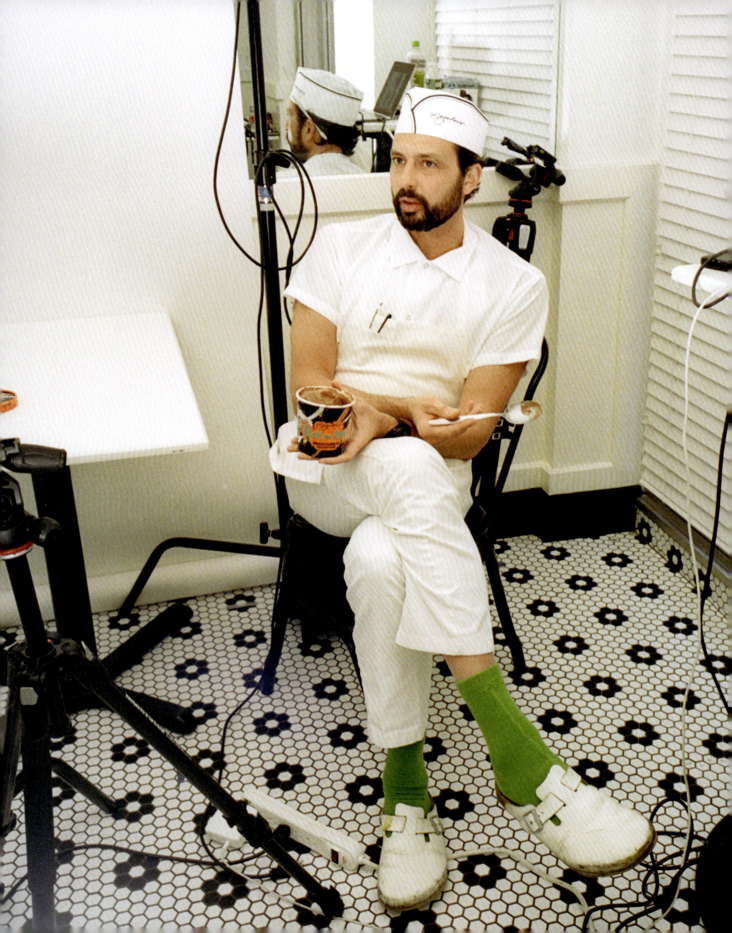

Nicholas Morgenstern is an ice cream operator.